BLACK
SAINTS
in a
WHITE
CHURCH

BLACK SAINTS

SAINTS

in a

WHITE

CHURCH

CONTEMPORARY AFRICAN AMERICAN MORMONS

JESSIE L. EMBRY

SALT LAKE CITY

1994

To
Alan Cherry
and
Roger Launius

Cover design by Randall Smith Associates.

Black Saints in a White Church was printed on acid-free paper
meeting the permanence of paper requirements of the
American National Standard for Information Sciences.
This book was composed, printed and bound in the United States.

98 97 96 95 94   6 5 4 3 2 1

Library of Congress Cataloging-in-Publication Data

Embry, Jessie L.
Black Saints in a white church : contemporary African American
Mormons / by Jessie L. Embry.
p.   cm.
Includes bibliographical references.
ISBN 1-56085-044-2
1. Afro-American Mormons. 2. Race relations—Religious aspects—
Church of Jesus Christ of Latter-day Saints. 3. Race relations—
Religious aspects—Mormon church. 4. Church of Jesus Christ of
Latter-day Saints—Membership. 5. Mormon Church—Membership.
I. Title.
BX8643.A35E42   1994
289.3'089'96073—dc20   94-13559
CIP

TABLE OF CONTENTS

ACKNOWLEDGMENTS

In 1985 when Alan Cherry suggested that I do an oral history project on LDS Afro-Americans, I had no idea that eight years later I would be publishing a book on the subject. At the time I was so wrapped up in finishing *Mormon Polygamous Families* that I was not sure what I would do once that project was finished. Because my mind was elsewhere, Alan's involvement in the new venture was essential. He developed the outline, contacted the people, and conducted the interviews. As I finished my first book and became more interested in the experiences of black Mormons, he spent hours talking to me. Whatever understanding I have of African Americans and especially LDS Afro-Americans developed from the spark that Alan lit.

Alan and his wife, Janice Marie Barkum Cherry, one of the people interviewed, have continued to encourage me. They never laughed at my cultural naivete; they patiently answered questions when I did not understand black American culture. Alan and Janice are treasured friends.

I am also grateful for all of the people who agreed to be inter- viewed as part of the LDS Afro-American Oral History Project. While not every one of them is quoted in this book, each helped me in developing my ideas. Since I have read through the interviews several times, I feel as though I know them well. When I visit the Oakland, California, 9th Branch, Rodney Carey laughs and says to whomever is around, "This is the person who knows my life story better than I do."

I have enjoyed meeting other women and men involved in the interviews. I gained new insights from the eight who spoke at the LDS Afro-American Symposium at Brigham Young University on the tenth anniversary of blacks receiving the priesthood. I have fond memories of meeting Burgess Owens, Nathleen Albright, Johnnie McKoy, Jerri Harwell, Robert Stevenson, Cleeretta Smiley, Cathy Stokes, and Emanuel Reid. I'll always remember giving a fireside in San Pedro, California, and prize my early morning telephone calls from Beverly Perry. Whenever I hear the hymn "Amazing Grace," I will remember Gabrielle Smith's wedding and then recall her accepting me into black circles as an honorary member. I could give numerous examples of where this project has broadened my horizons and enabled me to meet people and understand another culture.

The project not only gave me a chance to meet blacks, I also have had rewarding experiences with people who helped process the interviews. These included Natalie Ethington, Barbara Lyman, Irene Fuja, Kyra Larsen Swain, Rhonda Coursey, Kristine Judd Ireland, Elizabeth Robbins Austin, Julie Greenland, Paul Hillyard, Teresa Yancey Wilson, and Rebecca Ream Vorimo. And while I have not kept in contact with all of them, I value their contribution to the study.

A colleague at BYU once told me that another project I was working on fell in the cracks between sociology and history. I am discovering that much of what I do slips into those crevices. Yet I don't have the sociological training to pull the material out. I am indebted to Cardell Jacobson, a professor of sociology at BYU, for helping me with the survey, running cross tabs, and answering my questions. I especially appreciate his help in co-authoring two chapters in this book.

Although I am committed to more than simply placing oral history transcripts on the shelf in the BYU library, writing this book was difficult. I had reached a hurdle that I could not get over in 1991 and was ready to give up. Fortunately, Roger D. Launius came to speak at a Redd Center conference that year and encouraged me to keep working on the manuscript. Without his faith, this book would have died.

Once the rough draft was completed, my sister Janet, my ever-faithful friend and critic, edited the manuscript. Then I hired Lavina Fielding Anderson to go through the text. Once her work was completed, Cardell Jacobson, Kris Nelson, and Rebecca Ream Vorimo read the entire manuscript and offered valuable suggestions. Newell Bringhurst loaned me his collection of articles from the LDS *Church News*. He also read the complete manuscript and gave me suggestions.

John Sillito also helped improve the manuscript. In addition, Roger Launius and Armand Mauss read chapters and pointed out weaknesses. Rachel Nathan read the entire edited final copy, and Kris Nelson read the page proofs. They both found some embarrassing errors. Kris Nelson also helped with the index.

During winter semester 1994 at BYU I taught a class on LDS ethnic groups in the United States, and my students read the manuscript. I appreciate their support and encouragement, as well.

Since 1979 when I was hired as the Oral History Program Director at the Charles Redd Center for Western Studies at BYU I have had the opportunity to work with outstanding directors. Thomas G. Alexander and William A. Wilson have been extremely supportive. They have let me select my own projects and then supported me completely. This book is a product of that backing.

Yet when all is said and done, I am the one who wrote the book. I hope that I have done justice to all of these people—especially the men and women whose stories I retell. Several times people have told me that they have used my article in *Dialogue: A Journal of Mormon Thought* which explored the advantages and disadvantages of separate black branches or integrated wards to better understand the concerns of LDS African Americans. I hope this study will be as useful in promoting racial and ethnic understanding.

INTRODUCTION

I grew up in a small Mormon community in northern Utah where everyone belonged to the same church. I only realized that I lived in a "Mormon culture" when my family moved to Iran when I was in elementary school and later to Missouri when I was in junior high school. Even then my parents sought out the LDS church, and while I went to school with children from other backgrounds, my life still revolved around Mormonism.

It took years before I knew I spoke a different religious language than my non-Mormon acquaintances. For me a "stake house" was where Mormons meet in stake conference, not where "steaks" are eaten. I didn't realize that my definitions of bishop, baptism, and blessings differed from those of Catholic and Protestant Americans.

My contact with African Americans in Logan, Utah, was even more limited. The only blacks in the community were basketball and football players recruited to play for Utah State University. They were my heroes, and I could have qualified for "sports fan of the year." But I didn't realize that while I idealized them I also stereotyped them: "All blacks are good athletes." I didn't know that other Mormons in the community feared these students and believed that "all black men are oversexed and after white women."

I was so naive that in Missouri I did not understand why all the black students "got" to sit on the back row. The rest of us had to sit in alphabetical order. The school praised itself on being "liberal" and "integrated." After all they elected a black basketball player as student body president one semester. Yet as I look back, I realize that whites held all the other leadership positions. There were no blacks in the pep club (where I was readily accepted even though I was a newcomer). The school was integrated, but for the most part blacks were invisible.

I did not really get to know an African American until I met Alan Cherry in 1985. Later I met other blacks and started to see them as individuals rather than stereotypes. I began to feel a part of "them." I considered it a compliment when Gabrielle Smith implied that I was an honorary African American (although I am sure my Southern grandmother turned over in her grave).

I still knew nothing about African American culture when I attended a Pentecostal service in a black church in Oakland, California. I was the only white in the congregation; I had become the minority. I felt welcomed, but as I listened to the music and the sermon, I realized I had entered another world.

LDS African Americans face the same dilemma as they leave one culture and join a completely new one. Just as when I attended the Pentecostal church, it is not just that the people they meet are a different color. The Mormon church comprises a distinctive new culture. Black Mormons are essentially caught between two different worlds. How are Latter-day Saint African Americans able to make that transfer? How are they accepted into a new culture? What is the reaction of their black friends and relatives? And how do white Mormons respond?

These are not new questions for African Americans. Those who grew up prior to the 1960s dealt with segregated schools, restrooms, and drinking fountains and with designated seating on buses and in theaters. Civil disobedience led to political changes during the 1960s, but not automatically or necessarily to unequivocal acceptance. Integration and discrimination exist together as realities in their lives.

These may be old concerns for some, but they are new ones for Latter-day Saints. Although the Mormon church has expanded to all sectors within American society, its growth among African Americans would have been impossible two decades ago. Up until 1978 black men could not be ordained to the LDS priesthood, and black men and women could not be married in Mormon temples or receive the "temple endowment" ordinance. Mormon missionaries, normally encouraged to share their message with anyone who would listen, were discouraged from teaching blacks. Since the 1978 announcement lifting the restrictions, missionaries have actively sought out blacks, and many—though not statistically significant—African Americans have joined.

According to surveys, most African Americans are still more comfortable in traditional black churches. But the fact that their ranks in Mormonism have grown to thousands raises questions about what they see in a church that previously excluded them from full participation. This is a question not only for Mormons but for the sociology of religion as well. What changes are taking place in the black community that allow some black members to leave their traditional churches and join another church with such strong ties that it has been called an ethnic group?[1] How are blacks accepted, and how do they adapt to new religious teachings?

These questions are not easy to answer. First, it is impossible to find out exactly how many African Americans belong to the LDS church. Membership records do not mention race. But for those who are identifiable, how are they doing in what one historian has called the American *"Reader's Digest"* church,[2] and how willing are they to share their experiences?

The LDS church is growing outside the United States, most notably in Latin America. It has also grown in Africa, where missionary work was not started until after the 1978 revelation. In areas such as Africa where the majority is black, the number of black members is much easier to determine. This book could study the remarkable growth among blacks throughout the world, yet the experiences of blacks in Africa would be much different than those in the United States, the Caribbean, or Brazil.

This book could also discuss the whys and hows of priesthood restriction. Several important studies have already asked that ques-

---

1. Sociologists Armand L. Mauss and Keith Parry discuss the concept of Mormonism as an ethnic group. See Mauss, "Mormons as Ethnics: Variable Historical and International Implications of an Appealing Concept," and Parry, "Mormons as Ethnics: A Canadian Perspective," in B. Y. Card et al., *The Mormon Presence in Canada* (Logan, UT: Utah State University Press, 1990).

2. Jan Shipps, in Martin E. Marty, "The Protestant Experience and Perspective," *American Religious Values and the Future of America* (Philadelphia: Fortress Press, 1978), 40-41.

tion.[3] Instead this study is based on oral history interviews and a mail survey conducted with LDS African Americans. The underlying message of this book is that these black Mormons, though sharing a common ethnic group background, are separate individuals joining a religious movement. While they share some common experiences, each man and woman is unique.

This book could have been written as a faith-promoting study along the lines of Hartman and Connie Rector's *No More Strangers* (1971-90), and argue, "Look at how well blacks have been accepted into the church." Or it could come to the opposite conclusion: "Look at how blacks have been discriminated against." In this book there are elements of both because blacks have had mixed experiences. Many blacks feel that they are accepted by their white Latter-day Saint counterparts, but not necessarily understood or valued for their cultural differences. Some want more association with other LDS blacks; others want to blend in with the mainstream. I use historical and sociological theories to try to better understand these conflicting experiences. In the end there may be more questions than answers, but I try to provide insight into the experiences of African-American Mormons.

This study is based on two data sets: the LDS Afro-American Oral History Project interviews and the LDS Afro-American Survey responses. In 1985 Alan Cherry, a black Latter-day Saint, suggested that the Charles Redd Center for Western Studies at Brigham Young University conduct oral history interviews with LDS Afro-Americans. The Redd Center agreed and hired Cherry as a consultant. He interviewed a total of 224 black Latter-day Saints.

The interviews were valuable, but they revealed the need for a sample with more focused questions. Therefore, the Redd Center sent a mail survey to black Latter-day Saints throughout the United States. Approximately 200 people returned the survey. This book is a "group

---

3. See Newell G. Bringhurst, *Saints, Slaves, and Blacks: The Changing Place of Blacks Within Mormonism* (Westport, CT: Greenwood Press, 1981); and Lester E. Bush and Armand L. Mauss, eds., *Neither White Nor Black: Mormon Scholars Confront the Race Issue in a Universal Church* (Salt Lake City: Signature Books, 1984).

biography" of those who participated in the oral history project and the survey.

The perception of the Mormon church has been changing since the 1950s. It is generally no longer considered a "cult." But it has not completely broken out of its western American model, and blacks are not completely integrated. Consequently the story of African American Mormons is not without problems. Yet despite the dilemmas, most black Latter-day Saints look beyond the past to the role they can play in the church. The LDS African American experience is one of integration and discrimination, yet it promises hope for assimilation as black and white Mormons replace stereotypes with individual faces.

1.

BLACK CHURCHES IN AMERICA

Understanding African American Mormons requires an understanding of the broader history of black churches in the United States. Blacks organized the first separate congregations during the late eighteenth century. These churches remained separate for a century until the 1960s civil rights movement made religious discrimination an issue.

AMERICAN RELIGION IN CONTEXT

During the colonial and federalist periods, the American landscape seemed vast enough for a multitude of religious dreams alongside the many political and social scenarios. Although settlers colonized Virginia, Florida, Louisiana, and New Mexico primarily for economic reasons, New England immigrants sought religious freedom, a benefit Pilgrims denied later arrivals. Some of these, including Roger Williams, went west to form new colonies. Eventually Catholics of all nationalities, many Protestants, and groups of Jews from throughout Europe flocked to the New World and established communities. Each set of immigrants brought its own culture, and religious participation was an important part of ethnic identity. New American denominations and adaptations of European denominations increased the variety. Martin E. Marty, a historian specializing in religions, refers to the "bewildering pluralism" of American belief.[1]

---

1. Martin E. Marty, *A Nation of Behavers* (Chicago: University of Chicago Press, 1976), 18.

Throughout the eighteenth and nineteenth centuries evangelical churches kept Americans on the "strait and narrow" with series of revivals. Despite unremitting laments from orthodox leaders that religion was dying, visitors to the United States saw religion as an important part of American vitality. In 1820 Alexis de Tocqueville wrote, "There is no country in this world where the Christian religion retains a greater influence over the souls of men than in America."[2] Organized religion in America underlaid many educational and civic improvements and cultural events from the seventeenth century to the present.

Many groups proselyted, even among believing neighbors, but they paid special attention to "savage" native Americans and "heathen" Africans. How best to deal with blacks led to differences. In 1844 Methodist-Episcopal churches split over the issue of slavery; the next year the same question forced a division in the Baptist church. Though the Civil War ended slavery, the churches did not reunite.[3]

Based on models from other countries, one might predict that urbanization and industrialization would contribute to a decline in church participation,[4] but that did not happen in the United States. Theological distinctions faded until sociologist Max Weber observed in 1904, "The kind of denomination in American religion is rather irrelevant."[5] Marty commented, "What was remarkable about the scene in 1904 is that, while erosion of denominational separateness declined, denominations themselves survived, proliferated, and often prospered when secularization was supposed to be doing its undercutting."[6]

Religion retained importance and sometimes prickly boundary-guarding through such twentieth-century challenges as organic evolution, World War I, prohibition, the economic depression of the 1930s,

---

2. In Jackson W. Carroll, Douglas W. Johnson, and Martin E. Marty, *Religion in America, 1950 to the Present* (San Francisco: Harper and Row, 1979), 3.

3. C. Eric Lincoln and Lawrence H. Mamiya, *The Black Church in the African American Experience* (Durham, NC: Duke University Press, 1990), 60, 25.

4. Martin E. Marty, *Modern American Religion, Volume 1: The Irony of It All, 1893-1991* (Chicago: University of Chicago Press, 1986), 151.

5. In ibid., 156.

6. Ibid.

and World War II. During the post-war prosperity and the zeal of the Cold War of the 1950s, religious faith again surged. As historian Sydney E. Ahlstrom put it, "During the [Dwight] Eisenhower years [evangelists such as Norman Vincent Peale and Billy Graham] could link hands, as it were, and preside over an Indian summer of confident living and renewed religious interest. . . . Beneath the affluence and the abundant piety, however, a vast range of unresolved issues remained."[7]

During the 1960s old ways were challenged,[8] and traditional denominations were hit especially hard. According to Marty, "Mainline churches . . . suffer in times of cultural crisis and disintegration." He continued, "They receive blame for what goes wrong in society [and] are bypassed when people look for new ways to achieve social identity and location." In short, mainline churches looked as bad in the 1970s as they had looked good in the 1950s.[9]

AFRICAN AMERICAN CHURCHES

The founding of black churches occupies a peculiar niche in American religious history. Partially because of their desire to share the message of Jesus, northerners and southerners agreed that African slaves needed to be converted to Christianity. In addition, Christianity bred docility by promising a better afterlife and encouraging acceptance of their current existence. But where and how blacks should worship also concerned whites. Owners encouraged slaves to hold services on plantations under their personal supervision, using "orthodox" Christian forms of worship. However, slaves often met in secret, combining Christianity with native religion.

When a significant number of blacks were freed in the North in the 1780s, they sought churches where they could continue to worship Jesus but found they were not welcome in white churches. As a result they organized their own. The first became known as the African

---

7. Sydney E. Ahlstrom, *A Religious History of the American People* (New Haven, CT: Yale University Press, 1972), 1988.

8. See Wade Clark Roof and William McKinney, *American Mainline Religion: Its Changing Shape and Future* (New Brunswick, NJ: Rutgers University Press, 1987), 11.

9. In ibid., 22.

Methodist Episcopal (AME) church. Richard Allen, a freed black, joined the Methodist church in Delaware around 1780 and preached as a "licensed exhorter" in New Jersey and Pennsylvania. He arrived in Philadelphia in 1786 and attempted to establish a separate meeting place for blacks, but white Methodists objected.[10] Instead African Americans attended services at St. George Methodist Episcopal church with whites until, in Allen's words, "the colored people began to get numerous." Then the whites moved the blacks "from the seats [they] usually sat on, and placed [them] around the wall."

One Sunday in 1787 a black attempted to kneel during prayer in one of the galleries, and whites objected. A confrontation developed, and the conflict was resolved when the blacks "all went out of the church in a body, and they [the whites] were no longer plagued with us in the church." Allen no doubt reflected the feelings of many blacks when he bitterly noted that "we had subscribed largely towards finishing St. George's church. . . . Just as the house was made comfortable, we were turned out from enjoying the comforts of worshipping there." As a result, he continued, "We hired a store-room and held worship ourselves. Here we were pursued by threats of being disowned, and read publicly out of meeting if we did continue to worship in the place we had hired; but we believed the Lord would be our friend."[11]

Other churches developed in much the same way, with only reluctant sponsorship or downright hostility from parent congregations. In nearly all cases black Christians initiated these separatist organizations in response to white limitations. African American historians summarized, "The move toward racially separate churches was not a matter of doctrinal disagreement, but a protest against unequal and restrictive treatment."[12]

Initially black congregations shared denominational alliances with whites. For example, black Baptists were affiliated with white Baptist conventions from 1815 to 1880 though they were not accepted as

---

10. Lincoln and Mamiya, *Black Church*, 50-51.

11. Benjamin E. Mays, "The Black Experience and Perspective," in *American Religious Values and the Future of America*, ed. Rodger Van Allen (Philadelphia: Fortress Press, 1978), 117-18.

12. Lincoln and Mamiya, *Black Church*, 25.

equal parishes and usually assigned to the African Baptist Missionary Society.[13] White Alabama Baptists stated that blacks should "stay absolutely in [their] own sphere, and let us manfully, religiously and patriotically maintain our dignity, supremacy and social status in our own sphere."[14] When blacks decided to organize their own American National Baptist Convention, U.S.A., in 1901 to preserve the "integrity of the black church," the Southern Baptist Committee on Missions to the Colored People was "relieved," according to Marty. Southern Baptist bishops were pleased, expecting separation would prevent "needless jealousies and irritating and damaging complications," and the "mention of blacks largely disappeared in white Baptist church convention proceedings."[15] The result was an early "separate but equal" policy.

Several black churches had already formed their own associations prior to the Southern Baptists. After corresponding about mutual concerns, black Methodist Episcopal congregations, including Allen's Philadelphia group, met in 1816 to organize the African Methodist Episcopal church.[16] The African Methodist Episcopal Zion church (AMEZ) began in 1821 as a union of black congregations in New York City. Although these churches refused to join Allen's group and sought a separate identity, they also called themselves AME until 1848 when they added "Zion" to distinguish themselves from the Philadelphia movement.[17] The AME and the AMEZ initially affiliated with Northern Methodist Episcopalians, who had split from a Southern group over slavery in 1844. Some black Methodist Episcopalians stayed with the Southerners, but after the Civil War officials of the Methodist Episcopal South convention told blacks they could remain only on pre-war terms. According to historians, the convention was "unprepared to revise radically its conception of the proper place of

---

13. Ibid., 26.

14. In Marty, *Modern American Religion*, 102.

15. According to Lincoln and Mamiya (28), the American National Baptist Convention, U.S.A., was organized in 1886. It took several years for it to be completely organized. Quote from Marty, *Modern American Religion*, 102-103.

16. Lincoln and Mamiya, *Black Church*, 52.

17. Ibid., 57-58.

blacks" and blacks "would continue in an inferior and subordinate relation."[18] Many black congregations refused to accept this status and looked for another conference affiliation. Both the AME and the AMEZ sent missionaries to the South, resulting in "intense rivalry" and disputes over how to split the property previously held by the Methodist Episcopal South congregations. In 1866 the General Conference of the Methodist Episcopal South agreed to a petition by blacks allowing them to withdraw. The Colored Methodist Episcopal church (CME) was officially organized in 1870; the name was changed to Christian Methodist Episcopal church in 1954.[19]

In contrast to these separatist black churches, the Pentecostal movement was started and led by a black minister, William J. Seymour, who held revivals in Los Angeles between 1906 and 1909. Pentecostals traced their origins to Methodism through a subgroup, the National Camp Meeting Association of the Promotion of Holiness, organized in 1867 and later named the National Holiness Association. It stressed the principle of sanctification, held interdenominational camp meetings, and "sought to purify and preserve the faith believed to have been corrupted by the increasingly middle-class churches."[20] As historians C. Eric Lincoln and Lawrence H. Mamiya point out, "Both Holiness and Pentecostalism gained momentum in reaction to liberal tendencies at the turn of the century expressed in Darwinism, the ecumenical emphasis, and the Social Gospel movement." These "antiliberal" views eventually led to "separatist white denominations."[21] Marty explained that the split took place when Pentecostals "turned respectable"—in other words when it stopped being a radical sect and became a mainline religion. Following the split the black movement continued to grow. The largest black Pentecostal group today is the Church of God in Christ.[22]

THE SOCIAL ROLE OF BLACK CHURCHES

Whatever the denomination, black churches developed a theology

---

18. In ibid., 61.
19. Ibid., 60-63.
20. Ibid., 78-80.
21. Ibid.
22. Marty, *Modern American Religion*, 245-46.

based on social needs. Ministers preached that despite life's trials, the Lord would "deliver" his people from oppression just as he had saved Daniel and the Hebrews.[23] The need for consolation encouraged an emphasis on Jesus as savior, and black churches still look to him for deliverance, salvation, and holiness.[24]

Yet as Lincoln and Mamiya explain, "Past studies have overemphasized the other worldly views of black churches."[25] Their revisionist 1991 work shows how black churches have provided a "prophetic critique" of society and met the social, political, and economic needs of their members.[26] According to sociologists Wade Clark Roof and William McKinney, "Early on, the black church emerged as an important institution, second only to the family, as a symbol and embodiment of racial solidarity and the quest for freedom and justice."[27]

After the 1954 *Brown v. the Board of Education* U.S. Supreme Court decision providing for integrated schools, blacks moved forward aggressively to obtain long-denied civil rights. The movement was, assert Lincoln and Mamiya, "anchored in the Black Church, organized by black ministers and laity, and supported financially by black church members."[28] Historian Benjamin Mays claims that "the Montgomery bus boycott, the Birmingham and Selma marches, the battle against segregation in Albany, Georgia, [and] the non-violent march on Washington in 1963 were mainly the results of black people led by black preachers."[29]

Because black churches have been social, cultural, and political communities as well as religious groups, African Americans have been reluctant to enter white congregations. Doris Marie Wilson, a black

---

23. Mays, "Black Experience," 119.

24. Reverend M. Simmons, "Black Music in White Churches," Gospel Music Workshop of America Convention, 14 Aug. 1991, Salt Lake City; notes in my possession.

25. Lincoln and Mamiya, *Black Church*, 12.

26. Lincoln and Mamiya's chaps. 7-13 discuss the various roles of the black churches in their history.

27. Roof and McKinney, *American Mainline Religion*, 90.

28. Lincoln and Mamiya, *Black Church*, 165.

29. Mays, "Black Experience," 125.

Latter-day Saint from Williamsport, Pennsylvania, belonged to the Bethal AME church before she became a Mormon in 1981. "There is a cultural thing with the black churches," she explained. "If you leave the black church, you are also leaving the culture."[30] Another black Latter-day Saint, Reginald Allen, grew up in Harlem during the 1940s and attended St. Mark's Methodist church, one of the larger black churches in the area. For him church was a place for blacks to learn their "heritage" and to meet "prominent black leaders"[31] who combined political leadership with ministerial responsibilities.

The passage of Civil Rights laws during the 1960s gave blacks greater options in education, housing, and employment. Some had always been part of the middle class, but now more had real access to status. Black religious sociologist E. Franklin Frazier had predicted as early as the 1950s that blacks' upward mobility would take them out of black churches into white ones, at least "partly . . . to confirm their new status."[32] Instead, the 1960s "black is beautiful" movement kept most African Americans in black churches. The new middle class attended "elite" black churches or supported commuter churches, driving from middle-class suburbs to inner-city churches.[33]

Contemporary "black churches are, on the whole, still healthy and vibrant institutions," according to Lincoln and Mamiya. Despite some erosion, "particularly among unchurched underclass black youth and some college educated, middle-class young adults, black churches still remain the central institutional sector in most black communities."[34] Yet increased options resulted in increased diversity, and a split developed between the middle and lower classes and between rural and urban blacks.[35] As Lincoln and Mamiya explain, "The gradual

---

30. Doris Marie Wilson, Oral History, interviewed by Alan Cherry, 1986, 7, LDS Afro-American Oral History Project, Charles Redd Center for Western Studies, Harold B. Lee Library, Brigham Young University, Provo, Utah (hereinafter cited as LDS Afro-American).

31. Reginald Allen, Oral History, interviewed by Alan Cherry, 1986, 18, LDS Afro-American.

32. In Lincoln and Mamiya, *Black Church*, 159.

33. Ibid.

34. Ibid., 382.

35. Ibid., 113, 383-84.

emergence of two fairly distinct black Americas along class lines—of two nations within a nation—has raised a serious challenge to the Black Church." Historically black denominations were composed of the lower middle-class whose pastors "have had a difficult time in attempting to reach the hard-core urban poor, the black underclass." They conclude, "If the traditional Black Church fails in its attempt to include the urban poor, the possibility of a Black Church of the poor may emerge, consisting largely of independent, fundamentalist, and Pentecostal storefront churches."[36]

BLACKS IN WHITE CHURCHES

Some blacks have always belonged to traditionally white churches. Following the Civil War the Northern Methodist Episcopal church sent missionaries to the South, and by 1896 nearly 250,000 blacks had joined.[37] In 1900 they appealed to the national convention for black bishops, but the general conference did not respond. According to Marty, those who remained in the Methodist Episcopal church were essentially assigned to a "world-within-a-world," and were never fully accepted.[38] In 1939 the Methodist Episcopal, Methodist Episcopal South, and Methodist Protestant churches combined to create new divisions based on geography. All blacks, however, were placed in a separate black unit known as Central Jurisdiction. Under this arrangement blacks could elect their own bishops. This separate unit remained until 1966 when the church eliminated Central Jurisdiction. Even then complete integration failed to take place, and as a result, according to Lincoln and Mamiya, "The ambiguity of being neither members in an independent church nor full participants in a truly inclusive church was a factor in the organizing of Black Methodists for Church Renewal in 1968" to push for greater assimilation in the United Methodist church.[39]

Other churches also accepted black members only with strict limits. When northern Presbyterians and Cumberland Presbyterians of the mid-South discussed a merger in 1900, race was an issue.

---

36. Ibid., 384.
37. Ibid., 65.
38. Marty, *Modern American Religion*, 103.
39. Lincoln and Mamiya, *Black Church*, 67.

According to Marty, "Cumberlanders said that the northerners recognized the absolute necessity of a separation of the races in the South." Although a church publication, the *Africo-American Presbyterian*, denounced segregation as having no "just ground . . . in law, morals or Christianity," the Special Committee on the Territorial Limits of Presbyteries adopted a policy that blacks were "inferior to the whites in culture, mental and moral development" and needed "the stronger race for help and guidance."[40]

Catholics were also segregated or limited from full participation.[41] The church ordained few blacks to the priesthood until the 1920s, and those who were installed encountered prejudice and misunderstanding. Some dioceses voted against ordaining "colored" priests. Others, according to Dorothy Liptak's history of Catholic immigrants, simply had "an unwritten policy concerning the preparation of black men for the priesthood." She explains, "Had it not been for the commissioning in the 1920s of the Society of the Divine Word . . . specifically to train blacks for the priesthood (the first black priest trained by the society was ordained in 1934), there might not have been a single opportunity for Afro-Americans to advance ordination within the American Catholic church during the first half of the twentieth century." Black women who joined religious orders were segregated and allowed to work only with blacks.[42]

Some Catholics supported civil rights actions during the 1930s and 1940s. For example, John LaFarge, a Jesuit who worked with black missions in Maryland, became leader of the Federation of Colored Catholics. At first some blacks did not want whites included in the federation because they feared a white take-over. After two years of discussions, the Catholic Interracial Council was launched on 6 June 1934, and by 1959 there were thirty-five affiliates in the North and South.[43]

---

40. Marty, *Modern American Religion*, 104.

41. See Stephen J. Ochs, *Desegregating the Altar: The Josephites and the Struggle for Black Priests, 1871-1960* (Baton Rouge: Louisiana State University Press, 1990).

42. Delore Liptak, *Immigrants and Their Church* (New York: MacMillan Publishing Company, 1989), 174.

43. Ibid., 181-82.

Liptak summarized the history of black Catholics after the Civil War in these terms:

> A golden harvest had been predicted in 1866; a black layman looked with expectation toward what the Church offered his people in the 1890s; and the Federation of Colored Catholics rekindled the hopes of blacks in the period of the 1920s renascence. Yet, even in the mid-twentieth century, all too little seemed to have resulted. . . . Only when American society as a whole was forced to take up the question of racial justice in the 1960s did American Catholics seem to listen more seriously to the concerns of black Catholics.[44]

The Catholic and mainline Protestant experiences are not unique. Smaller denominations did not become entirely integrated until after the civil rights upheaval. The Reorganized Church of Jesus Christ of Latter Day Saints (RLDS), one of several groups that recognize Joseph Smith as their founding prophet, is not atypical. The RLDS church did not adopt a formal policy of priesthood restriction as did the Utah-based Church of Jesus Christ of Latter-day Saints, but its relationship with blacks was characterized by the conflicting ideals of universal brotherhood and *de facto* segregation. Historian Roger D. Launius concluded that the Reorganized church "was largely unwilling to move beyond the bounds of polite American ideas on the race question; it was wedded to the social norm, whatever it happened to be at the time."[45]

Joseph Smith III, president of the RLDS church beginning in 1860, spoke out against slavery and encouraged missionary work to blacks.[46] He presented a revelation to the church's general conference in 1865 in which the Lord stated, "It is expedient in me that you ordain priests unto me, of every race who receive the teachings of my law." But the revelation contained a restrictive clause, "There are some who are chosen instruments to be ministers to their own race."[47]

Throughout the rest of the nineteenth century, the RLDS church struggled with racial issues. While it expressed a commitment to send

44. Ibid., 183.
45. Roger D. Launius, *Invisible Saints: A History of Black Americans in the Reorganized Church* (Independence, MO: Herald Publishing House, 1988), 248.
46. Ibid., 116, 121-22.
47. Ibid., 127.

missionaries to blacks, limited resources, concern about race relations, and a limited black membership led to only "moderate success" among black Americans. The few who did join showed by "their willingness to unite with an unpopular, small, and basically Caucasian church" their willingness to "sacrifice" for what they believed.[48]

In 1866 the RLDS Quorum of Twelve Apostles decided blacks should worship with whites, declaring, "As the Author of Life and Salvation does not discriminate among His rational creatures on account of Color neither does the Church of Jesus Christ of Latter Day Saints."[49] This idealistic policy, however, ran into practical difficulties in a world divided by segregation. In the South RLDS blacks had separate congregations. Joseph Smith III conceded in 1893: "Custom and the natural barriers in the way must have their weight. . . . Any attempt to urge the unrestrained intercourse of all classes, races, and conditions will stir up strife and contention far more dangerous to the welfare and unity of the church, than the principle contended for will justify."[50]

This concession to custom guided RLDS policy through much of the twentieth century. In a 1943 article in the church's *Saints' Herald* magazine, the Presiding Patriarch called for an improved racial policy in the United States but restated the church's views, "If and when we make a real effort to proselyte among colored people we will find it wiser to keep congregations separated according to their color until there comes better general adjustment."[51]

An adjustment came during the Civil Rights movement. A church resolution passed in 1956 after *Brown v. the Board of Education* called for integrated congregations but did not dissolve the already segregated branches.[52] An official declaration in 1963 called for equal rights for blacks but gave no support to the civil rights movement. It downplayed difficulties, stating, "The internal racial problems in our church have been very minor."[53] In 1968 the church passed one

---

48. Ibid., 144-46.
49. In ibid., 148.
50. In ibid., 158-59.
51. Ibid., 199-200.
52. Ibid., 227-28.
53. Ibid., 138.

resolution in support of Martin Luther King and another entitled "Gospel to Racial and Ethnic Groups" which, according to Launius, "affirmed, once again, the traditional position of racial equality."[54]

Since 1970 the RLDS church has continued to re-define racial relationships. The RLDS Black Ministries Coalition, for example, attempted to create networking between black members by publishing a newsletter and sponsoring summer reunions. Church leadership continued to be faced with the problem of separate versus integrated congregations. There are still reasons for some separation to promote leadership and heritage. Yet there is also the desire to allow all Saints to worship together.[55] The RLDS church's dilemma, of course, is not unique. All religious organizations with minority members struggle with the same predicament.

Much has been written about the history of churches in the United States and the roles blacks have played. The civil rights movement of the 1960s was an important watershed which not only gave greater political equality to blacks but also provided an opportunity for all Americans to reexamine their racial feelings. During the 1980s both black and white Americans turned to conservative values. Progressive mainline churches lost members and "marginal" churches grew. In the black community, the greatest growth was in Pentecostal churches. One of the white churches which grew rapidly during this period was the Church of Jesus Christ of Latter-day Saints. Handicapped in dealing with racial problems by a policy that barred black men from priesthood ordination until 1978, it now has a worldwide multi-racial membership and the contemporary challenge of how to assimilate members of different cultures.

---

54. Ibid., 244.
55. Ibid., 259, 263-64.

2.

THE LDS CHURCH AND
AFRICAN AMERICANS

The Church of Jesus Christ of Latter-day Saints was rooted in the religious revivals of the nineteenth century. Many who moved to western New York sought a new spiritual life as well as economic improvement. The Second Great Awakening in 1799-1800 was followed by irregular waves of religious fervor. One surge occurred in the 1820s when various denominations held camp meetings, sent out traveling ministers, and encouraged Americans to return to faith.[1]

Joseph Smith, founder of Mormonism, and his family responded to this pious excitement. Smith's mother, two brothers, and a sister joined the Presbyterian church. Because of the "confusion and strife among the different denominations," Smith later recorded in his history, "it was impossible for a person as young as I was, and so unacquainted with men and things, to come to any certain conclusion who was right and who was wrong." As a result, "I kept myself aloof from all these parties, though I attended their several meetings as often as occasion would permit." He leaned toward joining the Methodist church, which would have brought the religious conflict directly into his home.

To resolve his confusion Smith turned to the Bible, prayed fervently for enlightenment, and, after a series of visions over the next decade, felt authorized to organize a new church—a restoration of

---

1. Leonard J. Arrington and Davis Bitton, *The Mormon Experience: A History of the Latter-day Saints* (New York: Alfred A. Knopf, 1979), 3, 7.

biblical faith. On 6 April 1830 he and a few people who had accepted his revelations organized a church in New York. Since the Book of Mormon, a new scripture Smith had dictated, was considered a history of the American Indians, some of the first missionaries were sent to preach to native Americans.

These missionaries were not successful, but they did interest and baptize a large number of white Americans in Ohio. As a result Smith and many of his followers moved there in 1831. Smith then received a revelation that a New Jerusalem was to be built in Missouri, and church members dutifully moved to that frontier.

Their attempt to live a communal lifestyle and their northern antislavery views led to conflicts with neighbors. Twice they were forced to leave Missouri, once in 1833 and again in 1838-39. The second time they found refuge in Illinois, where they established Nauvoo, "the City Beautiful," on the Mississippi River.

Four years later after a period of intensifying conflicts with neighbors, Joseph and his brother Hyrum were killed. In the ensuing confusion over succession, some Saints elected to follow the Quorum of Twelve, headed by Brigham Young, west. Others stayed in the Midwest and eventually formed other churches, the largest of which is the Reorganized Church of Jesus Christ of Latter Day Saints, headquartered in Independence, Missouri.[2]

Many of the early LDS church's conflicts stemmed from its theological innovations such as polygamy, communalism, and political unity. Mormonism was contemporary with such utopian religious groups as the Oneida community and the Shakers. In comparing these three groups, non-Mormon historian Lawrence Foster noted:

> These movements were either founded or attracted many followers in western New York State—an area similar to California [in the 1980s] as a source and magnet for all manner of religious and social causes.... These three movements were characterized by their unusually intense concern to overcome perceived social disorder, their intellectual and social roots in the Protestant Reformation, initial leadership by charismatic or prophetic figures, and a membership which may not have been significantly different from the generality of Americans of their period.[3]

---

2. For more history of the early LDS church, see ibid.
3. Lawrence Foster, *Religion and Sexuality: The Shakers, the Mormons,*

Rather than a short-lived experiment with an idealized lifestyle, Latter-day Saints adapted their beliefs to mainstream America, and by the early twentieth century, Mormons had abandoned polygamy and political separatism. Their economic communal attempts gave way to the Protestant work ethic. Sociologists Wade Clark Roof and William McKinney described Mormons as having risen from the lowest position on the bottom rank of the "status hierarchy of the denominations" in 1945 to the highest position of the middle rank by 1987.[4]

The church's most rapid growth came after World War II. From 1955 to 1965 it was the fastest growing church in the United States. From 1965 to 1975 it dropped to third behind the Assemblies of God and the Seventh-day Adventist churches.[5] Thus, it followed a pattern typical for the United States. Sociologist Andrew M. Greeley argued that earlier church membership had been determined by the "old lines of class, race, ethnicity, region" and family.[6] As these factors waned, mainline religions' membership dropped while churches that "strongly emphasized local evangelism, maintained a distinctive lifestyle and morality apart from mainstream culture, maintained a unitary set of beliefs, and de-emphasized social action and ecumenism . . . grew."[7]

These characteristics were all true of Mormons.[8] In a 1978 study

and the Oneida Community (Urbana: University of Illinois Press, 1984), v, 228.

4. Wade Clark Roof and William McKinney, *American Mainline Religion: Its Changing Shape and Future* (New Brunswick: Rutgers University Press, 1987), 110. This classification is based on income, education, profession, and social class. Their findings are discussed further in chap. 4.

5. Dean R. Hoge, "A Test of Theories of Denominational Growth and Decline," in *Understanding Church Growth and Decline, 1950-1978*, eds. Dean R. Hoge and David A. Roozen (New York: Pilgrim Press, 1970), 187.

6. Andrew M. Greeley, *Religious Change in America* (Cambridge, MA: Harvard University Press, 1989), 68.

7. Dean R. Hoge and David A. Roozen, "Sociological Conclusions about Church Trends," in Hoge and Roozen, *Understanding Church Growth and Decline*, 323.

8. Hoge, "A Test of Theories," in Hoge and Roozen, *Understanding Church Growth and Decline*, 192.

of seventeen denominations, the LDS church rated first in lack of ecumenism, first in central authority, first in distinctive lifestyle, third in emphasis on evangelism, and third in unwillingness to allow independent beliefs among its members.[9]

ETHNIC GROUPS

By the 1990s the LDS church was no longer a regional church with most members in the western United States. Eighty-one percent lived outside of Utah. The population also shifted away from Euro-Americans. In 1988 and 1989, for example, when a million converts were baptized, 60 percent came from Mexico and Central and South America.[10] Determining ethnic membership for the United States is difficult because like Catholics, the LDS church prides itself on not identifying race or ethnic origins on membership lists. Thus there is no practical way to determine how many Hispanic Americans, Asian Americans, Polynesian Americans, or African Americans are members.[11]

The church's policies toward its ethnic members have cycled over the years. A clear example is the LDS church's views of native Americans.[12] The Book of Mormon contributed to the nineteenth-century discussion about Indian origins and the nature of American identity, declaring native Americans to be descendants of the House of Israel. The Book of Mormon stressed that this continent had been reserved

---

9. Ibid., 185. The Southern Baptist Convention and the Seventh-day Adventist rated higher than Mormons in evangelism. The Seventh-day Adventist and the Lutheran Church-Missouri Synod demanded more rigid belief patterns.

10. "Y Official Tries to Calm Fears," *Deseret News*, 8 Sept. 1991, B-9.

11. According to Carl J. Fisher, an African American Catholic bishop in Los Angeles, "We do not really keep statistics by way of race, and many of the estimates are guess-timates." Interview in *America* 164 (13 Apr. 1991): 417.

12. See David J. Whittaker, "Mormons and Native Americans: A Historical and Bibliographical Introduction," *Dialogue: A Journal of Mormon Thought* 18 (Winter 1985): 33-64. Much of the general information in this section comes from this article.

for a righteous people (including the Pilgrim fathers) and recorded a visit to the ancestors of the native Americans by Jesus Christ.

The Book of Mormon also answered a dilemma facing Anglo-Saxon Protestants. As God-fearing people how should they relate to the native Americans? The Book of Mormon identified contemporary Indians as descendants of a rebellious branch of the family, lazy and violent, whom God cursed with a dark skin. This group, the Lamanites, was contrasted with the record-keeping branch of the family—the peace-loving, urbanized, agricultural Nephites. In the end the Nephites became more wicked, and the Lamanites annihilated them. The Lamanites then broke up into wandering tribes and continued their wicked lifestyle. Thus native Americans constituted a people opposed to and in disfavor with God.

One of the stated purposes of the Book of Mormon was to return the Lamanites to God. Although the first missionaries sent to native Americans were not successful, they demonstrated a philosophical commitment to "redeem" this "chosen" but "fallen" people. Mormons shared the common American view that Indians were savages to be either converted and redeemed or confined to reservations so that Christians could make better use of the land. Mormons had conflicts with Indians on more than one occasion, but they also attempted to convert and "civilize" them by teaching them western farming methods. These efforts were suspended during the later decades of the nineteenth century due to the church's struggle with the federal government's suppression of polygamy.

Native American missionary activities remained in limbo for almost half a century. Then during the 1930s exclusive native American missions were established in the American southwest and Dakotas. In the 1940s Apostle Spencer W. Kimball, later church president, supervised the Southwest Indian Mission. He not only worked closely with members and missionaries there but championed the cause of native Americans among all Mormons. In a 1949 talk, he urged members to care for Indians as the Good Samaritan cared for the wounded man on the road to Jericho. The only way that Euro-Americans could "justify our invasion of these Americas, and our conquest of this promised land," he said, was to care for the original inhabitants.[13]

A project started during this time was the Indian Student Placement Program. Children from reservations boarded with white Mormons and attended public schools. Church-owned Brigham Young University in Provo, Utah, sponsored special academic programs and support services for native Americans during the 1960s and 1970s. In 1975 George P. Lee, a Navajo, was called to be the first native American general authority. The time seemed ripe for Mormons to become the "nursing fathers and nursing mothers" prophecied by the Book of Mormon (2 Ne. 6:7).

Instead church emphasis on Lamanites dropped sharply during the 1980s. In 1989 Lee was excommunicated for "apostasy." Afterwards he distributed two letters to the First Presidency and Quorum of Twelve complaining about the lack of attention native Americans received in the church and the unjust treatment he had received as a general authority. Lee felt that the church was neglecting its Book-of-Mormon-mandated responsibilities.[14] He did not recognize other reasons for this deemphasis, including mounting resistance to the Placement Program from the American Indian Movement, improved educational and social service programs on reservations, and a dramatic surge in baptisms in Third World countries.[15]

Church policies toward other ethnic groups varied over the years. Like Catholics, Mormons went through cycles in their attempts to serve the needs of its ethnic members. Historian Jay Dolan explained that Catholic immigrants to the United States dealt with cultural differences by establishing ethnic-based parishes "to preserve the religious life of the old country." The local parish served a variety of purposes: "For some it was a reference point, a place that helped them to remember who they were in their adopted homeland. . . . It helped them cope with life in the emerging metropolis or the small town."[16]

During the twentieth century the Catholic church put greater

---

13. *Report of the Semi-Annual Conference of the Church of Jesus Christ of Latter-day Saints, April 1949* (Salt Lake City: Church of Jesus Christ of Latter-day Saints, 1949), 106.

14. See "Press Coverage of Lee's Excommunication Ambivalent," *Sunstone* 13 (Aug. 1989): 47-51.

15. Jessie L. Embry, "Reactions of LDS Native Americans to the Excommunication of George P. Lee," copy in my possession.

16. Jay P. Dolan, *The American Catholic Experience: A History from Colonial Times to the Present* (Garden City, NY: Doubleday and Company, 1985), 164, 207-208, 197.

emphasis on integration. Dolan explained that separate parishes "reinforced the ethnic differences of the people and enabled neighbors to build cultural barriers among themselves."[17] In 1980 the National Catholic Council of Bishops "urge[d] all Americans to accept the fact of religious and cultural pluralism not as a historic oddity or a sentimental journey into the past but a vital, fruitful and challenging phenomenon of our society." Rather than separate ethnic parishes, churches "that serve more than one nationality" were encouraged. Segregated parishes "were ill-conceived [and] were based on mistaken perceptions of cultural affinities." These new "dual purpose parish centers (based upon the notion that religion will bind the ethnically diverse newcomers)" were to "have the advantage of shared resources" and eliminate the "logistical problem for church authorities" of parishes with different languages and cultures.[18]

Mormon approaches to ethnicity varied from segregated congregations with some Euro-American leadership to full integration into the mainstream with and without translation support. In the 1960s, for example, Apostle Kimball actively organized Indian congregations (generally called Lamanite branches) and other ethnic groups, including a Chinese branch and a German-speaking ward. But in the early 1970s church leaders once again questioned the utility of separate congregations and urged wards and stakes to integrate ethnic members. However, before the end of the decade a Basic Unit plan again encouraged ethnic branches.[19]

These plans operated from mutually exclusive premises. Both met some of the needs of ethnic members and failed to meet others. Integration into multi-cultural, multi-lingual units was based on the ideal—and idealized—philosophy that gospel unity produces social unity. Paul H. Dunn, a member of the First Quorum of Seventy, articulated this view in 1988 when rededicating a chapel in Oakland: "Do you think when we get to the other side of the veil the Lord is going to care whether you came from Tonga or New Zealand or

---

17. Ibid., 21, 44.

18. Dolores Liptak, *Immigrants and Their Church* (New York: Macmillan, 1989), 191, 192, 202.

19. Jessie L. Embry, "Ethnic Groups in the LDS Church," *Dialogue: A Journal of Mormon Thought* 25 (Winter 1992): 83-84.

Germany or America? . . . No. That's why we call each other brothers and sisters. . . . The color of skin, the culture we represent, the interests we have are all quite secondary to the concept of the great eternal family."[20]

The contrasting philosophy of ethnic independence recognized language handicaps. John H. Groberg, an LDS area president in southern California, explained, "Our prime role . . . is not to teach people English or how to become American. Gospel principles . . . don't vary from language to language. We declare Christ, not English, our mission is not limited to culture."[21] Joyce L. Jones, a Euro-American stake Relief Society president supervising ethnic Relief Society units in Oakland, felt similarly that ethnic groups would "learn better in their own language surrounded by other members who shared the same ethnic/cultural background."[22]

In practice, church policy has vacillated because language and cultural barriers weaken the uniting ties of religion. Whether ethnic Latter-day Saints were Swiss-German immigrants to Logan, Utah, during the early twentieth century, Tongans settling in Oakland, or Navajos on the reservation, they have faced the same isolating barriers. The difference, however, is that Swiss-Germans were integrated in one generation; other ethnic groups were not.

THE PRIESTHOOD BAN

Mormons experienced a more fundamental problem in dealing with blacks—whether they were black Americans, black Brazilians, or black Africans. Whether blacks should be integrated into the regular wards and branches was almost a mute issue because there were few black members. This stemmed from the policy that until 1978 barred black men from the lay priesthood. After Joseph Smith's death a policy developed which prevented black men from holding certain church positions open to men of all other races. Black men and women were also excluded from receiving temple ordinances.

Like most Northerners, early Latter-day Saints opposed slavery. But like nearly all Euro-Americans, they believed that blacks were

---

20. Ibid, 84.
21. Giles H. Florence, Jr., "City of Angels," *Ensign* 22 (Sept. 1992): 36.
22. Embry, "Ethnic Groups," 84-45.

mentally and morally inferior. At least two black men, Elijah Abel and Walker Lewis, were ordained during Joseph Smith's lifetime. Religious discrimination can nonetheless be traced to Smith's early statements. In 1841 he said that biblical Ham had been cursed with a dark skin by his father Noah and that this curse continued to the "posterity of Canaan." The next year he identified "negroes" as "sons of Cain." In May 1844 just before his death, he declared, "Africa, from the curse of God has lost the use of her limbs."[23] Such rhetoric was not unique to Mormons. Southerners also linked blacks with Ham and Canaan as did Northerners who argued against abolition.[24]

After Smith's death in 1844, Mormon opinions about blacks became more prejudiced. A church newspaper, the *Times and Seasons,* reiterated Smith's statement in 1845 that blacks were "the descendants of Ham." Apostle Orson Hyde subsequently wrote that blacks "did not take an active part on either side" in a pre-earth life conflict between Satan and a pre-mortal Jesus. Anglo spirits, according to Hyde, supported Jesus, while those who sided with Satan were denied an earth existence. By the time Mormons had reached Winter Quarters, Nebraska, on their way west, Apostle Parley P. Pratt could declare that William McCary, a self-proclaimed prophet, had "the blood of Ham in him which linege [sic] was cursed as regard [to] the priesthood."[25]

These 1840s statements shaped Mormon views. No blacks were ordained after that period although previous ordinations were not rescinded. Although Elijah Abel was a faithful member the rest of his life, he was not allowed to receive temple blessings. Jane Manning James, a black woman who joined the church, moved to Nauvoo, and then traveled to Utah, also petitioned leaders to receive her temple endowment but was denied.[26]

Over the years Mormons continued to reinforce priesthood denial by attributing apocryphal statements to Joseph Smith. In 1879 Abraham O. Smoot, a former Southerner who served a mission there,

---

23. In Newell G. Bringhurst, *Saints, Slaves, and Blacks: The Changing Place of Black People Within Mormonism* (Westport, CT: Greenwood Press, 1981), 86.

24. Ibid., 43.

25. Ibid., 87.

26. Ibid., 147-48.

claimed that Joseph Smith had told him in 1843 "what should be done with the Negro in the South, as I was preaching to them. He said I could baptise them by consent of their masters, but not to confer the priesthood upon them."[27]

In 1887 Apostle George Q. Cannon asserted that "the Prophet Joseph Smith taught this doctrine: That the seed of Cain could not receive the priesthood nor act in any of the offices of the priesthood." In 1904 Joseph F. Smith, then church president, assumed the policy had come from Joseph Smith and, four years later, claimed that Abel's priesthood "ordination was declared null and void by the Prophet himself" because of his "blackness."[28] In fact, Abel had participated in the Third Quorum of Seventies up until 1883. Joseph F. Smith himself had even ordained Abel to go on a mission in 1884, a mission Abel was unable to complete because of illness.[29]

The First Presidency did not issue an official public statement of priesthood denial until 1949: "The attitude of the church with reference to the Negroes remains as it has always stood. It is not a matter of the declaration of a policy but of direct commandment from the Lord on which is founded the doctrine of the Church from the days of its organization, to the effect that Negroes may become members of the Church but that they are not entitled to the priesthood at the present time."[30] The statement was a reaction to the growing number of blacks moving to Utah during World War II.

In 1963 the First Presidency tried with limited success to separate priesthood exclusion from the Civil Rights movement. In an official statement, they said: "During recent months, both in Salt Lake City and across the nation, considerable interest has been expressed in the position of the Church of Jesus Christ of Latter-day Saints on the matter of civil rights. We would like it to be known that there is in this Church no doctrine, belief, or practice that is intended to deny the

---

27. Ibid., 144-46 (quote on 146).

28. Ibid., 149.

29. Newell G. Bringhurst, "Elijah Abel and the Changing Status of Blacks Within Mormonism," *Neither White nor Black: Mormon Scholars Confront the Race Issue in a Universal Church*, eds. Lester E. Bush, Jr., and Armand L. Mauss (Midvale, UT: Signature Books, 1984), 138.

30. Bringhurst, *Saints, Slaves, and Blacks*, 230.

enjoyment of full civil rights by any person regardless of race, color, or creed."[31] Church observers generally agree that this statement was made because the NAACP had threatened to picket Temple Square. The statement, a concession that prevented such action, continued by affirming equal opportunities in housing, education, and employment while still maintaining the right of the church to deny priesthood.

Just a few weeks after this statement was issued, Joseph Fielding Smith, the son of Joseph F. Smith and later church president, told *Look* magazine, "'Darkies' are wonderful people and they have their place in our church." The next year he stated that "the Lord" established priesthood denial.[32]

In 1965 the NAACP, noting that the church-owned *Deseret News* had not endorsed a state civil rights bill, threatened to picket the church's administration building. The newspaper responded by confirming the 1963 church statement, and the state legislature passed the public accommodations and fair employment acts.[33] Yet not all church leaders supported civil rights. Ezra Taft Benson, then an apostle and later church president, claimed that the movement was "fomented almost entirely by the communists."[34]

As the Civil Rights movement made gains nationwide, Mormonism's exclusionary policy came under repeated attack. In addition to NAACP action, universities refused to play Brigham Young University in athletic events. Black members of the New York City Planning Commission threatened to block construction of a Mormon-owned building near the Lincoln Center. The NAACP filed a suit against the Boy Scouts of America because a black could not be a scout leader in Mormon patrols. The Mormon Tabernacle Choir canceled an engagement in New England because black clergy opposed its appearance.[35]

Coupled with national pressure came growing dissent from within the church. Lowry Nelson, a Mormon sociologist, wrote to the church's leadership in 1947 protesting the exclusionary policy. In 1952 he announced his public opposition in *Nation*. Sterling McMurrin, a

31. Ibid., 231.
32. Ibid., 171.
33. Ibid., 181.
34. Ibid., 169.
35. Ibid.

philosophy professor at the University of Utah, also corresponded with LDS church leaders and spoke against the Mormon view of blacks during the 1960s.[36]

In 1969 the counselors of then incapacitated church President David O. McKay signed a statement confirming priesthood denial but omitting references to Cain and Ham and to a premortal life. "From the beginning of this dispensation," the statement read, "Joseph Smith and all succeeding presidents of the Church have taught that Negroes, while spirit children of a common Father, and the progeny of our earthly parents Adam and Eve, were not yet to receive the priesthood, for reasons which we believe are known to God, but which He has not made fully known to men."[37] This concession was insufficient. LDS historians and sociologists tracing the roots of the policy could find no historical evidence that it was based on revelation.[38]

At the same time some Mormon activists tried unsuccessfully to force the issue. Douglas A. Wallace, a Vancouver, Washington, attorney, baptized and ordained a black, Larry Lester, in 1976. The ordination was declared void and Wallace was excommunicated. In 1977 Bryon Marchant, a Boy Scout leader in Salt Lake City, was excommunicated for voting against Spencer W. Kimball as church president at general conference in protest of the church's racial policies.[39] Other members lobbied church leaders in other ways.[40] Still the church held firm, enduring bad publicity and refusing to engage in debate.

By 1978 most protests had died down. Doubtless many Mormons experienced increased social, educational, and professional contacts with blacks as a result of the Civil Rights movement. They sensed that the nation had moved to a new place and felt the gap between the

---

36. Ibid., 183-84.

37. Ibid., 233.

38. The articles in Bush and Mauss, *Neither White Nor Black*, are examples of these scholarly studies that were published during the 1960s and 1970s.

39. Bringhurst, *Saints, Slaves, and Blacks*, 185-86.

40. There is a small file of letters in archives, historical department, Church of Jesus Christ of Latter-day Saints, Salt Lake City, Utah, which were written to members about the priesthood policy.

nation's and church's positions. However, few if any expected the policy to change soon, which may explain the shock that accompanied the First Presidency's 9 June 1978 declaration:

> As we have witnessed the expansion of the work of the Lord over the earth, we have been grateful that people of many nations have responded to the message of the restored gospel, and have joined the Church in ever-increasing numbers. This, in turn, has inspired us with a desire to extend to every worthy member of the Church all of the privileges and blessings which the gospel affords.
>
> Aware of the promises made by the prophets and presidents of the Church who have preceded us that at some time, in God's eternal plan, all of our brethren who are worthy may receive the priesthood, and witnessing the faithfulness of those from whom the priesthood has been withheld, we have pleaded long and earnestly in behalf of these, our faithful brethren, spending many hours in the Upper Room of the Temple supplicating the Lord for divine guidance.
>
> He has heard our prayers, and by revelation has confirmed that the long-promised day has come when every faithful, worthy man in the Church may receive the holy priesthood, with power to exercise its divine authority, and enjoy with his loved ones every blessing that flows therefrom, including the blessings of the temple. Accordingly, all worthy members of the Church may be ordained to the priesthood without regard for race or color. Priesthood leaders are instructed to follow the policy of carefully interviewing all candidates for ordination to either the Aaronic or the Melchizedek Priesthood to insure that they meet the established standards for worthiness.
>
> We declare with soberness that the Lord has now made known his will for the blessing of all his children throughout the earth who will hearken to the voice of his authorized servants, and prepare themselves to receive every blessing of the gospel.

CAUSES OF THE REVELATION

Most observers agree that foreign trends had more impact on the policy change than external pressure or internal debate. Non-Mormon historian Jan Shipps, writing in *Christian Century*, explained: "The June 9 revelation will never be fully understood if it is regarded simply as a pragmatic doctrinal shift ultimately designed to bring Latter-day Saints into congruence with mainstream America. . . . This revelation came in the context of worldwide evangelism rather than . . . American social and cultural circumstances."[41]

At least two pressure points can be identified. First, since at least 1946 blacks in Nigeria had been asking for missionaries to come to that country and had organized churches using the Book of Mormon.[42] At one point in 1963 missionaries were called, but the Nigerian government refused to admit them after learning of the priesthood restriction. Some general authorities also questioned committing resources to Africa at all. Still, LaMar Williams, an employee of the missionary department, visited the would-be Mormons in Nigeria several times and was impressed with their spirit and eagerness to accept the church, including priesthood restriction.[43]

Second, church membership in Brazil had grown enormously during the 1960s and 1970s. Determining who was black had always been a sensitive issue in the racially mixed country. In 1978 a temple, from which blacks would be excluded, was under construction. Complicating the problem was the perplexity of determining which deceased men were "eligible" (that is, not black) for proxy ordinations to priesthood.[44] (Mormons believe in vicarious proxy baptisms, priesthood ordinations, and marriages for the dead.)

A third important ingredient in the timing of the revelation was the personality of church president Kimball. Long viewed as the "Lamanite apostle," Kimball also supported other ethnic groups. At general conference in April 1954, he commented, "It pleases me greatly to notice that at each succeeding conference there is a larger sprinkling of Japanese and Chinese brothers and sisters; of Hawaiians and other islanders; of Indians, Mexicans, Spanish-Americans, and others." Kimball explained his talk would be "on behalf of those minorities." While most of the talk focused on Native Americans as part of the tribe of Israel, he denounced racial prejudice as "a monster.

41. Jan Shipps, "The Mormons: Looking Forward and Outward," *Christian Century*, 16-23 Aug. 1978, 762.

42. For a complete description of the events leading to missions in West Africa, see James B. Allen, "Would-Be Saints: West Africa before the 1978 Priesthood Revelation," *Journal of Mormon History* 17 (1991): 207-47.

43. Ibid.

44. For more information, see Mark L. Grover, "The Mormon Priesthood Revelation and the Sao Paulo, Brazil Temple," *Dialogue: A Journal of Mormon Thought* 23 (Spring 1990): 39-53.

. . . Often we think ourselves free of its destructive force, [but] we need only to test ourselves. Our expressions, our voice tones, our movements, our thoughts betray us. . . . Until we project ourselves into the very situation, we little realize our bias and our prejudice."[45]

Kimball was well acquainted with black Mormons. For example, when he went to Brazil, he often visited with black members there. Helvecio Martins, who became a general authority in 1990, was present at the cornerstone laying for the Brazilian temple in 1977. Kimball called him to the podium, embraced him, and told him, "Brother, what is necessary for you is faithfulness. Remain faithful and you will enjoy all the blessings of the Church."[46] According to Edward L. Kimball, "My father always had a personal feeling for minorities, deprived people."[47]

President Kimball's own discussion of the announcement focused on human needs of church members. Speaking to missionaries in South Africa in October 1978, he confided:

> I remember very vividly that day after day I walked to the temple and ascended to the fourth floor where we have our solemn assemblies and . . . our meetings of the Twelve and the First Presidency. After everybody had gone out of the temple, I knelt and prayed. I prayed with much fervency. I knew that something was before us that was extremely important to many of the children of God. I knew that we could receive the revelations of Lord only by being worthy and ready for them and ready to accept them and put them into place. Day after day I went alone and with great solemnity and seriousness in the upper rooms of the temple, and there I offered my soul and offered my efforts to go forward with the program.[48]

During one of the sessions at the dedication of the Brazilian temple, Kimball mentioned his extended pleadings in prayer. He said that the policy of priesthood exclusion was one he had always de-

---

45. Spencer W. Kimball, "The Evil of Intolerance," *Improvement Era* 57 (June 1954): 423-24.

46. In Grover, "Mormon Priesthood Revelation," 48.

47. "All Worthy Males," KBYU-TV Special, 9 June 1988, video in my possession.

48. Edward L. Kimball, ed., *The Teachings of Spencer W. Kimball* (Salt Lake City: Bookcraft, 1982), 450-51.

fended and supported. He pledged to the Lord that he would continue to support it but sought to know "if there was any way at this time that the destiny of [black] people in the Church could be changed." It was after that long petitionary process that he received the answer.

Other general authorities were touched by the plight of Brazilian members. During Kimball's prayer dedicating the Brazilian temple, Gordon B. Hinckley, Kimball's first counselor, wept and during his address spoke tenderly about the revelation. He said the First Presidency had been aware that black members in Brazil had given financial support to the temple, never expecting to enter the building themselves.[49]

Apostle James E. Faust, who supervised church activities in Brazil, recalled in an oral history interview how black members had worked alongside whites to construct the temple. He told the First Presidency that black members helped "to make blocks for the temple just like anybody else." He remembered that church leaders had discussed the priesthood revelation prior to its public announcement.[50]

Apostle Bruce R. McConkie provided the most detail. Speaking to a group of Church Educational System employees, he set the scene as the first Thursday in June, a day when the First Presidency and apostles regularly met in the Salt Lake temple. Except for those ill or out of town, everyone was present. They had come fasting, which was also customary, and after a three-hour meeting also attended by the Seventies, the Twelve and the First Presidency remained in session. McConkie recalled: "When we were . . . by ourselves in that sacred place where we meet weekly . . . , President Kimball brought up the matter of the possible conferral of the priesthood upon those of all races. That was a subject that the group of us had discussed at length on numerous occasions in the preceding weeks and months."

Kimball told about his prayers. McConkie continued: "He said that if the answer was to continue our present course of denying the priesthood to the seed of Cain, as the Lord had theretofore directed, he was prepared to defend that decision to the death. But, he said, if the long sought day had come in which the curse of the past was to be removed, he thought we might prevail upon the Lord so to indicate."

---

49. Grover, "Mormon Priesthood Revelation," 50-51.
50. Ibid., 47, 49.

Kimball then asked for comments, and McConkie recalled those present "all [responded] freely. . . . There was a marvelous outpouring of unity, oneness, and agreement in the council."

After two more hours Kimball asked if they could have a formal prayer and if he could be the voice. McConkie continued, "It was during this prayer that the revelation came. The Spirit of the Lord rested mightily upon us all; we felt something akin to what happened on the day of Pentecost and at the dedication of the Kirtland Temple." The message was that the priesthood was to go to all, regardless of color or race, "solely on the basis of personal worthiness. And we all heard the same voice, received the same message, and became personal witnesses that the word received was the mind and will and voice of the Lord."[51]

Ten years after the revelation, Elder Hinckley spoke at a "fireside" sermon for teenage boys. Looking back ten years he recalled his feelings during that "remarkable" experience and clarified the sequence. The meeting described by McConkie had occurred a week before the revelation was announced on 1 June 1978. On the first Thursday of each month, the general authorities gather for a testimony meeting. After the Seventies left, President Kimball offered a prayer. Hinckley did not recall the exact words but said he felt the heavens open. "The spirit of God was there, and by the power of the Holy Ghost" he was assured that all men should receive the priesthood. There were no rushing winds, "but there was a pentecostal experience because the Holy Ghost was present." A week later on 8 June 1978, the announcement was made to the Seventies and other general authorities. A statement was issued to the press on 9 June 1978. Hinckley added, "Gone now was every element of discrimination; extended was every power of the priesthood of God."[52]

Heber Wolsey, director of the LDS Public Communications Department, was assigned to make the dramatic announcement that stopped presses across the nation. *Time* magazine initially planned to run the news as its cover story.[53] There was a rush to collect the

---

51. Bruce R. McConkie, "The New Revelation on Priesthood," *Priesthood* (Salt Lake City: Deseret Book Co., 1981), 126-28.

52. Gordon B. Hinckley, Aaronic Priesthood Restoration Fireside, 15 May 1978, video in my possession.

reactions of black Mormons, scholars of Mormonism, leaders of other religious groups, and black leaders.

Most of the responses were positive. Jimmy Carter, then president of the United States, wrote President Kimball, "I welcome today your announcement. . . . I commend you for your compassionate prayer-fulness and courage in receiving a new doctrine. This announcement brings a healing spirit to the world and reminds all men and women that they are truly brothers and sisters."[54] Sterling McMurrin called "it the most important day for the church of the century."[55]

When one non-Mormon ecclesiastical leader called it simply an internal matter, the non-Mormon newspaper, *The Salt Lake Tribune*, editorialized: "If Salt Lake City and Utah were not so closely identified with the LDS church and all Utahns not in some way affected by its policies, this significant action could be called a strictly Mormon matter. But it is much more than that. In a very real way a burden has been lifted from all Utahns, whether members of the LDS faith or of other beliefs."[56] The *Church News*, a weekly tabloid insert in the church-owned *Deseret News*, carried a story entitled "Priesthood News Evokes Joy" in its 17 June 1978 edition that included reactions from black members.[57]

The excitement continued as ordinations immediately began. Joseph Freeman, Jr., who lived in Salt Lake City at the time, reportedly the first black elder ordained, was interviewed repeatedly. Robert Lang, who joined the church in 1970 after talking to a Mormon store owner, recalled that, besides calls from friends, "someone from the Salt Lake newspaper called to interview me. . . . The following weekend Channel Two [in Los Angeles] called and wanted to interview me and

---

53. "All Worthy Males."

54. "Carter Praises LDS Church Action," *Deseret News*, 10 June 1978, A-1.

55. Ibid., A-3.

56. "A Burden is Lifted," editorial, *Salt Lake Tribune*, 11 June 1978.

57. *Church News*, 17 June 1978, 3-4. Since then the *Church News* has occasionally carried articles about black members, focusing more on conversion stories and positive service than on their experiences as blacks per se or possible problems. Most articles have focused on international rather than American blacks. Newell Bringhurst has kept a clipping file of such articles, which he kindly loaned me.

my wife down in front of the temple."[58] Lang later became president of the Southwest Los Angeles Branch in the Watts area.

Ironically, Douglas Wallace called the development "a revelation of convenience" like the 1890 manifesto banning polygamy. He thought the change would have "very little impact unless the church begins to work among minorities,"[59] which it did in fact.

ATTITUDES TOWARD EQUALITY

What had been Mormon attitudes towards blacks, and did those views change with the policy? The Salt Lake branch of the NAACP issued a statement of mingled congratulation and reproof in response to the announcement: "We have been of the opinion for many years that your prior practice of exclusion of blacks from progression . . . has extended into secular affairs and has done much to sustain discrimination in areas of employment, education, and cultural affairs."[60] It is difficult to prove or disprove this statement. It is true that Marian Anderson was not allowed to stay at the church-owned Hotel Utah when she toured Utah in concert during World War II.[61] Marion D. Hanks, retired from the First Quorum of Seventies, recalled that after World War II blacks from the Phoenix College in Arizona stayed at his mother's because they could not find other lodgings when their group performed in Salt Lake City.[62] Anecdotal reports of blacks begin discriminated against at Brigham Young University and at Utah State University in Logan, Utah, occasionally still surface.

These experiences are not unique to Mormons. Mirroring national attitudes, most Mormons held pro-Civil Rights views. Using material gathered by Charles Y. Glock and Rodney Stark, Mormon sociologist Armand L. Mauss argued as early as 1966 that Mormons'

58. Robert Lang Oral History, interviewed by Alan Cherry, 21 Oct. 1985, 4, LDS Afro-American Oral History Project, Charles Redd Center for Western Studies, Archives and Manuscripts, Harold B. Lee Library, Brigham Young University, Provo, Utah (hereafter LDS Afro-American).

59. "Carter Praises LDS Church Action," A-1.

60. Ibid., A-3.

61. Bringhurst, *Saints, Slaves, and Blacks*, 168.

62. Marion D. Hanks Oral History, 5, interviewed by Jessie L. Embry, 1989, LDS Afro-American.

"secular attitudes towards Negroes" were similar to those of the nation as a whole. Using three LDS congregations in northern California, Mauss found "no systematic differences in secular race attitudes . . . between Mormons and others." The differences he did find were related more to education, occupation, and rural/urban settings than Mormon orthodoxy.[63] Over two decades later Roof and McKinney reached a similar conclusion. Mormons as a group were slightly more willing to accept minority rights than national averages and were considerably more willing to do so than white fundamentalist/pentecostal churches.[64]

An important exemplar of changing attitudes was Apostle McConkie, who had become a prolific theologian. His 1966 *Mormon Doctrine*, used by some members as a dictionary of theology, contained the following justifications for the black exclusion policy: "Those who were less valiant in pre-existence and who thereby had certain spiritual restrictions imposed upon them are known to us as the negroes. Such spirits are sent to earth through the lineage of Cain." He went on: "Negroes in this life are denied the priesthood; under no circumstances can they hold this delegation of authority from the Almighty."[65] Two months after the announcement, he declared to a group of church-employed teachers:

> There are statements in our literature by the early brethren which we have interpreted to mean that the Negroes would not receive the priesthood in mortality. I have said the same things. . . . All I can say to that is that it is time disbelieving people repented and got in line and believed in a living, modern prophet. Forget everything that I have said, or what President Brigham Young or President George Q. Cannon or whomsoever has said in days past that is contrary to the present revelation. We spoke with a limited understanding and without the light and knowledge that now has come into the world. We get our truth and our light line upon line and precept upon precept. We have now had added a new flood of intelligence and light on this particular subject, and it erases all the darkness, and all the views and all the thoughts of the past. They don't

---

63. Armand L. Mauss, "Mormonism and Secular Attitudes Toward Negroes," *Pacific Sociological Review* 8 (Fall 1966): 99.

64. Roof and McKinney, *American Mainline Religion*, 199-200.

65. Bruce R. McConkie, *Mormon Doctrine* (Salt Lake City: Bookcraft, 1966), 527.

matter any more. It doesn't make a particle of difference what anybody ever said about the Negro matter before the first day of June of this year [1978]. It is a new day and a new arrangement, and the Lord has now given the revelation that sheds light out into the world on this subject. As to any slivers of light or any particles of darkness of the past, we forget about them. We now do what meridian Israel did when the Lord said the gospel should go to the gentiles. We forget all the statements that limited the gospel to the house of Israel, and we start going to the gentiles.[66]

SUMMARY

The LDS church, which arose at the same time as other nine-teenth-century utopian organizations, survived far beyond the others. As it eliminated polygamy and other practices viewed as un-American, it moved closer to mainstream U.S. churches. Like other religions it has not been sure how to deal with ethnic groups who are not a part of that middle-class upperwardly mobile image. As a consequence policies concerning native Americans, Hispanics, and others have varied over the years, driven simultaneously by Christian feelings and procedural awkwardness. The policy towards blacks was stable during the long period in which they were denied priesthood ordination, an exclusion explained at various extremes as God's curse and a mystery with reasons known only to God. In actuality the Mormon policy was not much different from that of other white churches.

An important and unique barrier for blacks was lifted in 1978 when the First Presidency announced a revelation allowing priesthood for all men regardless of race, and proselyting began among blacks worldwide. Though responses have varied, most of those by Mormons and non-Mormons have generally been positive, even celebratory.

---

66. Bruce R. McConkie, "All Are Alike unto God," an address to a Book of Mormon Symposium for Seminary and Institute teachers, Brigham Young University, 18 Aug. 1978, copy in my possession.

3.

IMPACT OF THE LDS "NEGRO POLICY"

Research on LDS African Americans has often focused on priesthood denial and ignored the limitations other churches have placed on blacks even when they did not have a public policy of overt discrimination. Perhaps a greater omission is the impact on individual LDS African American members before and after 1978. Why were blacks willing to join the Mormon church knowing they could not have all the privileges of other members? How did they view this policy, and what difference did the change in policy make? How do blacks who have joined since 1978 view that historic restriction?

EARLY BLACK LATTER-DAY SAINTS

After the LDS church was organized in 1830, missionaries taught the "restored" gospel to blacks who sought them out and baptized a few. It was impossible then, as it is now, to know how many blacks joined the new church. The only indication comes from a frequently quoted remark by Apostle Parley P. Pratt, "One dozen free negroes or mulattoes never have belonged to our society in any part of the world, from its organization [in 1830] to this date, 1839."[1] Historians have pieced together the histories of a few early black members.

---

1. Quoted in Newell G. Bringhurst, "Elijah Abel and the Changing Status of Blacks Within Mormonism," in *Neither White Nor Black: Mormon Scholars Confront the Race Issue in a Universal Church,* Lester E. Bush, Jr., and Armand L. Mauss, eds. (Midvale, UT: Signature Books, 1984), 132. For more information, see the short biographical information in Kate B. Car-

Elijah Abel

Born in Maryland in 1810, Elijah Abel was baptized into Joseph Smith's church in 1832. He moved to Kirtland, Ohio, to be with the rest of the Saints, and in June 1836 he was ordained an elder, a position in the Melchizedek priesthood. Six months later he became a seventy and received a patriarchal blessing from Joseph Smith, Sr. Rather than declaring Abel to be a descendant of one of the tribes of Israel, as was common practice, Abel was told he was "an orphan." He was promised, "Thou shalt be made equal to thy brethren, and thy soul be white in eternity and thy robes glittering."[2]

Like many early priesthood brethren, Abel worked as a missionary during the late 1830s in New York and Canada. In 1839 he moved from Kirtland to Nauvoo, Illinois, where he performed baptisms for the dead and, according to Abel's accounts, was appointed by Joseph Smith, Jr., to be an undertaker.[3] He worked in Nauvoo as a carpenter until 1842 when he moved to Cincinnati, continuing in the same profession. There he married a black woman, Mary Ann Adams.

During this time Joseph Smith spoke highly of Abel. In 1843 Smith explained, "Go to Cincinnati . . . and find an educated negro (sic), who rides in his carriage, and you will see a man who has risen by the power of his own mind to his exalted state of respectability."[4] Just six months later, however, three apostles, a "Traveling High Council," visited the Cincinnati branch and questioned Abel's high profile as a black Mormon. John E. Page explained that he "respects a coloured Bro" but "wisdom forbids that we should introduce [him] before the public." After some discussion a resolution was adopted which stated that to accommodate the "duty of the 12 [Apostles] . . . to ordain and send men to their native country Bro Abels [sic] was advised to visit the coloured population" of Cincinnati in his missionary work.[5]

---

ter, *The Story of the Negro Pioneer* (Salt Lake City: Daughters of Utah Pioneers, 1965); other articles in *Neither White Nor Black*; and Newell G. Bringhurst, *Saints, Slaves, and Blacks: The Changing Place of Black People Within Mormonism* (Westport, CT: Greenwood Press, 1981).

2. Quoted in Bringhurst, "Elijah Abel," 131.

3. Quoted in ibid., 133.

4. Quoted in ibid., 133.

5. Quoted in ibid., 88.

In 1853 Abel moved to Utah. By the time he arrived, LDS church leaders had already taken steps to prevent blacks from being appointed to the priesthood. However, there were no attempts to take away Abel's priesthood authority. He settled in Millcreek in Salt Lake Valley where he was rebaptized in 1857 during the "Mormon Reformation." He continued to be an active member of the Third Quorum of Seventies. In 1883 Apostle Joseph F. Smith set apart Abel, then in his early seventies, as a missionary to Ohio and Canada. However, Abel became ill and returned to Utah where he died in December 1884.

Abel continued to participate in quorum activities. But when he asked Brigham Young if he could be sealed to his wife and children in the temple, he was denied. A later appeal to Young's successor, John Taylor, was referred to the Council of the Twelve and also denied.[6]

As the church's Negro doctrine developed, Abel's ordination became an embarrassment and caused a debate in the hierarchy. In 1879 Zebedee Coltrin insisted that Abel had been ordained a seventy because he had worked on the Nauvoo temple, but Smith had "dropped [Abel] from the quorum" because of his lineage. Joseph F. Smith denied Coltrin's claim, pointing out that Abel had two certificates listing him as a seventy, one issued in Salt Lake City. Other church leaders such as John Taylor explained that Abel had been given the priesthood, which had later been removed. By 1908 Joseph F. Smith had reversed his 1879 stand, saying that even though Abel had been "ordained a seventy . . . in the days of the Prophet Joseph Smith . . . this ordination was declared null and void by the Prophet himself." In 1920 Andrew Jenson explained in his *Latter-day Saint Biographical Encyclopedia* that an exception had been made in Abel's case and the "general rule of the Church" was against ordaining blacks. In 1955 in a letter to a member of the church, Apostle Joseph Fielding Smith suggested there had been two Elijah Abels—one white and one black. However, just as Smith was trying to "bury the ghost of Elijah Abel,"[7] others were discovering his unique position as a priesthood holder. He remains an obstacle to those who try to trace priesthood denial to Joseph Smith.[8]

---

6. Ibid., 137.

7. Ibid., 139-40.

8. Ibid.

Jane Manning James

A free-born servant, Jane Elizabeth Manning was born in the late 1810s or early 1820s and grew up in Connecticut during the 1820s, earning her living as a domestic. When Mormon missionaries came to the area, she listened and along with other family members joined the church. In 1843 eight members of the Manning family started toward Nauvoo but became separated at Buffalo, New York, when they were refused passage on a boat because they were black. The Mannings set out on foot and, after experiencing illness, threatened imprisonment, and extreme cold, finally arrived in Nauvoo where Joseph Smith welcomed them into his home. Before the Latter-day Saints left Nauvoo, Jane Manning married another black Mormon, Isaac James. James, a native of New Jersey, had converted to Mormonism in 1839 at the age of nineteen and immigrated to Nauvoo. Their first son was born at Winter Quarters in 1846. The couple had six more children in Utah. In 1869 Isaac left the family, selling his property to Jane. He returned to Salt Lake City approximately twenty-one years later just before he passed away. When he died in 1891, Jane held his funeral in her home.

Jane Manning James was a member of the female Relief Society and donated to the St. George, Manti, and Logan temple funds. She repeatedly petitioned the First Presidency to be endowed and to have her children sealed to her. During the time that Isaac was gone, Jane asked to be sealed to Walker Lewis who, like Elijah Abel, had been ordained during Joseph Smith's lifetime.

After Issac died, Jane asked that they be given the ordination of adoption so they would be together in the next life.[9] She explained in correspondence to church leaders that Emma Smith had offered to have her sealed to the Smith family as a child. She reconsidered that decision and asked to be sealed to the Smiths. Permission for all of these requests was denied.

Instead the First Presidency "decided she might be adopted into the family of Joseph Smith as a servant, which was done, a special

---

9. For discussion of the law of adoption, see Gordon Irving, "The Law of Adoption: One Phase of the Development of the Mormon Concept of Salvation, 1830-1900," *Brigham Young University Studies* 14 (Spring 1974): 291-314.

ceremony having been prepared for the purpose." The minutes of the
Council of Twelve Apostles continued, "But Aunt Jane was not satisfied with this, and as a mark of dissatisfaction she applied again after
this for sealing blessings, but of course in vain."[10]

Jane Manning James bore a testimony of Mormonism to the end
of her life: "My faith in the gospel of Jesus Christ, as taught by the
Church of Jesus Christ of Latter-day Saints, is as strong today, nay, it
is if possible stronger than it was the day I was first baptized. I pay my
tithes and offerings, keep the word of wisdom, I go to bed early and
rise early, I try in my feeble way to set a good example to all." When
she died in 1908, church president Joseph F. Smith spoke at her
funeral.[11]

Samuel D. Chambers

Another early black Mormon, Samuel D. Chambers, first heard
about the Mormon church as a thirteen-year-old slave in Mississippi
in 1844. He was baptized secretly and then lost contact with the church
until after the Civil War. "Tho' lacking age and experience yet God
kept the seeds of life alive in me," he reported. As a free man,
Chambers worked as a shoemaker and a sharecropper to save money
to emigrate. When he was thirty-eight years old, he moved with his
wife and teenage son to Utah. Although he could not receive the
priesthood, Chambers assisted deacons in the Salt Lake City 8th Ward,
attended meetings, prayed, and bore testimony in public meetings. In
1873 forty-two-year-old Chambers expressed his feelings about the
LDS church: "I know we are the people of God, we have been led to
these peaceful vallies of the mountains, and we enjoy life and many

---

10. "Excerpts from the Weekly Council Meetings of the Quorum of
Twelve Apostles, Dealing with the Rights of Negroes in the Church, 1849-
1940," George Albert Smith Papers, University of Utah, quoted in Henry J.
Wolfinger, "A Test of Faith: Jane Manning James and the Origins of the
Utah Black Community," 18, Manuscript Collection, Harold B. Lee Library,
Brigham Young University, Provo, Utah. Wolfinger's study was also publish-
ed in *Social Accommodations in Utah* (Salt Lake City: American West Center
occasional papers, University of Utah, 1975).

11. Linda King Newell and Valeen Tippetts Avery, "Jane Manning
James," *Ensign* 9 (Aug. 1979): 26-29.

other blessings. I don't get tired of being with the Latter-day Saints, nor of being one of them. I'm glad that I ever took upon me the name of Christ. . . . I've been blest from youth up, although I was in bondage for 20 years after receiving the gospel, yet I kept the faith. I thank God that I ever gathered with the Saints." Chambers died in 1929 at the age of 98.[12]

Mary Lucile Bankhead

Most early black converts were strengthened by such compelling spiritual experiences that they overlooked prejudice and discrimination. Their children did not always share their parents' enthusiasm. In fact rarely did a second or third generation of African Americans remain in the church. Mary Lucile Perkins Bankhead is an exception. She is a fourth generation descendant of the pioneer blacks who came to Utah. Her ancestors include Green Flake, who drove Brigham Young's wagon into the Salt Lake Valley in 1847, and Jane Manning James. Bankhead recalled having asked to be baptized: "my mother didn't have to tell me." She faithfully attended the Wilford Ward in Salt Lake City, sang duets with her brother for events in the stake house, and states, "We have never been ostracized."[13]

Mary Lucile was courted by Roy Bankhead, whom she married. The Bankheads were from Cache Valley, and according to Mary Lucile, the family "were all Mormons," but Roy and his immediate family were not. The newlyweds settled in Salt Lake City where they raised six sons and two daughters. Mary Lucile recalled that she and the children "would all go to church together every Sunday morning," although none of her children or grandchildren were active Mormons at the time of the priesthood announcement in 1978. Although their decision pained her, she accepted it. "When they get older in their thirties and forties, it is their responsibility, not mine."[14]

---

12. William G. Hartley, "Samuel D. Chambers," *New Era* 4 (June 1974): 47-50 (quote on 48-49).

13. Mary Lucile Bankhead Oral History, 11, interviewed by Alan Cherry, 1985, LDS Afro-American Oral History Project, Charles Redd Center for Western Studies, Harold B. Lee Library, Brigham Young University (hereinafter cited as LDS Afro-American).

14. Ibid., 15, 20.

Mary Lucile talked about the church's stand during the Civil Rights movement of the 1960s. Church leaders "were not doing much speaking out about civil rights. Only a few of them would say that the Lord is no respecter of persons. They would say that once in awhile. I think they were quite slow in giving advice and saying what they felt." She acknowledged racism in Salt Lake City: "I cannot understand why people cannot live and why some of them have to be racist. . . . My blood is just as red as theirs even if my skin is dark. The Lord made us all."[15]

When asked about priesthood restriction, she replied, "I don't know as it affected me. I knew about it, and I knew that they did not want us to have it. But I prayed that they would. I told people in the ward, . . . 'It is coming, and we are going to have it. I do not know what day.'" She continued, "It surely came, but when it came and they called me . . . I did not believe it at first because it had been so long in coming." It took a second phone call to convince her, and she concluded simply, "It is nice. I am glad."[16] However, she recognized that this would not cure racism, explaining for "deep dyed Mormons in the South . . . that have had [racism] dealt in them from childhood . . . it is going to be hard for them to take a black bishop or priest."[17]

BLACK CONVERTS BETWEEN 1900 AND 1960

Elijah Abel, Jane Manning James, and Samuel Chambers are among the best documented black church members between 1840 and about 1900. Stories of other blacks who converted after the pioneer period are more difficult to reconstruct. While the Charles Redd Center was conducting oral history interviews, relatives and acquaintances provided information about deceased members who joined around the turn of the century.

Len Hope, Sr., and Mary Lee Pugh Hope

Len Hope, Sr., was born on 10 October 1892 in Magnolia, Alabama. Accounts vary about how he came in contact with the

---

15. Ibid., 18, 11.
16. Ibid., 17-18.
17. Ibid., 18.

Mormon church, but he was baptized in Alabama on 22 June 1919. After he served in France during World War I and returned to the United States, non-Mormon whites reportedly threatened him unless he removed his name from the records of a "white" church. However, he remained a committed Latter-day Saint. On 25 January 1920 he married Mary Lee Pugh, a woman ten years his junior. She was born 11 October 1902 in Lamison, Alabama. Five years after their marriage, she was baptized on 15 September 1925.[18]

While they were in the South, they were unable to attend church because of resentment of other Latter-day Saints. They eventually moved to Cincinnati, Ohio, with their children (ultimately six) seeking better employment in the industrial North and fewer Jim Crow laws. At first the Hopes attended the LDS branch in Cincinnati but soon made their own arrangements for worship. Some sources say they were asked not to attend. Others report they made the decision on their own.[19]

When I interviewed Marion D. Hanks, who had served a mission in Ohio and stayed with the Hopes once when he was ill during the 1940s, I asked, "Do you know of any particular case of someone going and telling them they couldn't go to church?" Hanks replied, "No, I think it was more subtle than that. It was just understood. It had been made known to them that they were not to be there." [20]

---

18. Len and Mary Hope membership records, archives, historical department, Church of Jesus Christ of Latter-day Saints, Salt Lake City, Utah (hereinafter LDS archives).

19. Loran Stephenson, Mary Hope's bishop at the time she passed away, recalled her story of a visit from the Cincinnati branch president. "I don't know anything about him other than the fact that she called him Brother Anderson," he said. "Brother Anderson was red-eyed; he was just crying. He told them that this was the hardest visit that he had ever made to anybody in his life. He would rather give up his right arm than to have to make this call, but there were objections in the branch to them attending church just because they were black." The branch president then offered to come to the Hopes' home once a month to bring them the sacrament and to have a meeting with them. See Loran Stephenson Oral History, 2, interviewed by Jessie L. Embry, 1989, LDS Afro-American.

20. See Marion D. Hanks Oral History, 7, interviewed by Jessie L. Embry, 1989, LDS Afro-American.

But they did not lose faith. In 1936 future LDS apostle Mark E. Petersen, who was then working for the *Deseret News,* was assigned to study newspaper practices at the *Cincinnati Enquirer.* He attended a missionary-organized meeting in the Hopes' home. Petersen recalled that the branch president showed him Len Hope's tithing receipts. He faithfully paid $1.50 per week. Hope told Petersen that he often had to peddle berries to earn the money, adding that he was the only black he knew in his neighborhood with a job during the 1930s depression and attributed the blessing to paying tithing.[21] Mary Hope's last bishop said, "I never sensed any kind of frustration, impatience, or resentment of any kind" about those years of restricted activity, although "I could tell from Sister Hope's expression that she was disappointed that they could not attend church. They would have loved to have been Latter-day Saints in a full sense."[22]

Marion D. Hanks recalled that in the early 1940s the Hopes were allowed to attend district conferences. On those occasions the whole family lined up at the door and greeted the missionaries' special guests. He recalled that some visitors and members "were not advanced in their sense of the value of other human beings but geared that to their own sense of ethnic purity and color." These people avoided greeting the Hopes. Hanks, however, felt "some defensiveness. I used to go stand by them while the guests arrived with other missionaries. . . . I was not able to accommodate other people's sense of propriety in trying to keep black people away."[23] Hanks continued, "One interesting thing about the Hopes not being accepted at the normal worship service in the Cincinnati, Ohio, branch of the one true church was they held a meeting at the Hope home every first Sunday of the month. There would be a testimony meeting and an instruction period followed by a meal which the Hopes would prepare for those who came. . . . When I learned of that, I began attending immediately. For nearly a year in Cincinnati, I spent my first Sunday afternoons at the Hope home. They would bear testimony in order from Len, Mary, Rose, down to Vernon who could barely talk."[24]

---

21. Carter, *Story of the Negro Pioneer,* 61.
22. Stephenson Oral History, 6-7.
23. Hanks Oral History, 2.
24. Ibid., 4.

Len Hope was forced to take early retirement because he developed a form of black lung from working on a fiberizing machine. In 1947 after he retired, the Hopes visited Utah and stayed with Hanks and his mother. They were so well received that they decided to move to Utah. Hanks explained, "I tried to dissuade them. They had a nice home. The branch by now was treating them more courteously. Their children were there. . . . It just looked like they would be better off where they were with friends and associates."[25] However, one day he received a call that the Hopes had arrived.

The Hopes were members of the Millcreek Ward where Len attended high priest group meetings and Mary went to Relief Society. Hanks explained, "As far as I am aware, they were treated well in the church. They were curiosities, but out in the Millcreek area were the descendants of the Flake family and other black folks who were church people."[26]

The Hopes had not been in Salt Lake City long when Len became ill and was admitted to the Veteran's Hospital. Hanks gave him a blessing, sensing that "he was not long for this world." One Sunday in September 1952 when Hanks was supposed to speak at a sacrament meeting, he felt uneasy. Instead of going to the meeting, he called the Hopes and was told that Len had just passed away.[27]

Following her husband's death, Mary moved to Philadelphia, where some of her children were living. She received church welfare assistance. Joseph T. Lindsey, who served as her bishop, recalled taking her supplies in 1955.[28] After Lindsey was released, Loran Stephenson, Hope's home teacher, was called to be bishop. He continued his monthly visits and explained, "I think during that period of time, outside of the members of her family, I probably knew her better than anyone else in the world."[29] When asked how Mary was accepted in the ward, Stephenson replied,

---

25. Ibid., 5.

26. Ibid., 9.

27. Ibid., 6.

28. Joseph T. Lindsey wrote me a letter in 1989 describing his experiences with Mary Hope.

29. Stephenson Oral History, 1.

There was no problem there. . . . I think she felt comfortable with all the members of the church there. I never heard anybody from the time that I was bishop or any other time express any negative views towards her or her family. I did not see any indication whatever of social or personal ostracism. She was never asked to serve in any calling that I know of, but I did not think as bishop that she was physically able to perform much of anything or that it was wisdom to give the responsibility to her. Sister Hope was such a non-threatening personality that it would be difficult for anybody to respond negatively to her.[30]

Stephenson told of Mary's faith. "I've heard her bear her testimony a number of times in testimony meeting about the truthfulness of the gospel, the heart-felt way she felt about the Lord Jesus Christ, the truthfulness of the Church, the divinity of the mission of the prophet Joseph Smith, and the truth and proper authority of the priesthood."[31] When Mary died in 1971, Stephenson made arrangements to fly her body to Salt Lake City, where she was buried next to her husband.

Regarding the priesthood, Hanks remembered: "Brother Hope in bearing his testimony always said that the day would come and that they could wait. They knew the Lord knew their hearts. I think he said it maybe with a smile and a hint now and then that when the white people were ready the time would come."[32] According to Hanks, "He had found the gospel and found it in a miraculous way. He was content to wait patiently for the day when the full blessings of the gospel were available through the priesthood."[33] As with many early black members, such patience was not passed on to their children. Most of the Hope family eventually converted to Islam.[34] During the June 1978 meeting in the Salt Lake temple, Hanks, now a general authority, bore his testimony about Len Hope, whom he described as a "pure, beautiful, patriotic, heroic man who was ready to give his life rather than surrender his membership."[35]

---

30. Ibid., 7.
31. Ibid., 7.
32. Hanks Oral History, 8.
33. Ibid., 9.
34. Ibid., 5-6.
35. Ibid., 7.

Three Generations of Sargents

In 1895 Mormon missionaries knocking on doors in a rural area of Caroline County, Virginia, contacted the Sargents. For the next ten years missionaries stopped at this home where they shared their gospel message, and Nellie Gray Patron Sargent fed them, washed their clothes, and mended their shoes. On 19 August 1906 the mother and all seven children were baptized. According to a daughter, Novella Sargent Gibson, her father John "wasn't a member, but he was administered to. He liked the Mormons, but he was never baptized."[36] Although others in the area listened to missionaries and joined the church, they were white and emigrated to Utah. Soon the Sargents were the only Latter-day Saints left in the area. Although isolated from other members, ridiculed, and excluded by the black community, the mother remained faithful.

One at a time the Sargent children moved to Washington, D.C., seeking employment. Novella moved in 1908 when she was sixteen years old. Two years later she found members of the LDS church meeting in a rented hall. After that she attended as often as her work schedule permitted. She recalled one incident of racial discrimination. It was a conference so the room was "filled up with people. I don't know who this man was, whether he was a Mormon or whether he wasn't. There was a seat left by me. I was sitting there, and there was one seat here. The place was crowded. He wouldn't sit down. He just stood there. It was very noticeable. Everybody was bound to see it. Sister [Alpha Mae Eldredge] Smoot [wife of LDS apostle and Utah senator Reed Smoot] got up from her seat and came back and sat by me. He went there and sat in her seat." Novella added, "Those things don't hurt me. Just pray for them. That's all because they really don't know what they are doing."[37]

Novella Sargent married Joseph Milton Gibson on 18 June 1913.

---

36. Novella Gibson Oral History, interviewed by Chad Orton, 1985. Gibson was interviewed as part of the Mormon Outward Migration program conducted by G. Wesley Johnson, a professor of history at BYU, and his students. Due to mechanical problems with the tape, I only have a partial transcript in my possession.

37. Ibid.

He did not discourage her involvement in the church. After he died in 15 October 1966, she had him vicariously baptized and ordained. Novella commented, "I hope he is [a member] by now."[38]

One of Novella's sisters, Mary Virginia Sargent, stayed in Caroline County, Viriginia, and married Julius Keys. Like her mother, Mary Virginia's only contact with Latter-day Saints was literature and rare missionary visits. According to her daughter Ethel Keys Kelly, she once became ill. While her husband went for the doctor, the Mormon missionaries arrived and gave her a blessing. When Julius returned, she was sitting up in bed preaching. After this miraculous recovery, her husband joined the LDS church.

The Keys had little contact with the church because as Ethel Kelly said it was "too far to travel . . . and we had no transportation." The children were baptized in a Baptist church, but Virginia Keys Wright recalled that her mother "never stopped telling us about the Mormons and the Mormon church. She never would try to force it on us. But if anything would happen, she wanted us to get in touch with the Mormons."[39]

Even without attending church three of the children—Ethel, Virginia, and Raymond—later became interested and were baptized. Ethel moved to Washington, D.C., where she married James Kelly and then moved to New York City. She wrote to her aunt Novella asking for a copy of the Book of Mormon and was referred to the church in New York. She was baptized in 1961.[40] Her sister Virginia lived with Ethel at the time and took the missionary lessons. Later she returned to her home in Richmond, Virginia, became very ill, and after a series of miraculous experiences decided to be baptized in 1976.[41] Ethel asked missionaries to visit her brother Raymond, who was baptized in 1981.

---

38. Ibid. The dates are from Novella Sargent Gibson's membership records in Deceased Membership Records, LDS archives. Gibson died on 28 April 1986.

39. Ethel Kelly Oral History, 3, interviewed by Alan Cherry, 1987, LDS Afro-American; Virginia Wright Oral History, 2, interviewed by Alan Cherry, 1986, LDS Afro-American.

40. Kelly Oral History, 3-5.

41. Virgina Wright Oral History, 3-14.

Samuel Magee and Ardella Bickham Magee

Samuel and Ardella Bickham Magee were taught and baptized by a white neighbor, John Israel, in their rural village of Tylertown, Mississippi. The couple traveled by wagon about fifteen miles to Darbun to attend quarterly district conferences whenever possible, held morning and evening family prayers, and read the scriptures together. Freda, their fourth of eight children, was baptized in a creek near Tylertown in 1908 at the age of nine. Freda divorced her first husband, and on 3 February 1938 married Rudolph Beaulieu. Although Beaulieu was not a member, he encouraged her to pay tithing and once telephoned the branch president in New Orleans to administer to her.[42]

Freda Beaulieu described the effects of the Mormon church on her life. "I feel I have been blessed with good health all these years from living the Word of Wisdom, as my parents taught me many years ago." She was "really excited when the blacks were given the opportunity to receive the priesthood in June 1978." She felt the announcement opened up new opportunities for her: "July 21, 1978 was the happiest day of my life. I went to the Washington Temple for my own endowment and to be sealed to Rudolph [who had passed away] for time and eternity."[43]

BLACK CONVERTS BETWEEN 1960 AND 1978

White missionaries in the 1960s and 1970s, sensitive to discrepancies between black and white Mormon experiences, were cautious about proselyting blacks. The stories of some of these black members have been published; others are available in libraries and archival collections.

---

42. The information regarding Freda Lucretia Magee Beaulieu is from a talk she wrote and was read at a stake conference and from a letter to James Kimball from Robert B. Evans, 20 Feb. 1982, both in LDS archives; see also Katherine Warren Oral History, 10, interviewed by Alan Cherry, 1987, LDS Afro-American; and Elder Parker P. Warner, "Negro Members of the Church Display Great Faith," *Church News,* 16 Dec. 1944, 4.

43. Beaulieu talk.

Alan Cherry

Alan Cherry joined the LDS church on 9 May 1968 at age twenty-two. His published autobiography is entitled *It's You and Me, Lord.*[44] Cherry grew up in New York City with his mother, father, and half-sister. After he graduated from high school, he attended Howard University in Washington, D.C., for one year. He enlisted in the air force just before he would have been drafted. In 1966 he was stationed in Texas where he reported: "I was at my permanent duty station, already engrossed in a unique plan called 'Boredom, And How to Eat Ten Meals a Day.'"[45] After several months of "my experience with the immorality of downtown Abilene, the view I was developing of race, relationships and how this seemed symbolic of the nation, . . . I wondered if that was what America was really all about—what life was about, or if there was perhaps something more. . . . Was there any truth?"[46]

For several months he searched for "absolute truth." After reading philosophy and scripture he decided, "I had to dedicate my life to Christ."[47] With this new resolve, "I decided that the next day I would stop work. I knew I would probably be apprehended and then placed in confinement, but if that was what was necessary to sever connections with the world in which I found myself, then I was most willing to do it."[48] On 19 January 1968 when he refused to report to work, he was placed in the base confinement facility. In mid-February he found the LDS pamphlet *Which Church Is Right?* He requested information and was eventually referred to the Mormon missionaries. The missionaries came to the confinement facility on 13 April 1968. When they arrived, he defused any apprehensions by announcing, "I already know the doctrine of Negro and the priesthood." He had read about it in a *Reader's Digest* article about Mormons.

Cherry was released from confinement twelve days after his first meeting with the missionaries and had all of the lessons in the next

---

44. Alan Gerald Cherry, *It's You and Me, Lord!* (Provo, UT: Trilogy Arts Publication, 1970).
    45. Ibid., 5.
    46. Ibid., 16.
    47. Ibid., 25, 28.
    48. Ibid.

ten days before he was baptized. He was discharged from the military on 24 May 1968 and returned to New York City. After working and attending church there, he decided to enroll at BYU the fall of 1969. For the next ten years he worked, performed with several BYU and Mormon-related groups, and started an acting career.

Following the 1978 announcement he was ordained an elder. In 1982 he accepted a call to serve in the California Oakland Mission. I met him soon after he returned from his mission. At his suggestion the Charles Redd Center for Western Studies conduct interviews with LDS African Americans, and he donated four years to completing the interviews. One of the people he interviewed was Janice Barkum of Gulfport, Mississippi, whom he married in the Salt Lake temple five months after they met.

When Cherry published his book in 1970, he explained his reaction to the priesthood ban: "I guess when it all comes out in the end the important thing in God's Kingdom will not be who leads us there, but simply who gets there."[49] In 1985 he reflected on his experiences: "Priesthood restriction was culturally administered very poorly. It turned me and perhaps many black Latter-day Saints into shadowy figures who in effect were asked to languish in the shadows to minimize discomfort of other Latter-day Saints. . . . It was an inequality born out of ignorance and mismanagement rather than deliberate disenfranchisement."[50]

Helen Kennedy

Helen Kennedy, who grew up in Pocatello, Idaho, was working at Hill Air Force Base near Ogden, Utah in 1969 when her co-workers gave her some Mormon church literature. When the forty-eight-year-old single mother showed interest, other fellow employees sent missionaries to her home. She recalled, "The first thing they told us was the blacks could not have the priesthood and that we were going to get a greater blessing later in life. It wouldn't happen in our lifetime, but there would be a greater blessing." When the missionaries asked if they could return, Helen's daughter Candace, who had attended

---

49. Ibid., 38, 50, 52, 64.

50. Alan Cherry Oral History (in process), interviewed by Jessie L. Embry, 1985, LDS Afro-American.

LDS religion classes adjacent to her high school, told her to say yes because "the gospel's beautiful."[51]

Helen took the lessons and prayed. She recalled, "Pretty soon one night I was praying. I went to sleep with just a really good feeling, but I didn't know if the church was true. Then during the night I woke up, and I was saying, 'It's true.'"[52] She was baptized on 19 May 1969.[53] Candace was baptized in 1979 when she was in her twenties and living in California.[54]

Before Helen's conversion she had sung in the New Zion Baptist church choir. Candace recalled that members of their former congregation "said things like, 'The Kennedys always thought they were too good for everyone. They've joined Mormonism. They're too good for the New Zion Baptist church now. Mormons don't like blacks. I don't know what they are doing in that religion.'"[55]

Helen was elated but shocked when she heard about the 1978 announcement. "I thought the world was going to come to an end because the missionaries said that we wouldn't get that in my lifetime. . . . It was just a beautiful surprise. No bells rang, no stars started down, but it was just really something." Elaborating, she said: "Sometimes I think, 'Why did the Lord wait so long?' I had a kind of a rough time with my kids. I know that the gospel really helped me. . . . My kids would always say, 'My mom has really changed.' And I know that I did. . . . I am proud of the things that I have learned about the Lord, about forgiveness, about the plan of salvation, and about love."[56]

James Henry Sinquefield

James Henry Sinquefield's first contact with Mormons came in 1970 when he was twenty-seven years old and living in Chicago. He enjoyed the weekly broadcasts of the Mormon Tabernacle Choir, and

---

51. Helen Mae Thompson Kennedy Oral History, 4, interviewed by Alan Cherry, 1986, LDS Afro-American.

52. Ibid., 5.

53. Ibid., 4-5.

54. Candace Kennedy Oral History, 3, interviewed by Alan Cherry, 1986, LDS Afro-American.

55. Ibid., 3.

56. Helen Kennedy Oral History, 16-17.

when he heard in 1970 that two black women had joined the choir, he wrote to Salt Lake City applying to sing. The choir public communications department wrote back explaining that members of the choir had to be Mormons. Sinquefield recalled, "For some reason that did not discourage me or dampen my enthusiasm for wanting to know more."[57]

When someone from the choir asked if the missionaries could come by, Sinquefield agreed. He listened to the missionaries and believed them. "I thought, 'These young men have brought an answer to my prayer.'" As a result of his faith and his acceptance of Mormon doctrine, Sinquefield moved to Utah in 1972 where he was baptized in January 1974. He began taking private music lessons, and five months later he auditioned and was accepted into the choir.[58]

When the missionaries told him about priesthood restriction, Sinquefield commented: "My immediate feeling was that this was something that Father in Heaven himself had allowed. . . . I joined the Church feeling that after I had accepted the principles and the teachings of the gospel and lived them it would make me worthy of the priesthood in the life hereafter."[59]

Katherine Warren

Katherine Warren first came in contact with the LDS church in 1968 in Connecticut when someone gave her a copy of the Book of Mormon. She was then a single mother working as a nurse's aide and living with an aunt. Returning to her home state of Louisiana, and eventually locating in New Orleans, she decided: "I wanted to find the church of Jesus Christ, so I looked in the telephone directory. I found the ward and started going there. I investigated the church for about three years. They were prejudiced in that church. They didn't want any blacks. There weren't any blacks there. Yet I felt good when I would go. I kept going, even though nobody said anything to me."[60]

---

57. James Henry Sinquefield Oral History, 3-4, interviewed by Alan Cherry, 1985, LDS Afro-American.

58. Ibid., 5-7.

59. Ibid., 11.

60. Warren Oral History, 5.

Confused about how she could join the church, she wrote to church president Kimball.

Soon she received a visit from the missionaries who, with painful candor, explained: "It's hard to become a member of this Church. Have you heard Joseph Smith said that it wasn't time for the blacks as yet? . . . [But] if the blacks come to us, we will receive them. We can't cast them out."[61] Warren took all of the lessons in 1975, but her husband refused permission for baptism until late 1976. Eager to share her church with her brothers and sisters and their families, she started holding Bible study with them on Sundays in Baker, near Baton Rouge. Since then four generations of relatives have followed her lead.[62]

When asked about priesthood restriction, Warren replied: "The bishop came to visit my house one day and told me that the blacks would never receive the priesthood, but they will when Jesus comes in his glory. I said, 'They're going to receive it before then.' About two weeks later the bulletin came over that the Lord had told President Kimball that now was the time."[63]

Riccardo Wright

Riccardo Wright recalled that he first learned about Mormons in 1974 when two missionaries came to his dog ranch in Aldie, Virginia. He was busy but invited them back that evening. Wright was twenty-eight years old, divorced, and remarried. He recalled: "I think now that I had been prepared spiritually in a lot of ways for their coming. In retrospect I can see a lot of things where it was just a question of timing, and I was ready. The elders did come back. We did a lot of challenging them, and we made them go home and do a lot of homework."[64] After a year and a half of studying, Wright and his wife Nancy were baptized on 4 July 1976.

The priesthood doctrine "bothered Nancy [his white wife] more

---

61. Ibid.

62. Ibid., 5-6; Roger W. Carpenter, "13 of Convert's Relatives Join Church," *Church News,* 17 Feb. 1979, 13.

63. Warren Oral History, 14.

64. Riccardo Wright Oral History, 3, interviewed by Alan Cherry, 1986, LDS Afro-American.

than it bothered me. For me," he explained, "the priesthood wasn't in itself the issue. Once I got to the point where I could accept that Joseph Smith . . . did translate the Book of Mormon and started to appreciate what I considered the major principles of the gospel as a priority, then the black issue became actually a secondary thing."[65]

Linda Reid

Linda Reid was in her twenties and living in Denver, Colorado, when she was contacted by missionaries. The topic of the priesthood restriction did not come up until about a week before her scheduled baptism. Then the uncomfortable senior companion, not sure how to bring the subject up, began "going in circles." Finally the junior companion interrupted: "The Lord loves you very much. He wants you to be baptized. . . . We don't understand everything. The Lord hasn't revealed to us why. But at the present time the blacks cannot hold the priesthood."

Reid's response was immediate: "I politely asked them to leave my house. I said, 'Go away for a while because I need to think about this.' I stayed up all night and tried to figure it out." While she felt convinced that she had found the right church for her, she could not understand why it was "separate but equal." She continued, "They came over the next day after I called them. Unbeknownst to me, they had been up praying and fasting all night in my behalf."

The missionaries gave Reid a copy of Alan Cherry's book and told her of another black member in the stake. They felt she would not want to attend church the next day, but she assured them she needed a ride. Unsure how she would react, they told her that it would be a fast and testimony meeting, a monthly meeting where members stand and express their beliefs. She remembered: "I was sitting in this fast and testimony meeting, and these people were talking like they ate breakfast with Him. . . . They talked about how they knew the Savior and how much they loved Him." When an eight-year-old child said, "I know this Church is true," Reid wondered how. She said she then realized, "I've got to accept some things on faith because the Lord's not going to reveal everything to me." After the meeting, "I went home, got down on my knees, and had a long talk with the Lord.

---

65. Ibid., 3.

Basically it was my decision as it always has been. . . . I just said, 'Yes, I'm willing to sacrifice.' I have no regrets. It is the hardest thing that I have ever done."[66] She was baptized on 9 April 1977.

Later the missionaries confessed that the mission president had told them, "It would be easier to just tell her to continue to reinforce her beliefs in her religion whatever it is and tell her to stay close to the Lord. But don't encourage her. Don't return." The missionaries felt that they should continue to teach Reid and that "the Lord would provide a way." Reid said she was grateful the missionaries did not give up.[67]

MISSION POLICY ON PROSELYTING

As these examples illustrate, prior to 1978 missionaries were reluctant to teach blacks. Some did not tell prospective converts about the priesthood restriction until late in the teaching process. Church members were not free of prejudice, and black members felt stigmatized. Yet despite these odds, those who joined felt they were where God wanted them to be. Although they did not come to the same understanding of why the church discriminated, most felt they were obeying God's will and that present restrictions would not limit their opportunities to receive full rewards in the next life.

H. Selby Berry who served as a missionary in the South during the 1930s recalled that when he met blacks: "I just spoke to them and passed on, because we were instructed not to proselyte the blacks because it wasn't their day. Now if one persisted and was very persistent, then we'd take the time to talk with him. But our mission was not to the black race, we were told."[68] Historian Newell G. Bringhurst collected typical statements about missionary instructions during the 1940s and 1950s. One mission president instructed missionaries to avoid areas "where it is known that color does actually exist," and in 1947 the First Presidency wrote to another mission president, "No special effort has ever been made to proselyte among the Negro race."

---

66. Linda Reid Oral History, 7-9, interviewed by Alan Cherry, 1987, LDS Afro-American.

67. Ibid., 11.

68. H. Selby Berry Oral History, 107, interviewed by David Boone, 1984, LDS archives.

In 1958 Bruce R. McConkie wrote, "The gospel message of salvation is not carried affirmatively to black people."[69] In 1961 Apostle Joseph Fielding Smith told a mission president in South America to "avoid seeking out the Negro."[70]

Most of these instructions were given to individuals. No doctrine was announced. Yet this idea percolated through informal discussions. J. Kenneth Davies, in the New England Mission from 1946 to 1948, recalled asking his mission president, S. Dilworth Young, about working with a black minister who was interested in the church. He was told that he should not attempt to convert him.[71] A missionary who served in New York City during the 1960s recalls telephoning referrals from the World's Fair. If a black family made an appointment, missionaries gave a brief overview of Mormon beliefs and practices but did not return unless the family insisted. With families of other races, missionaries would press for a return invitation.

This was the informal policy in the Canada Halifax Mission where I served from 1974-76. When we knocked on the door of the only black family I encountered in Fredericton, New Brunswick, my companion gave them a pamphlet and encouraged them to attend the church of their choice. After we left she explained that the mission policy was not to teach blacks. I never heard my mission president discuss the issue nor did a missionary ever ask about it in any meeting I attended.

Given this policy, the few blacks who did join usually had to take the initiative. The unofficial aloofness had many causes. Church leaders probably assumed that blacks would not be interested in light of such clear racial bias. It may be that leaders were also concerned about how blacks would be treated by other members. Many Latter-day Saints were unacquainted with, uninformed about, and ambivalent about black people. Leaders also reflected the common prejudice of the period. Even those uncomfortable with the policy could not challenge such a basic teaching without appearing to question their church's unique claims.

---

69. In Newell G. Bringhurst, *Saints, Slaves, and Blacks,* 167.

70. Ibid.

71. J. Kenneth Davies Oral History, 11, interviewed by Yvette Young, 1992, LDS Missionary "Without Purse or Scrip" Project, Charles Redd Center for Western Studies, Archives and Manuscripts, Lee Library.

The willingness to proselyte blacks after 1978 was so dramatic that it suggests that there had been personal discomfort with the policy. The priesthood announcement opened up new neighborhoods and missionaries were quick to work there. Many felt that black Americans were more willing to discuss religion than whites. Those who had no interest in joining a new church were often willing to talk about religion. "Elder Pinnock," a missionary in the North Carolina Charlotte Mission interviewed by KSL Television in 1988, described blacks he talked with as "very religious people. They are willing to talk about the Bible and Jesus Christ at any time. So we find it really open to us."[72] Bryan Waterman, who served a mission in Newark, New Jersey, affirmed that they had "the most success" in the black community.[73]

LDS AFRICAN AMERICAN CONVERTS AFTER 1978

With increased missionary efforts among African Americans, blacks are joining the Mormon church. In large metropolitan areas this often means a return to neighborhoods that Mormons had abandoned with the white flight to the suburbs. Examples of inner city growth include Charlotte and Greensboro, North Carolina; Birmingham, Alabama; Newark, New Jersey; New York City; Los Angeles; Chicago; and Detroit, Michigan. Educational backgrounds of black converts range from graduate school to less than sixth grade. There is no typical black Mormon convert.

Joan and Daniel Mosley

Joan Mosley, an attorney, and Dan Mosley, a businessman, were in their thirties and living in Phoenix when they were interviewed in 1985. They had been looking for a church when they adopted their son Danny in 1974 but were not satisfied with any they attended. In 1978 they moved from New York to California because of Dan's poor health. Two years later while in California, neighbors sent over Mormon missionaries. Joan let them in initially because she was interested

---

72. "Blacks and the Priesthood," KSL Prime Time Access, 8 June 1988, video in my possession.

73. Bryan Waterman Oral History, 2, interviewed by Jessie Embry, 1991, LDS Afro-American.

"not from a religious point of view but basically from an intellectual, being informed on what Mormons thought."[74] Dan joined the church in 1981. Joan and Danny attended church with him for two years. Then Joan joined.

Joan's views on the 1978 change in policy were clear: "I feel that probably the denial of the priesthood to black males was part of the times. I think it was just plain out racism, however else it may be justified by the Church."[75] Dan saw more reason for the policy. He stated: "I feel that it is unique that such emphasis on priesthood restriction is announced with regards to Latter-day Saints. If a person would be clinical, every Christian denomination in America has discriminated against the blacks even for walking in the doors of the church, having a membership, being buried in the church."[76]

James Johnson

James Johnson's first memories are of working in his hometown of Charlotte, North Carolina, because his mother was single and was ill. As a small boy he polished shoes to help meet expenses. Later he caddied at a golf course. When he was eighteen he married and joined the military at the end of World War II. He served for two and a half years. Shortly after he was released, he and his wife separated. He worked in the textile industry for over nineteen years. Then health problems forced him to retire, and he received military disability. In the meantime he remarried but was separated at the time he was interviewed in 1986. He had been a member for less than a year.

He told about giving his $65,000 home in Charlotte to his second wife and living in a "front" house in Monroe, North Carolina, that sold "bootleg liquor by the drink." He had been praying for help to quit drinking and saw the missionaries' visit as an answer to his prayer. When they invited him to meetings, he started attending regularly, stopped drinking, and prepared for baptism. When the elders came to interview him on a Saturday, he talked to them in the car because

---

74. Joan Mosley Oral History, 6, interviewed by Alan Cherry, LDS Afro-American.

75. Ibid., 16.

76. Dan Mosley Oral History, 16-17, interviewed by Alan Cherry, 1985, LDS Afro-American.

he did not want to invite them into the liquor house on its busiest day of the week. He told Alan Cherry he had never heard of the priesthood restriction, which had been lifted eight years earlier. In answer to the question, "What are your feelings about priesthood?" he replied, "I love being a part of the priesthood. I want to learn more about it and get stronger in it, so I can voice myself in it. I think that the more I learn the more I am able to voice myself in it."[77]

Thomas Harrison Johnson

Thomas Harrison Johnson was born in 1907 and grew up in a middle-class family in Philadelphia. He was active in sports: "I was a class athlete in my day. I chose track because of the discrimination in the other sport events." He "just missed being on the Olympic team in 1936."[78]

Johnson was active in bands during World War II, became an accomplished musician, and was a volunteer music teacher at Temple University when he was interviewed in 1986.

As a Catholic, Johnson was part of "one of the highest orders of the Catholic church . . . twenty years." He recalled, "Then I began to realize there was something missing in Catholicism. . . . I began running into some discriminatory problems that bothered me."[79]

Still, he was not thinking of leaving Catholicism when he accepted the invitation of some neighbors to see a film on Mormonism in 1979. As a result he met the missionaries and converted in January 1980. While investigating the church, he "heard all these adverse rumors about the Mormons. One of them was that they didn't allow Negroes . . . to have any offices. . . . I knew that if I was to be a part of something, I would like to be in it with my whole heart and soul. . . . There was no sense of my jumping into another religion where I was going to have trouble with discrimination." Reading the announcement eliminated his fears.[80]

---

77. James Johnson Oral History, 25, interviewed by Alan Cherry, 1986, LDS Afro-American.

78. Thomas Harrison Johnson Oral History, 4, interviewed by Alan Cherry, 1986, LDS Afro-American.

79. Ibid., 5.

80. Ibid., 6.

Ollie Mae Lofton

Ollie Mae Lofton was in her twenties and working as a computer operator for the federal government in South Carolina when she first came in contact with the LDS church in 1978. Two years earlier she had a dream in which an angel told her "the Lord had a work" for her. When missionaries started to teach her, she recognized her angel as Moroni in an illustrated copy of the Book of Mormon. Ollie's father was a Baptist minister, and her parents were concerned when she told them she was going to be baptized again. "They didn't think that was right because they believed in one faith, one Lord, and one baptism." However, she pursued her decision and was joined a year later by her sister Rose.

Racial equality was important to her: "I have always said that if I had heard [about priesthood restriction] before joining the Church I am sure it would have been very difficult to join. I know that the Lord would have had to touch my heart in that way to accept [the church]." Lofton served a mission to California and was attending Brigham Young University at the time she was interviewed in 1985.[81]

Emma Williams

Emma Williams, feeling that her Methodist and Presbyterian baptisms were inadequate, visited several ministers when she was in her sixties asking them to baptize her. They refused because she did not want to join their churches. Williams had already lived a full life, having survived two husbands and was married to a third, Bill Williams. When he died she began traveling but always felt as if "someone was speaking to me saying, 'Repent, believe, be baptized.'" Three years later in 1984 she was praying for a resolution to her question and "in walked the missionaries." When she asked them if they would baptize her, they said, "The Lord sent us here." After quitting smoking, she was baptized even after her son threatened not to speak to her. (He later accepted her decision.) Williams shared her testimony with others in her hometown of Hickory, North Carolina, a number of

---

81. Ollie Mae Lofton Oral History, 8-9, 22, interviewed by Alan Cherry, 1985, LDS Afro-American.

whom converted.[82] She received her temple endowments in November 1985.

REACTIONS TO PRIESTHOOD RESTRICTION

Missionaries faced a dilemma after 1978: What should they tell black investigators about the past? Some blacks had never heard of the priesthood restriction, and young missionaries, eager to share their message and lacking a clear explanation of why blacks had not been ordained historically, often avoided the subject. Bryan Waterman, from Snowflake, Arizona, said most of the blacks he taught during his 1989-91 mission in Newark, New Jersey, had never heard they could not be ordained to the priesthood prior to 1978. He and his companions did not mention it unless they were asked. He said that some blacks were uncomfortable with the Book of Mormon description of the Lamanite curse of dark skin. They wondered what this implied about their own skin tone. Waterman confessed that he felt relieved that most investigators did not read that far. In fact he suggested to other missionaries that they "razor" out the page in the children's Book of Mormon reader when they used it with less literate investigators.[83]

Carl Angelo Simmons, a black football player at Utah State University in Logan, Utah, was born in Oakland in 1963, where he was raised Baptist. By the time he went to junior college, he had no formal religious affiliation. He learned about the Mormon church while he was at USU and joined in 1984. A year later he drew a blank when Alan Cherry asked him about priesthood restriction. After Cherry's brief explanation, Simmons replied laconically, "None of the missionaries ever told me about that at all."[84]

This became a problem for Edwin Allen Burwell, who grew up in Richmond, Virginia, and lived in Greensboro, North Carolina. In 1975 when he was in his early twenties, Mormon missionaries often came into a sandwich shop where he worked, ordered a single sandwich

---

82. Emma Williams Oral History, 3-8, interviewed by Alan Cherry, 1986, LDS Afro-American.

83. Waterman Oral History, 12.

84. Carl Angelo Simmons Oral History, 15, interviewed by Alan Cherry, 1985, LDS Afro-American.

between them, and drank only Sprite. He befriended them, expressing interest in the church. He recalled: "At that particular time they told me I couldn't [join]. They said, 'There are not that many blacks in the church and you would not feel comfortable. There are certain things in the church blacks cannot do.' They never explained it to me. I thought, 'I do not want to be a member of your church anyhow.' They said that they did not want to offend me. They tried to explain it the best they knew how. They stopped coming."[85]

After the revelation Burwell came in contact with Mormon missionaries again. He and his wife Retha were baptized in February 1985. The next month the first counselor in the mission presidency was ordaining Edwin to the priesthood, but he first gave a "little speech" about how he "was getting ready to do something that blacks were not allowed to at one time." Burwell added analytically, "It was like Satan just took that, and he used it to his best advantage. At that particular time I said, 'If blacks were not allowed to have it, I don't want it [now].'"[86] Retha corroborated, "He just felt like . . . walking out because it seemed like some of the missionaries or somebody would have told him this before."[87]

Misunderstandings about what priesthood restriction really meant led to further complications. A few early converts had been told not to attend priesthood meetings even though nonmember males investigating the church were allowed to attend.[88] Robert Lang, who

---

85. Edwin Allen Burwell Oral History, 10, interviewed by Alan Cherry, 1986, LDS Afro-American.

86. Ibid., 14.

87. Retha Burwell Oral History, 21, interviewed by Alan Cherry, 1986, LDS Afro-American.

88. Later a First Presidency letter to "All General Authorities, Regional Representatives, Stake and Mission Presidents, Bishops, and Branch Presidents," 21 Apr. 1980, explained that with the consolidated meeting schedule there would be nonmembers and those who had been disciplined by a church court who would want to attend priesthood meeting during that block of time. The letter stated, "While attendance at priesthood meeting has generally been limited to those who hold the priesthood, it is felt that men in the categories mentioned may well be invited to attend the priesthood meeting with the understanding that they not participate in the discussions, or any business transacted." Copy of letter in my possession.

was baptized in 1970, attended a ward in Inglewood, California. The bishop made him the secretary of the Senior Aaronic priesthood group because Lang was at the meetings every week. In a later reorganization, the bishop told Lang he could not attend. Lang commented wryly: "That was my time to quit then, but apparently I had a testimony. . . . I continued to go to church." Lang decided to find out why the change had been made and found out that the stake president had "misunderstood" the instructions of a general authority. "I sent a letter, and they straightened it all out. They said, 'This man can attend the quorum meetings. Even though he does not hold the priesthood, he is a member of the Church.' The next Sunday the bishop called me up and asked me if I would come back in the quorum meetings they would appreciate it. It had all been straightened out."[89] Alan Cherry had a similar experience in Queens, New York, in 1969. The bishop requested that he not attend priesthood meeting. Cherry did not contest the decision, but when he moved to Provo to attend BYU later that year, he asked the bishop about attending priesthood meeting and was welcomed.[90]

Prior to the announcement black women faced other forms of confusing regulation. Black men could not serve missions, but white women served full time as missionaries without being ordained. Were black women also eligible for missions? Jerri Allene Thornton Hale (later Harwell), half black and half native American from Detroit, joined the church as a college sophomore in 1977. She asked if she could serve a mission and was told she could when she was twenty-one. However, a counselor in the bishopric was subsequently told that this would not be possible.[91]

Mary Frances Sturlaugson, who grew up in Tennessee, went to Dakota Wesleyan University in South Dakota during the 1970s. She joined the church her second year in college. Later she transferred to BYU, where she continued her studies. "A few of the young men I'd grown really close to," she wrote in her autobiography, "were prepar-

---

89. Robert Lang Oral History, 3, interviewed by Alan Cherry, 1985, LDS Afro-American.

90. Alan Cherry Oral History.

91. Jerri Hale Oral History, 15, interviewed by Alan Cherry, 1985, LDS Afro-American.

ing for their missions. Seeing their joy each time one of them received his mission call made my heart ache to receive a similar call." She confided her desire to her bishop, who made an appointment with the stake president, BYU professor Jae Ballif. Sturlaugson recalled that Ballif "told me he would discuss it with the Brethren in Salt Lake City." The reply came back no. And although Sturlaugson repeated her request "after a period of time," she continued to be told, "The time is not yet."[92]

Joelle Margot Aull, who was born in 1968 and raised Catholic in Lake Forest, Illinois, felt that the priesthood restriction had not been fully explained when the family joined the church in 1976. "I don't think we knew that blacks weren't allowed in the priesthood because when my mom found out I remember she went into the bishop's office one Sunday and was talking to them. She came out crying and full of tears. . . . She wanted to go to the temple and be sealed. The bishop told her no, that blacks weren't allowed in the temple." Joelle could not understand why her white stepfather could go to the temple while she, her mother, and her sister could not.[93]

These were shattering experiences for black members. Hale was "upset" when she was told she could not serve a mission. "I just told [the member of the bishopric] I felt the church was prejudiced, and I didn't want anything more to do with it. I was not [coming] back." When he suggested that she pray, she retorted that she would not pray to a God she felt was prejudiced. "I went home that Sunday resolving not to pray. I didn't for two or three days. It seemed like it was on a Wednesday when all of a sudden I found myself on my knees praying and saying, 'Why can't blacks hold the priesthood?' A comforting feeling came over me saying, 'I have not given a reason why, but eventually blacks will hold the priesthood with all the blessings.' . . . That calmed me down."[94]

Mary Frances Sturlaugson came to a similar resolution: "No one, except my Father in heaven, will ever be able to know how I hurt

---

92. Mary Frances Sturlaugson, *A Soul So Rebellious* (Salt Lake City: Deseret Book Co., 1981), 62-64.

93. Joelle Margot Aull Oral History, 4, interviewed by Alan Cherry, 1987, LDS Afro-American.

94. Hale Oral History, 15.

during that time. All I wanted to do was to go forth, but because of the color of my skin, I had to wait." But she added: "Don't misunderstand me. I hurt at being rejected for a mission, but I never once failed to accept the will of the Lord."[95] Both Hale and Sturlaugson served missions after the priesthood revelation.

Joelle Aull reacted similarly. "I think in my days when I was really confused about what I really thought the truth was, that question always came up. I was bitter about it, and I thought that was a silly rule. If this was the truth, why? Someone said no one knows, and we're just going to have to accept it the way . . . it was. It's sad that it had to be that way. I've just learned to accept it."[96] She added, "When we got the news that we could be accepted in the temple, it was a happy time for my family, and we went as soon as possible."[97]

THE ANNOUNCEMENT

As would be expected the 1978 announcement was a great relief to black members. Gilmore Chappell, an American working in Holland, had been a church member for six months and had never been invited to priesthood meeting. One morning he impulsively decided to go. As part of his faith Chappell had previously assured other members that he ultimately expected to receive the priesthood. As matters turned out the announcement had been made that week. One of the members read the announcement aloud and then added to Chappell, "You told me it was going to be this way." Overcome, Chappell "immediately . . . turned around, walked out, sat in my car and laughed and cried until I got myself back together again. Then I went back into priesthood and they welcomed me in with open arms."[98] Most black Latter-day Saints recalled hearing about the announcement in much the same way. It was a time for personal reflection and introspection.

Darrin Bret Davis, a high school student from Summit, New Jersey, was baptized in 1977. He hesitated joining because he was not

---

95. Sturlaugson, *A Soul So Rebellious*, 64.

96. Aull Oral History, 16.

97. Ibid., 4.

98. Gilmore H. Chappell Oral History, 5, interviewed by Alan Cherry, 1986, LDS Afro-American.

sure he wanted to make the commitment. His girlfriend Sharon did not want to join because of prejudice. Later she began investigating the church more seriously and decided to join in 1978. The newly ordained Darrin was able to baptize her.[99]

Barbara Ann Pixton, serving with the U.S. military in Italy, planned to marry a white Latter-day Saint. At the time of their engagement, "he told me that he wanted to make sure that his sons would be able to hold the priesthood. Out of the clear blue sky that year the prophet had the revelation that gave the priesthood to all men."[100] Barbara joined the church in January 1979.

Gehrig Leonard Harris, a high school principal in White Castle, Louisiana, said the announcement was made the summer he was taking the missionary discussions. "I was excited because I wasn't limited [by not holding the priesthood] and it was good not to be limited."[101] He was baptized in December 1978.

The announcement also interested blacks who did not join the church at the time. Elizabeth Taylor Baltimore, born in 1943, was working for a company owned by a Mormon in Washington, D.C., at the time of the announcement. Some of her co-workers had not known about priesthood restriction until the announcement. They were upset that they had been working for someone whose church denied equal rights. Baltimore told them crisply, "You should be saying, 'Thank God there's somebody governing the church that will listen to God.'"[102]

Catherine M. Stokes, a nurse in Chicago, was flying to Hawaii. The pilot, after pointing out the Mormon temple from the air, told about the announcement and suggested the passengers visit the Polynesian Cultural Center. Stokes remembers that the announcement "kind of

99. Darrin Bret Davis Oral History, 13, interviewed by Alan Cherry, 1985, LDS Afro-American; Sharon Davis Oral History, 11, interviewed by Alan Cherry, 1985, LDS Afro-American.

100. Barbara Ann Pixton Oral History, 12, interviewed by Alan Cherry, 1986, LDS Afro-American.

101. Gehrig Leonard Harris Oral History, 14, interviewed by Alan Cherry, 1987, LDS Afro-American.

102. Elizabeth Taylor Baltimore Oral History, 15, interviewed by Alan Cherry, 1986, LDS Afro-American.

caught our attention, but I didn't have any feelings one way or another about it." She did, however, visit the church-owned Polynesian Cultural Center and the visitors' center at the temple, where she filled out a referral card. She was impressed how promptly the missionaries came to her home in Chicago. She was baptized in 1979.[103]

Rosa Lee Green Taylor, a grandmother at the time she was interviewed in 1985, remembered seeing a movie about Mormons when she was fourteen. She came home and told her mother that she was going to be a Mormon when she grew up. Her mother retorted, "They don't have black Mormons." In 1978 she was living in Phoenix. Acting on an impulse, she went to the visitors' center at the temple in Mesa and filled out a referral card. She was leaving on vacation when the missionaries called but promised to telephone when she returned. The missionaries were flabbergasted when she did. She was baptized six weeks later.[104]

Some black members were disappointed that there were not more baptisms following the policy change. Hale stated: "I got a lot of static about why blacks couldn't hold the priesthood. I ran into so many blacks who did not even know they could be members in the Mormon church. . . . When the revelation came, I thought maybe there were thousands and thousands and thousands of blacks in the church, and they would all come out of the woodwork when the revelation was announced. None came. There were still very few." Hale assumed it was because blacks did not know that they could be members.[105]

Mavis Odoms, a Baptist during her childhood in Fremont, California, joined the LDS church in 1980. She felt that African Americans did not join because they did not want to belong to a church that had previously restricted them.[106]

Robert Lang, who had little religious training growing up in

---

103. Catherine M. Stokes Oral History, 16, 6, interviewed by Alan Cherry, 1988, LDS Afro-American.

104. Rosa Lee Green Taylor Oral History, 3, interviewed by Alan Cherry, 1985, LDS Afro-American.

105. Hale, 18.

106. Mavis Odoms Oral History, 12, interviewed by Alan Cherry, 1985, LDS Afro-American.

Mississippi and lived in the Los Angeles area, disagreed. On the basis of his experience in the Southwest Los Angeles Branch, which was nearly all-black, he explained most African Americans "did not know anything about the priesthood being withheld from blacks. They had never heard of the LDS church before." He added that he did not think priesthood was going to make people flock to the church. For most it had never made a difference.[107]

THEORIES ABOUT PRIESTHOOD RESTRICTION

Why blacks were not given the priesthood has never been clear. Early LDS church leaders linked blacks to Adam's son Cain, who the Bible says killed his brother Abel, as well as to pre-earth decisions. The 1969 First Presidency statement simply said the restriction was "for reasons which we believe are known to God, but which He has not made fully known to men."[108] About three-fifths of African-American Mormons interviewed (63.5 percent) accepted the policy as "the Lord's will." Of the rest 29.4 percent were "concerned" about the policy's implications, while 7.1 percent were "appalled."

For those who saw priesthood restriction as God's will, there was no need to seek further explanation. They felt that just as they did not understand God's actions in other areas, they should accept the principle on faith. Sarah Kaye Gripper, a single mother from Spring-field, Illinois, who became a Mormon in 1987, asked both her home teacher and another member why there had been a restriction. Neither had an answer.

> All they could tell me basically was the blacks had the priesthood, it was taken away, and then it was given back. From my understanding, a lot of people could not accept that, white or black. It was coming from the prophet, so that was the reason for it. They don't know what the reason was, but there was a reason why they got it back too. No one can really answer that question. You just have to go on faith is what the bottom line is on that.[109]

---

107. Lang Oral History 19.

108. Newell G. Bringhurst, *Saints, Slaves, and Blacks: The Changing Place of Black People Within Mormonism* (Westport, CT: Greenwood Press, 1981), 2.

109. Sarah Kaye Gripper Oral History, 10, interviewed by Alan

Sherrie Honore Franklin first learned about the LDS church when she and her husband were vacationing in Hawaii in 1984. Then they visited Temple Square during a layover in Salt Lake City and were delighted when missionaries came to their home in New Orleans. They joined the church in 1984. "All we knew was that we believed in what the church teaches and Heavenly Father had some reason for it being that way," Franklin summed up. "No one understands, so why question it, because you're not going to get an answer. I don't think the prophet understood why. All they knew was the revelation said to."[110]

Emanuel Reid, originally from Roopville, Georgia, joined the LDS church there in 1979, served a mission to Oakland, and then attended BYU. Although he accepted the church's position, he still had questions. "Was it Heavenly Father? Were the members not ready? I still had no solid answers, but I had no reason to doubt what went on."[111]

Annie Wilbur grew up in a black neighborhood in Pennsylvania as one of thirteen surviving children. After high school she moved to New Kensington, Pennsylvania, a largely white area, where she joined the Mormon church in 1983 at the age of forty-four after missionaries came to her home. She explained, "I do not know what the true story is, but I do know that there is more to it than meets the eye. But our Heavenly Father will let us know one of these days. He has the right to do whatever He wants."[112]

Burgess Owens, a professional football player, and his wife Josephine, an airline stewardess, joined the Mormon church in 1982. When their first daughter was born, they began looking for a family religion. Fellow Oakland Raider Todd Christensen and his wife Kathy introduced them to the Mormon church. Burgess privately questioned the priesthood doctrine at first. But his question was resolved when a mission president spontaneously counseled him to accept the church and its teachings on the basis of his present knowledge, promising that

---

Cherry, 1988, LDS Afro-American.

110. Sherrie Honore Franklin Oral History, 20, interviewed by Alan Cherry, 1987, LDS Afro-American.

111. Emanuel Reid Oral History, 19, interviewed by Alan Cherry, 1985, LDS Afro-American.

112. Annie Wilbur Oral History, 25, interviewed by Alan Cherry, 1985, LDS Afro-American.

he would receive more. Burgess felt at peace and accepted the policy as the will of the Lord: "I realize that it is the Lord's wisdom, not mine, that counts. As long as I see the fruit and I know how it is going to impact my kids and my wife and my family and it does a good job, I am not going to concern myself over it. That is really the bottom line."[113]

James Henry Sinquefield, who had become a member of the Mormon Tabernacle Choir, summarized: "I never [had] a feeling that the priesthood was something that was withheld from my race of people because of discrimination or some of the negativeness that man has tried to make it be. I really believed that it was of God, that it was His will to be that way. That is just my personal opinion. I feel it is right."[114]

Others felt a need to explain the restriction at least to themselves. Some, like Kenneth Bolton, Sr., a twenty-seven-year-old resident of Jackson, Mississippi, pointed out that the priesthood had not always been available to everyone. During much of the Old Testament, only the tribe of Levi was eligible.[115]

Some hypothesized that nineteenth-century prejudice made it impossible for the church to give priesthood to blacks. For example, Doris Nelson Russell, who joined the church in the Los Angeles area in 1980, felt first that it "was a very unpopular thing for" white Mormons "to be so closely connected with the black men in the church." She explained that "the majority of black men up to that point were slaves and had the mentality of slaves. . . . If you have been a slave all of your life, you hardly feel worthy of anything else but the experience of a slave."

She added,

I felt that the church was growing and had gone through some very traumatic experiences as far as being driven from the east coast to the west, to a barren place like the wastelands of Utah. They didn't need to deal with more than they could handle at the time. They had already been

---

113. Burgess Owens Oral History, 18, interviewed by Alan Cherry, 1986, LDS Afro-American.

114. Sinquefield Oral History, 11.

115. Kenneth Bolton Oral History, 9, interviewed by Alan Cherry, 1987, LDS Afro-American.

chased out of everything they had and had been killed and persecuted. The issue of the black people had to wait until the church could become stronger and more established, to give time to the rest of the nation to catch up with the idea that we were emancipated, we are God's children, and we do have a right to be considered God's children just like everyone else. The mentality of the American whites was not really ready for that—and still isn't to a great extent.[116]

Peter Tabani Gillo, a Ugandan immigrant converted in 1983 in Chicago, held the same view:

My personal understanding in that regard is in the first place the gospel was true for the Jews first. After the Jews it was for Gentiles. That's what Jesus Christ Himself said. Many people did not question that. But people question about the Mormon church. . . . Maybe God did not think that black people were ready to join the church. . . . When the church was established, . . . many white people had an attitude toward the black people. They did not accept them. . . . Maybe the white people would have left and the church would not have grown. Maybe it was right in the beginning to keep the blacks out and allow the church to grow and become strong and then allow the blacks in. We never know what God had in His mind, what plans He has.[117]

Others saw the LDS position as being little different from that of other churches which, while not denying priesthood, had discriminated in other ways. For example, J. Joseph Faulkner, a member of the Mount Pilgrim Baptist church in Gadsden, Alabama, before he became a Mormon in 1983, stated: "I had no problem with blacks in particular and other races also not holding the priesthood in the church. In other denominations you could not only not hold the priesthood, but you could not attend the so-called white churches. . . . If you attempted to go, you would get lynched." When other blacks asked why he would join a church that had denied his race, he rejoined:

I was in the Baptist church for forty-five years and never did hold the office of deacon. . . . I never was found worthy by the pastors that I was under to even be mentioned to hold the office of deacon. Deacons in the

---

116. Doris Russell Oral History, 28-29, interviewed by Alan Cherry, 1986, LDS Afro-American.

117. Peter Tabani Gillo Oral History, 8, interviewed by Alan Cherry, 1988, LDS Afro-American.

church only serve at the pleasure of the pastor. I have many problems with that. . . . Within two months after I was baptized in the Church, by my age . . . and being found worthy, I was ordained a deacon, teacher, and priest.[118]

Finally many felt the restriction was human in origin. Brenda Elaine Combs, a divorced single mother from St. Louis who joined the Mormon church in 1981, phrased her position gently: "I'll put it this way. I haven't seen a perfected person yet. . . . Sometimes we say God told us to do this, and God didn't tell us to do it. Let's put it that way. A lot of times we listen to the imaginations of our own hearts and not that of God's."[119]

William T. Johnson, who first came in contact with the LDS church from talking to some Mormons on a plane in 1978, recalled: "One day in the newspaper in 1978 on the front page was a story about the revelation that blacks were to be received into the priesthood in the Mormon church. That really upset me. I thought, 'What an insult.'"[120]

He talked to a Mormon who gave him LeGrand Richards's *A Marvelous Work and a Wonder* to read. He read that and started reading the Book of Mormon, but the passages about dark skin upset him. He was about to return the book, but somehow he was still interested. Johnson continued to have contact with Mormons and joined the church a year later.

Priesthood restriction was a concern. He told Alan Cherry when he was interviewed in 1987, "That has been the greatest obstacle that I ever had to overcome in order to get into the church, and it has been something that I have struggled with to this day. . . . I wonder sometimes if they [church leaders] had not really inquired of the Lord back during the 1800s or even in the early 1900s would they have not received that same revelation."[121] Jerry Willis, a Methodist minister,

---

118. J. Joseph Faulkner Oral History, 15-16, interviewed by Alan Cherry, 1987, LDS Afro-American.

119. Brenda Elaine Combs Oral History, 8, interviewed by Alan Cherry, 1988, LDS Afro-American.

120. William T. Johnson Oral History, 7, interviewed by Alan Cherry, 1987, LDS Afro-American.

121. Ibid., 16-17.

then pastor of a nonaffiliated church in St. Louis, joined the Mormon church in 1982. He expressed the same feelings, "I know even if church fathers were off-centered. They didn't verbally put themselves in a position of prayer to receive the answer, or if they received the answer, they didn't act on it."[122]

Others were more direct. Ruffin Bridgeforth, who joined the LDS church during the 1950s, summarized crisply: "Priesthood restriction was a church doing. The Lord tolerated it."[123] Catherine M. Stokes was equally forthright: "We don't believe that the church made a mistake. Yet we don't profess to believe that any of us are infallible. We don't believe in the infallibility of the prophet. I have to tell you that I think it was a mistake. That's based on my belief that the gospel of Jesus Christ is inclusive, not exclusive. I'm glad that it's remedied."[124]

Priesthood aside, many were uncomfortable with Cain-Ham, pre-earth life explanations. Annette E. Reid, who joined the church when she was attending college in 1980, was initially satisfied when a Mormon counselor at her college told her no one knew exactly why there had been priesthood restriction. But during her mission, she said: "I started to get angry about the whole situation. I didn't understand why so many church leaders were coming out making statements on something they knew nothing about, something that had not been revealed." Not having an explanation "meant more to me than any explanations that you get from people—being neutral in the spirit world, playing basketball during the war in heaven, not being worthy enough to be born white."[125]

Crystal Gathers Clark, whose parents joined in 1981 in North Carolina, was married in a Mormon ceremony in the ward meeting-house. She and her husband Matthew converted in 1985. When she asked about priesthood restriction in a Raleigh Sunday school class

122. Jerry Willis Oral History, 9, interviewed by Alan Cherry, 1988, LDS Afro-American.

123. Ruffin Bridgeforth Oral History, 17, interviewed by Alan Cherry, 1985, LDS Afro-American.

124. Catherine Stokes Oral History, 16.

125. Annette E. Reid Oral History, 27, interviewed by Alan Cherry, 1985, LDS Afro-American.

she said "they didn't really answer the question. . . . They went on the curse thing."[126] Janis R. Garrison decided as a high school student in Arkansas that she wanted to attend Brigham Young University. She joined the Mormon church in 1979. "When I first became a member, I was told everything about blacks and the priesthood as far as from being a bench sitter to descendants of Cain. I thought, 'This is just absolutely ridiculous.' I do not think I have ever been a bench sitter in my life, and I do not think I could have been one in the pre-existence either."[127]

CHANGING VIEWS

The issue of priesthood exclusion affected people in different ways before and after the announcement. Those who were baptized before 1978 came to terms with it. After June 1978 converts dealt with it as a historical condition that had signaled a change in their status. Some felt that nothing changed. Robert Lee Stevenson, who converted as a serviceman in Germany in 1971 and was elected to a BYU student body office in the mid-1970s, told people that "the gospel is just as true without priesthood as it is with the priesthood."[128] Tom Porter first met Mormons in Europe as a serviceman in the 1950s. He was baptized in the states in 1958. When asked why he would join a church which denied him priesthood, he replied, "I could not get excited about not having the priesthood because if Heavenly Father wanted me to have it, He would make arrangements for me to have it."[129]

Ruffin Bridgeforth's pre-1978 position was: "We are going to see this priesthood restriction as a blessing and therefore man cannot curse you. He can try to put restrictions on you, but because of the Lord above, you will be blessed and you will not lose any blessings for

---

126. Crystal Gathers Clark Oral History, 10, interviewed by Alan Cherry, 1986, LDS Afro-American.

127. Janis R. Garrison Oral History, 26, interviewed by Alan Cherry, 1985, LDS Afro-American.

128. Robert Lee Stevenson Oral History, 9, interviewed by Alan Cherry, 1987, LDS Afro-American.

129. Tom Porter Oral History, 4-5, interviewed by Alan Cherry, 1988, LDS Afro-American.

anything if we have been denied anything."[130] Robert Coleman Brown, who joined in the 1970s after he had trained to be an AME minister, pointed out one possible blessing of not having the priesthood: "I think I appreciated the priesthood a lot more when I didn't have it. When I didn't have the priesthood, I depended on it and called on other people to help me, to use it, and to exercise it. At the same time I wanted it so badly . . . that I appreciated it more." He wondered if he appreciated it as much after his ordination.[131]

Some of those who joined after the announcement expressed doubts about whether they would have considered affiliating with Mormonism before priesthood became available. David E. Gathers, an automobile sales representative, moved from New York to a white neighborhood in North Carolina where missionaries found him in 1981. He mused: "It is a good thing that the elders came when they did because I never took a back seat to anything. If they had come and said that they had a priesthood but I could not get it then, although I knew I was joining the church of Jesus Christ, there is no way at all I would have been there. I would have probably chased them out of the house."[132]

Joan Mosley, who worked for the Peace Corps in Africa and for the NAACP when she met her husband Dan, expressed the same concern: "I am glad I did not have to face . . . joining the church in that period of time. It would have been a lot harder for me, I am sure, than it was."[133] Melvin D. Mitchell of Columbus, Ohio, baptized in 1985, said he was happy he found the LDS church later. If he had joined and then learned about the ban he would have "gone insane."[134]

Ollie Mae Lofton said that being black in a largely white church is still difficult, but she saw herself as a pioneer, one of the first

---

130. Bridgeforth Oral History, 17.

131. Robert Coleman Brown Oral History, 12, interviewed by Alan Cherry, 1986, LDS Afro-American.

132. David E. Gathers Oral History, 24, interviewed by Alan Cherry, 1986, LDS Afro-American.

133. Joan Mosley Oral History, 17.

134. Melvin D. Mitchell Oral History, 13, interviewed by Alan Cherry, 1988, LDS Afro-American.

post-1978 black members. "I know that it is the will of the Lord that gives me strength and understanding to stay and be involved where I am a minority."[135]

SUMMARY

For LDS African Americans who converted prior to the lifting of the priesthood ban, each had to deal not only with discriminatory restrictions but also with blatant prejudice in a white church whose members had little contact with any ethnic group. Those who joined since 1978 have had to deal with similar concerns, conceding much of their heritage to world view where isolation more than conflict has shaped their expectation. Mormons have not been hostile as much as ambivalent—and sometimes intimidated—by racial differences. Contact with people who stayed when they did not seem wanted softened many members of the church. Though the priesthood change did not open mission floodgates to thousands of ethnic converts, the change had a tremendous impact on those who had prayed for its coming and even more so on the white majority whose theologically-based prejudice quickly evaporated.

---

135. Lofton Oral History, 22.

4.

THE ORAL HISTORY PROJECT
AND SURVEY

LDS African Americans are not a homogenous group. They vary in age, educational background, and occupation. Some live in black inner-city neighborhoods; others live in affluent, primarily white communities. The unavailability of church records and impossibility of targeting the total black population made statistically random sampling impossible. Consequently the profile presented in this chapter cannot be generalized to all LDS African Americans.

ORAL HISTORY PROJECT

In 1984 Alan Cherry proposed that the Charles Redd Center for Western Studies pursue the history of blacks in the Mormon church. He believed that unless the stories of current black Mormons were collected, they would continue to be omitted from history books. His experience with white Latter-day Saints indicated that most accepted the stereotypes. Without a clear picture of the diversity of the black experience, people had asked Cherry if he hated whites as much as Mary Frances Sturlegson, who wrote a book about her conversion. Cherry made a convincing argument that studying LDS African Americans would be valuable.

The interview questions focused on religious experiences. Recognizing that most black Mormons are converts and that the majority became acquainted with Mormonism after the 1978 announcement, the interviews first included open-ended questions about early family life, church attendance, personal religiosity, and educational and work experiences. There was no attempt to gather uniform data on each person. As a result information differed greatly. Some people told about conversion in great detail; others gave only sketchy accounts. The rest of the interview focused on experiences in the LDS church. Questions included the difference the church had made in the person's life. A section of the interview also focused on how blacks felt they were accepted in a predominately white church, their relationships with black and white Mormons, and the effects of their membership on associations with other blacks. There were also questions on the priesthood restriction.

Cherry gathered names from a variety of people, and compiled a shorter list of people from different walks of life: married and single, professional and blue collar, longtime members and recent converts. Some of these men and women could not be interviewed because of schedule conflicts. Usually people who had been in the church for less than a year were not included because it was assumed they had not had enough experience as Latter-day Saints to answer some of the questions. Occasionally Cherry did not realize that they had only been members for a short time until he started the interview.

Over the succeeding four years, Cherry interviewed 224 men and women; I interviewed Cherry himself and Charles W. Smith, Jr., a retired Chicago pharmacist living in southern California who was visiting Utah when Cherry was out of town. We hoped a black interviewer would be able to solicit information and attitudes the narrators would not tell someone from another cultural and racial background. Although I have no evidence to support this conclusion, I feel the interviewees were open about their feelings and talked about both positive and negative experiences they had as Mormons.

Cherry conducted the initial interviews in Utah. He and I recognized that being around people who shared their beliefs and accepted them as "fellow Saints" was reinforcing for these black members. Sometimes they were treated as a novelty. People wanted to get to know them because they were different. This type of attention was simultaneously flattering and embarrassing. Since most Utah Mormons had little contact with blacks, those in Utah inevitably dealt with prejudice, discrimination, and, most of all, ignorance. It also meant losing contact with African American culture. According to the 1990 census, less than 1 percent of Utah's population is black. Even in Salt

Lake City and Ogden, which had the highest concentrations of blacks, African Americans numbered only 1-1.5 percent of the population.[1] Most clung to their black churches as a refuge from what they perceived as a hostile, dominant Mormon society. Some viewed black Mormons as traitors to black culture.

As Cherry continued his interviews, the Redd Center secured grants and donations from the BYU College of Family, Home, and Social Sciences and from the Silver Foundation to continue the interviews. As a result he was able to travel throughout the United States. This included trips to northern and southern California and Arizona in October 1985 and to North Carolina in 1986. In the Charlotte area he had difficulties scheduling interviews. He had made initial appointments with twenty people before he left Utah, but nearly all decided not to be interviewed. One woman told him she was going back to her black church; she preferred its music. In Greensboro, 100 miles northeast of Charlotte, he found a completely different situation. Johnnie McKoy, a quiet, unassuming brick mason, had been a member since 1980 and was responsible for many others joining the Mormon church. Cherry found faithful Latter-day Saints in other areas across the state.

A third trip in September and October 1986 took Cherry to New York City, where he had grown up, and other areas in the northeast. Cherry then traveled to the Washington, D.C., area and Richmond, Virginia. Seeking blacks in an area of ethnic diversity, he conducted the next set of interviews in Hawaii in November 1986. Finding blacks in Hawaii was more laborious. In 1989 African Americans made up 1.7 percent of Hawaii's population.[2] But contacts through friends and church leaders produced nine interviews.

A fifth research trip took Cherry back to the South in June 1987. He traveled from Atlanta, Georgia, to Gulfport, Mississippi, with stops in Birmingham, Alabama, Jackson, Mississippi, Baker, Louisana, and New Orleans. A sixth trip in March 1988 took him to the Midwest, where thousands of blacks had moved in search of work in the 1920s.

---

1. 1990 Census; Bob Bernick, Jr., "Minorities Told Not to Fear Redistricting," *Deseret News*, 8 Sept. 1991, B-1.

2. Wanda L. Pete, "The Remarkable Preddy Family," *Afro-Hawa'i News*, 1-30 Nov. 1989, 5.

In Chicago's Hyde Park Ward near the University of Chicago, he found a diverse blend of lifetime Mormons from the West and local members, including converts from half a dozen ethnic groups. He also went to several towns in Ohio, St. Louis, Missouri, and Springfield, Illinois.

Oral history interviews ask open-ended questions that people can answer however they wish. They can express feelings and bring up related issues without being controlled. This format worked well for LDS African Americans, allowing them the freedom to share a variety of experiences. Most people were anxious to participate. In every area except Hawaii Cherry had more potential interviews than he could accommodate. Only in Charlotte did people agree to be interviewed and then cancel their appointments. Although not all interviews contained the same information, basically the same questions were asked each time. With this in mind Cardell Jacobson, a professor of sociology at Brigham Young University, analyzed the basic characteristics of the sample. The results of this and other statistical analyses are presented throughout the rest of this book.

THE SURVEY

As Cherry conducted interviews, he talked about how he wanted a more exact profile on some issues. For example, gospel music was important to some, but others did not mention it. He felt that a survey that asked more direct questions would help appraise the position more accurately. He wondered if being Mormon meant black members spent more time with whites, especially visiting in their homes. With just a few questions in a survey, he could ascertain information that would require leading and hence possibly biasing questions. In addition Cherry wanted to know if blacks perceived prejudice as intentional or simply because of ignorance. He had encountered uncomfortable situations when people assumed he was in the wrong place when he walked into an LDS chapel. He wanted to know if other blacks had experienced the same things and if these experiences bothered them. Finding answers to these questions required a different format. A survey would also allow us to increase our sample size without having to travel and held the advantage of anonymity—people could respond without using their names.

With the assistance of A. LeGrand Richards, a friend who had worked on surveys, Cherry developed target areas and Richards put them into standard format. The survey covered seven areas: (1) interaction with non-blacks at church functions, (2) self-initiated socializing outside of church meetings, (3) inclusion or exclusion because of cultural conditioning, (4) perceptions of prejudice, (5) peer pressure from nonmember blacks, (6) ability of black and white Latter-day Saints to communicate and understand cultural language, and (7) acceptance by white Latter-day Saints.

We also added questions from standard religiosity surveys so that blacks could be compared to other Latter-day Saints and to Americans in general. One set of questions measured orthodoxy regarding the divinity of Jesus Christ, God's existence, life after death, whether the Bible is the word of God, and Satan's existence. A second focus was distinctive LDS theology. Did respondents feel the president of the LDS church was a prophet, if the Book of Mormon was the word of God, if the LDS church was the only true church, and if Joseph Smith actually saw the Father and the Son? Other questions asked about religious commitment, closeness to God, the significance of the Holy Ghost, love for God, and willingness to do God's will, as well as belief and adherance to Mormon doctrines, programs, and restrictions. Church attendance before and after joining the LDS church and the importance of family religious practices before and after the respondents were Mormons were also of interest.

The survey included questions about general demographic information. What religion did they belong to before joining the Mormon church? How important was religion in their lives? Where do they live in the United States? What kinds of cities do they come from? What social and economic classes do they feel they belong to? How old were they when they became Latter-day Saints? All of these questions fit well into a written survey form.

Again there was no way to randomly sample LDS African Americans. We solicted information through the weekly *Church News* that is mailed throughout the United States. We asked those who responded if they knew of other black Mormons in their area. Eventually approximately 500 people received the survey, and 201 were completed and returned for a response rate of 40 percent.

The survey was also mailed to all those who had been interviewed, so there was some overlap. A comparison of survey responses and interviews shows that those surveyed were less likely to attend church than those interviewed. A criticism of the interviews had been that they represented mainly practicing Latter-day Saints and not lapsed members. The surveys may help explain why black Mormons disaffiliate. We also assumed a higher degree of candor in the anonymous surveys. In reporting results in this and subsequent chapters, I identify whether the information comes from oral histories, surveys, or both. Each has strengths that the other lacks: specific responses from the survey and detailed examples from oral histories. These data sets are used throughout this study.

STATISTICAL PROFILE OF PARTICIPANTS

Who responded to the survey and participated in the oral histories? How do the results compare with other surveys with black Americans or with Latter-day Saints? Table 4.1 helps in answering the first question. Slightly more women than men participated in both the interviews and survey. Those interviewed were on average approximately five years younger than survey respondents (41 compared to 46). The General Social Survey (GSS) samples 1,500 Americans conducted annually since 1972. Because random sampling methods sometimes include only a small percentage of blacks, for example, occasionally the GSS has conducted an additional survey which "oversamples" blacks. Our LDS sample was similar in most respects to the GSS samples. For example, just under a quarter (22.2 percent) were in their thirties and three-quarters (74.8 percent) were between ages twenty and fifty in both our LDS surveys and the GSS surveys.[3]

Nearly half of both the LDS survey respondents and interviewees were married. More never-married persons appeared in the oral history interviews. A higher percentage of widowed individuals responded to the survey. The GSS included almost the same proportion of divorced people as the LDS Afro-American Survey, but it included a category for "separated" which the LDS survey did not. The LDS respondents were more likely to be married than the GSS sample.

Historically most blacks have lived in the South. However, since World War I they have migrated north. Those responding to the

---

3. James Allen Davis and Tom W. Smith, *General Social Surveys, 1972-1987: Cumulative Codebook* (Chicago: National Opinion Research Center, 1987), np.

TABLE 4.1
DEMOGRAPHIES OF SURVEY RESPONDENTS AND INTERVIEWEES

Variable	Categories	Survey	Interviews
Gender	women	62.2	58.8
	men	37.3	44.2
Age	under 20	1.5	1.4
	20-29	11.5	23.3
	30-39	26.5	24.5
	40-49	25.5	24.5
	50-59	17.5	13.8
	60 and over	16.0	7.6
Marriage	single, never married	1.0	20.2
	divorced	20.4	17.4
	widowed	19.9	3.2
	married	34.8	49.5
	remarried	9.6	16.4
Geography growing up	deep south	42.4	33.5
	near south	17.6	14.5
	northeast	11.0	7.6
	midwest	17.5	19.9
	intemountain west	.5	1.8
	far west	7.5	8.6
Geography now	deep south	30.4	31.7
	near south	16.0	8.0
	northeast	11.0	7.6
	midwest	19.0	18.3
	intermountain west	3.5	17.4
	far west	16.4	17.0
Size of community growing up	under 2,500	11.4	
	2,500-10,000	12.4	
	10,000-25,000	8.5	
	25,000-100,000	11.9	
	1000,000-250-000	11.9	
	over 250,000	28.4	
	no response	15.4	
Size of community now	under 2,500	4.0	
	2,500-10,000	3.5	
	10,000-25,000	11.9	
	25,000-1000,000	19.4	
	over 250,000	38.2	
	no response	12.4	

survey reflect that movement. Although over 40 percent grew up in the Deep South, only 30 percent live there now. Many have moved to the Pacific Coast. The survey respondents were most likely to have grown up in urban areas, and most continued to live in large cities. However, the LDS Afro-Americans were less likely to live in urban areas than the black oversample in the GSS.

We wanted to know whether geographical locale made a difference in how blacks felt about being members of the LDS church. We also wanted to know if younger or older black members were more likely to be active. We tried to determine if coming from a fundamentalist or a denominational religious background influenced their experiences in the Mormon church. To answer these questions we computed cross tabulations, breaking down the survey responses into several categories. Region, age, gender, and education were not influential factors in any of these areas. Older people from the South and younger people from California generally gave the same responses. For example, in response to the question, "in general white members of the church are aware of the needs and problems of black Latter-day Saints," there was no significant difference in the responses given by age or education. Older people—who had grown up during segregation—were slightly more likely to feel misunderstood, but the difference was not significant. Those who agreed "when I am with my black friends I speak almost a different language than when I am with non-black friends" was not affected by educational level. We compared a number of items in this way, but most were not affected by education, region, age, or gender.

The most significant variable was church attendance. Those who attended sacrament and priesthood/Relief Society meetings were more likely to feel that their church leaders and other church members understood them. A similiar correlation holds between church attendance and positive relationships with whites. Those who attend church regularly did not feel that white Mormons "expect me to forget my 'blackness' and to fit into a 'white world.'" Likewise they were not likely to feel that "non-black members are often insensitive to blacks because of culture." Those who attend church irregularly were more likely, however, to feel "when I am with my black friends I speak almost a different language than when I am with non-black friends"; those who regularly attend church were less likely to feel this way.

It is impossible to know whether those who do not attend sacrament and priesthood/Relief Society meetings shun these gatherings because they feel unaccepted. It is clear, however, that the majority of the survey respondents attending formal church meetings do feel accepted, and this was generally true for both the educated and the uneducated. It was also true for those living in both the North and the South, for men and women, and those of all ages.

RELIGIOUS BACKGROUND

Mainline Protestant churches have been losing members since the 1950s—especially during the 1970s and 1980s—while proselyting churches with a unique lifestyle have continued to grow since the 1950s. Black mainline churches have held their ground in most cases but have not grown significantly, while black Pentecostal and Holiness churches such as the Church of God in Christ have had marked increases in membership. Most American blacks have belonged to and continue to be members of black denominations. For example, a 1920 study found 88 percent of African Americans in black churches. In 1987 sociologists Wade Clark Roof and William McKinney estimated that 85 percent of American blacks still attend black denominations. The remainder belonged to white churches, but most attended segregated congregations.[4]

Most LDS converts who returned a survey came from denominational rather than fundamentalist backgrounds. Almost 60 percent of interviewees and nearly 50 percent of survey respondents had been Baptists. Only a small proportion—15 percent of those interviewed and 9 percent of survey respondents—had been Catholics. Less than 5 percent in both the survey and the interviews were former black Methodist Episcopalians. However, 11.5 percent of those surveyed and 15.5 percent of those interviewed came from traditional white Methodist and Presbyterian churches.

More than two-thirds of both LDS black samples were former members of black congregations, but in 65 percent of the cases their new LDS congregations were all white. In over 80 percent of cases their new wards were mostly white. However, black Latter-day Saints

---

4. Wade Clark Roof and William McKinney, *American Mainline Religion: Its Changing Shape and Future* (New Brunswick, NJ: Rutgers University Press, 1987), 140-41.

in both data sets had substantial contact with whites before joining the LDS church. Their contact with whites in other settings may have made joining a majority white church a more comfortable process for them.

ECONOMIC AND SOCIAL BACKGROUND

Sociologist Wade Clark Roof and theologian William McKinney have examined the social and economic classes of members of various religions. Members of the Mormon church rose from the bottom of the lowest scale in the 1940s to the highest portion of the middle category by the 1980s. Black mainline churches, on the other hand, remained in the lower half of the bottom rank. According to Roof and McKinney, in the 1980s only 41 percent of U.S. blacks had incomes over $10,000. Over 77 percent of Mormons had incomes above that level.

In determining economic classes of various denominations, Roof and McKinney examined the "mean occupational prestige." (These ratings were first determined in the 1960s by the National Opinion Research Center. Respondents were asked to estimate the social status of 23,000 occupations. These ratings were updated in 1989 by the GSS. Based on their responses numerical prestige ratings were assigned to each profession. For example, a physician rating would be 86; most professors, 74; a chemical engineer, 73, an elementary school teacher, mid-60s; a janitor, 22; and a food preparer, 17.) The mean score for black Protestants in the 1980s was 30.9; the mean for Mormons was 38.8. The index also places 69 percent of black Protestants in the lower/working class with 31 percent as middle/upper class. In comparison 52 percent of Mormons are lower/working class and 48 percent are middle/upper.[5]

The profile of LDS African Americans more closely resembled other Mormons than it did black Americans. Of those responding to the survey, 72 percent had incomes of over $10,000. Using the prestige scale, we found that black African American interviewees had a prestige score of 47 compared to a national black rating of 32 as measured by the 1982 and 1987 GSS. Note that black Mormons score

---

5. Ibid., 112-13.

higher than Mormons generally on the prestige scale, though this may be due in part to our sampling methods.

Evidence of selectivity in proselyting appeared in the oral histories. Fifty-five-year-old Reginald Allen, active in a drug prevention program in New York City when he was interviewed in 1986 and a former federal government employee, told Alan Cherry that when he was a ward mission leader, he and the missionaries "would discuss the fact that many of our black brothers and sisters who were converts were of higher caliber than the whites. Most of them were better employed and had more education. They presented themselves as being more sincere and more spiritually guided."[6] Allen implied, and our analysis supports him, that African Americans who join the Mormon church and remain active are usually middle-class and well-educated. They have had significant contact with whites at work and in school and feel at ease in an integrated setting.

A self-rating by those responding to the survey shows that: 22.4 percent classified themselves as lower/working class; 66.2 percent were middle/upper; 1.5 percent rated themselves upper class. Our analysis of interviewees found that most were middle-class as well (1.5 percent, upper; 23.4 percent, upper middle; 51.5 percent, lower middle; 35.1 percent, working class). These ratings, once again, were closer to Mormons in general than to other black Americans.

Black Latter-day Saints like other Latter-day Saints were more educated than blacks and Americans generally. According to Roof and McKinney, 7 percent of black Protestants were college graduates; 18 percent of black Mormons surveyed had graduated from college. In 1984 BYU sociologists Stan L. Albrecht and Tim B. Heaton found that over half of Mormon men (53.5 percent) had some post-high school education compared to 36.7 percent of American men in general; 44.3 percent of Mormon women had similar training, contrasting with only 27.7 percent of American women.[7] Nearly three-quarters of black Mormons surveyed had some post-high school education.

6. Reginald Allen Oral History, 20, interviewed by Alan Cherry, 1986, LDS Afro-American Oral History Project, Charles Redd Center for Western Studies, Archives and Manuscripts, Harold B. Lee Library, Brigham Young University, Provo, Utah (hereafter LDS Afro-American).

7. Stan L. Albrecht and Tim B. Heaton, "Secularization, Higher Edu-

RELIGIOUS SWITCHING

Sociologists have identified a variety of reasons why people leave one religious tradition to join another. Roof and McKinney identified three movements in the "circulation of the saints." The first pattern is the "upward movement" where as people move up socially and economically, they switch to a religion which more closely matches their new status. According to Roof and McKinney, upward "switchers" are usually over forty-five. The second pattern is a conservative movement that occurs in reaction to secular trends in the society and religion. These people, usually younger, less educated, and of a lower social standing, take conservative positions on such social issues as abortion and gay rights. The third movement is away from church affiliation and usually consists of young people in their teens or twenties.

Moving from black Protestant churches to the Mormon church could be viewed as an upward movement. Those interviewed exemplify the upper mobility described by Roof and McKinney. Although 60 percent grew up in working class homes, only 35 percent remained in that category. Though not wealthy, more than half are solidly middle class. Over 40 percent of the survey respondents classified their childhood homes as lower middle class. More than 70 percent now have white collar jobs.

Roof and McKinney also pointed out that almost all converts who are part of the upward stream are over forty-five. Only 27 percent of black Mormons were over forty-five when they converted. Thus blacks who join the LDS church may be part of an upward stream, but they are not typical.[8]

The Civil Rights movement provided equal access to blacks in many areas of American life and changed the racial landscape dramatically. A social motive for the religious reaffiliation experienced by some men and women during the 1960s might be that reaffiliation represented a form of integration resisted by traditional black churches. In addition, during a time of changing values Mormonism's conservative doctrines, literal interpretation of the scriptures, strict

---

cation, and Religiosity," *Review of Religious Research* 26 (Sept. 1984): 49 (total pages, 43-58).

8. Roof and McKinney, *American Mainline Religion,* 172-77.

TABLE 4.2

"I feel understood by my church leaders" compared to sacrament meeting attendance.

	attends monthly or less	attends a few times a month	attends weekly
Strongly agree, agree	9	9	118
Not sure, disagree, strongly disagree	11	7	45

"I feel understood by my church leaders" compared to priesthood/Relief Society attendance.

	attends monthly or less	attends a few times a month	attends weekly
Strongly agree, agree	13	11	109
Not sure, disagree, strongly disagree	19	7	37

"I feel understood by my ward/branch" compared to sacrament meeting attendance.

	attends monthly or less	attends a few times a month	attends weekly
Strongly agree, agree	8	9	111
Not sure, disagree, strongly disagree	13	7	52

"I feel understood by my ward/branch" compared to priesthood/Relief Society attendance.

	attends monthly or less	attends a few times a month	attends weekly
Strongly agree, agree	11	10	104
Not sure, disagree, strongly disagree	21	8	42

moral code, and traditional family structure may have appealed to black converts. For example, one interviewee, Burgess Owens, mentioned that the LDS church taught him the role of the husband in the family. It may have been essentially a Victorian view of the man's role, but it appealed to him.[9]

PERSONAL REASONS FOR CONVERSION

As missionaries confirm, only a small percentage of convert baptisms result from a door-to-door canvassing (tracting).[10] But because few blacks have contact with Mormons, the statistical profile for them is different: 59.7 percent of those interviewed were contacted by tracting; 36.6 percent from referrals.

People cited a number of reasons why they found the Mormon message appealing. A significant group was searching for something they felt was missing in religion. For example, Delphrine Garcia Young was born in Oklahoma in 1937, where he attended the CME church. He moved to Kansas after high school and went to a Methodist church. Yet he did not find religious satisfaction. "I was in and out of different churches because I could not get a fullness of the gospel," he told Alan Cherry. "There was something always missing, and there was something that I could never understand about the gospel of Jesus Christ because of the way they were teaching."[11] Randolph E. Latimer, an attorney active in politics in New York City, said, "My wife, Beverly [a school teacher involved in drug prevention programs], was very interested in making a church a home. . . . I knew we needed to go to church because of the children. The children needed structure."[12]

For some, the missionaries were an answer to prayer. James

---

9. Burgess Owens, "Experiences of Black Latter-day Saints," LDS Afro-American Symposium, 8 June 1988, Charles Redd Center for Western Studies, videotape in my possession.

10. While I was on a mission in New Brunswick, I was told by the mission office that only one in one thousand people join as a result of knocking on doors.

11. Delphrine Garcia Young Oral History, 3, interviewed by Alan Cherry, 1985, LDS Afro-American.

12. Randolph E. Latimer, Jr., Oral History, 10, interviewed by Alan Cherry, 1986, LDS Afro-American.

Johnson, a heavy drinker, was praying for religion to come into his life. Those who were already religious often prayed for additional guidance and felt that the missionaries were an answer. Barbara Lancaster, a nurse in Massillion, Ohio, was confused about religion. Her husband Charles, the pastor of the Massillion's St. Luke African Methodist Episcopal church, was unsure about his continued ministry. Both recalled praying separately that their lives would be more fulfilled by religion. As Barbara recalled in her interview: "Within the last several weeks before they [the missionaries] approached me, my husband and I had been praying about some problems. . . . This particular day . . . I remember that at the end of my prayer I was saying, 'Lord, there must be something more to what we should be doing here. . . . Would you just send somebody or show us the way?' . . . It was a matter of minutes when the doorbell rang."[13]

For another significant group initial contact with missionaries was negative. Eva Willis grew up in the St. Louis area as a Baptist, then joined the Catholic church, and attended a non-denominational church where her husband Jerry was pastor. She "didn't like it at all" when Jerry invited the missionaries to discuss religion "because they had denied the blacks the priesthood." In fact she described her reaction as "quite hostile." She "thought I was satisfied where I was." Because her mother had taught her to be "at least cordial" to guests, she sat through the discussions with her husband. When Jerry decided to be baptized, Eva initially joined only because her husband did.[14]

Oddly enough, verbal attacks from former church members and her children helped to confirm her decision. In earlier religious discussions with her husband, she recalled she had commented: "In the days of old, Christians were thrown to the lions just for their beliefs. I don't see that happening today. I don't see the persecution of the saints, and I don't understand it. Something's wrong." The day after they were baptized, someone called, demanding to know if she had become a Mormon. "By the time we could turn around, it had spread through the community like wild fire. I was director of the choir

---

13. Barbara Lancaster Oral History, 2, interviewed by Alan Cherry, 1988, LDS Afro-American.

14. Eva Willis Oral History, 4, interviewed by Alan Cherry, 1988, LDS Afro-American.

at the time, and we were discharged from the church." A daughter "said she wasn't going to talk to us anymore." Willis added: "That's where my conversion really began, not with the baptism and not with the reading of the Book of Mormon but with the persecution."[15]

SUMMARY

While neither the surveys nor the interviews are representative samples, they suggest that LDS African Americans more closely resemble LDS Americans than black Americans. This match suggests that they may be part of an upward mobility stream. But the characteristics of the target church, the one they joined, are also important. The remaining chapters will use these two sets of data to study the experiences of African Americans as Latter-day Saints.

---

15. Ibid., 4.

5.

RELIGIOUS COMMITMENT

Sociologists Rodney Stark and Charles Y. Glock state in their 1968 study, "Both organizationally and theologically, the heart of religion is commitment."[1] They described five categories of commitment: belief, religious practice (public ritual and private devotions), experience, knowledge, and consequences. "Belief" is an individual's views of God and theology. Public ritual includes such public religious acts as baptism, worship, and communion. Private devotions are personal prayer and scripture reading. Most religions anticipate that members—whether new converts or lifetime members—will have a religious experience in which they receive a spiritual confirmation of the church's tenets. Churches also assume that members have some knowledge of their teachings. According to Stark and Glock, "The knowledge and belief dimensions are clearly related since knowledge of a belief is a necessary precondition for its acceptance. However, belief need not follow from knowledge, nor does all religious knowledge bear on belief." Finally, the "consequences" dimension is the working of the other four categories in a person's daily life.[2]

The LDS Afro-American Oral History Project and Survey collected information on two of these categories: belief and religious practices. This chapter compares the responses of black Mormons to three other groups: (1) white Mormons, (2) general U.S. samples, and

---

1. Rodney Stark and Charles Y. Glock, *American Piety: The Nature of Religious Commitment* (Berkeley: University of California Press, 1970), 1.

2. Ibid.

(3) black Americans. The general American information comes from the works of several sociologists who have examined religious beliefs in the United States. The Stark and Glock study, published in 1970, is the oldest. Wade Clark Roof and William McKinney's study of *American Mainline Reli- gion* is dated 1987.[3] Andrew N. Greeley published *Religious Change in America* in 1989.[4] Greeley's and Roof and McKinney's studies examine religious views in general. Stark and Glock questioned the value of looking at all Americans together by studying active members of congregations in northern California in the 1960s.

Black Latter-day Saints can be compared to LDS survey data published in an article in *Review of Religious Research* by Marie Cornwall and others. The authors used 1986 "data collected as part of a large-scale project on individual and family religious behavior among . . . Mormons in the United States." The thirty-two-page survey was mailed to 2,160 people. The study went to eighty people—thirty-two practicing and forty-eight nonpracticing Mormons selected at random from twenty-seven randomly selected wards (parishes).[5] Since the survey was drawn from the general membership of the LDS church, essentially all respondents were white. Religiosity questions included in the LDS Afro-American Survey were identical to questions used in this survey.

BELIEF

Despite an apparent decline in religious beliefs, sociologist Andrew M. Greeley found in his 1989 study that people who responded to various surveys from 1944 to 1981 had strong basic convictions of Christian values. Their answers to questions about the existence of God and life after death were positive and varied little.[6]

---

3. Wade Clark Roof and William McKinney, *American Mainline Religion* (New Brunswick, NJ: Rutgers University Press, 1987).

4. Andrew M. Greeley, *Religious Change in America* (Cambridge, MA: Harvard University Press, 1989).

5. Marie Cornwall et al., "The Dimensions of Religiosity: A Conceptual Model with an Empirical Test," *Review of Religious Research* 27 (Mar. 1986): 233.

6. Greeley, *Religious Change in America*.

In their 1970 study Stark and Glock critically pointed out that the Gallup polls did not differentiate among denominations. In their own surveys Stark and Glock found belief in the existence of God varied from 22 percent among Unitarians to 93 percent among Southern Baptists.[7] Liberal Protestants scored the lowest on orthodox Christian convictions, while more conservative Protestant groups such as Southern Baptists and Pentecostal churches had the highest. This finding, although dated, is similar to results from more recent surveys. According to Roof and McKinney's 1987 study, conservative Protestants were likely to respond positively to the query, "Do you believe in life after death?"[8]

Stark and Glock also reported that among those studied in northern California, those who went to churches were more likely to accept traditional Christian beliefs than other randomly selected respondents.[9] In other words, those who actively associated with a congregation held more established beliefs than those who simply claimed church affiliation.

Respondents to the LDS Afro-American Survey most closely resemble Stark and Glock's 1960s conservative Protestants who were actively affiliated with a congregation. In response to general questions about their religious views, black Mormons were extremely positive. Ninety-five and a half percent "agreed strongly" with the statement, "I have no doubts that God lives and is real"; 4.5 percent simply "agreed." The intensity dropped slightly when the questions became more specific. To the statement "I love God with all my heart," 87 percent "strongly agreed"; 10.5 percent "agreed." A few less, 84.4 percent, "strongly agreed" and 11.1 percent "agreed" with the statement, "I am willing to do whatever the Lord wants me to do."

In response to all the general religious belief questions, LDS African Americans surveyed rated higher than the national samples and only slightly lower than the 1960s Southern Baptists. For example, 99 percent of church-attending Southern Baptists in northern California accepted the divinity of Jesus Christ; 97 percent of black Latter-day

---

7. Stark and Glock, *American Piety*, 30-31.

8. Ibid., 30-39.

9. Ibid.

TABLE 5.1
MEANS AND STANDARD DEVIATIONS OF RELIGIOSITY
FOR BLACK AND WHITE MORMONS

	MEANS BLACKS		STD DEV WHITES	
TRADITIONAL ORTHODOXY				
Believe in the divinity of Jesus Christ	4.92	4.64	.35	.75
Have no doubts that God lives.	4.96	4.61	.21	.97
Life after death	4.88	4.62	.44	.72
Satan exists	4.84	4.56	.54	.79
Bible is the word of God	4.92	4.51	.27	.72
PARTICULARISTIC ORTHODOXY				
President is prophet	4.80	4.44	.51	.90
Book of Mormon is word of God	4.82	4.42	.50	.80
LDS is true church	4.61	4.21	.82	1.11
Joseph Smith saw God and Christ	4.75	4.37	.63	.86
SPIRITUAL COMMITMENT				
Relationship with the Lord important	4.93	4.34	.29	.94
Holy Ghost important influence	4.94	4.04	.26	1.19
Love God	4.84	4.53	.45	.82
Willing to do God's will	4.80	4.15	.53	1.04
Life has no meaning without faith	4.72	4.08	.69	1.26
CHURCH COMMITMENT				
Some doctrines hard to accept	3.53	3.40	1.48	1.49
Don't care about the church	4.74	4.32	.72	1.23
Do not accept standards	4.33	3.91	1.02	1.40
Too many restrictions	4.43	3.91	.95	1.12
Programs and activities important	4.27	3.28	.99	1.46
HOME RELIGIOUS OBSERVANCE				
Family Prayer	3.73	3.60	1.61	2.45
Family Religious discussion	3.86	3.63	1.40	1.85
Read Bible or other scripture	3.53	3.10	1.61	1.96
Family discussion of right/wrong	4.37		1.90	

Saints (93.9 percent "strongly agreed"; 4.5 percent "agreed") agreed with the statement, "I believe in the divinity of Jesus Christ." Similarly, 97 percent of Southern Baptists believed in life after death, and 96 percent of LDS African Americans accepted the concept (92.4 percent "strongly agreed"; 4 percent "agreed").

A comparison can also be made between blacks in the LDS Afro-American sample and U.S. Mormons. Black Mormons were more likely to agree with each item than those in the larger U.S. Mormon survey. Furthermore they were not only more orthodox on standard religious items about the Bible and so on, they were also more orthodox than the Mormon sample about their particular religion, the LDS church. However, black Mormon survey respondents expressed less conviction about unique Mormon doctrines. Compared with the general sample, black Mormons were more committed to both religion in general and to the LDS church in particular. The only area of agreement was the statement "Some LDS doctrines are hard to accept." Even there blacks gave more orthodox answers than U.S. Mormons in general, but the differences were not significant.

The intensity of conviction drops off for more distinctive Mormon claims. For instance, survey respondents accepted Joseph Smith's first vision and the Book of Mormon, but their rate of acceptance was lower than their beliefs in the existence of God: 94.5 percent believed Joseph Smith saw God the Father and Jesus Christ, but only 82 percent "strongly agreed." Again while 96.1 percent believed the Book of Mormon was "the word of God," only 86.1 percent "strongly agreed."

Religion has always played a meaningful role in the lives of black Latter-day Saints in this sample. Before they converted, 57.7 percent said religion was "very important"; only 17.5 percent said it was "not important." Not surprisingly, considering the emotional weight attached to changing religion, conversion to Mormonism made religion even more central to these respondents. About three-quarters of the survey respondents (76.1 percent) "strongly agreed" religion was "now more central" to their lives; 88.5 percent "agreed" or "strongly agreed" that the LDS church "greatly enhanced their views of religion."

PUBLIC RITUAL

As Stark and Glock point out, ways of expressing religious beliefs vary. For some denominations weekly attendance at church is essential. For others regular attendance is less important than key rituals such as marrying in church and having one's children christened.

The importance of "going to church" has changed for Mormons over time. Historian Jan Shipps described how modern-day Mormons would be surprised by nineteenth-century observances. For example, during the 1880s, individual congregations in Salt Lake City and other cities often did not hold sacrament meetings. Instead those interested attended a citywide afternoon meeting in the local tabernacle. She continued, "Hypothetical Saints . . . in a time machine would have been astonished to find so few Saints at sacrament meeting because the twentieth century sacrament meeting is a visible worship sign, whereas in the pioneer era more expressive worship signs were irrigation canals or neatly built or nicely decorated houses or good crops of sugar beets."[10] As Mormons gave up such distinctive practices as polygamy and communal cooperatives, the responsibility of "boundary maintenance" shifted from the church to the individual. According to Shipps, "The LDS dietary, behavior, and dress codes" are now important boundary markers, and, similarly, "worship activity . . . seems almost mandatory."[11]

The importance of attending worship services is reflected in contemporary Mormon church statistics. For example, a 1980 and 1981 study shows that 68 percent of lifetime Mormons in Utah attend church weekly. Converts are even more devout: 74 percent attend weekly. Roof and McKinney's survey of black Americans showed that attending worship services was also a measure of institutional commitment. Conservative Protestants were rated number one in terms of church attendance, black Protestants were second, and Catholics were third.[12] Other studies of randomly selected national populations show blacks attend weekly religious serv-

10. Jan Shipps, "In the Presence of the Past: Continuity and Change in Twentieth-Century Mormonism," in *After 150 Years: The Latter-day Saints in Sesquicentennial Perspective*, eds. Thomas G. Alexander and Jessie L. Embry (Provo, UT: Charles Redd Center for Western Studies, 1983), 23.

11. Ibid., 27-28.

12. Roof and McKinney, *American Mainline Religion*, 101.

ices more than white Protestants (44 percent compared to 40 percent) and are also more likely to attend midweek meetings (37 percent versus 31 percent).[13]

LDS African Americans surveyed were in general already committed church-goers. Before joining Mormonism, almost three-fifths (58.7 percent) attended services weekly. An additional 14.4 percent went a few times a month, 8 percent went monthly, and 11.9 percent went a few times a year. Only 2.5 percent never attended church. Information compiled from interviews were similar: 59.8 percent went weekly, 22.4 percent went somewhat frequently (monthly), 12.8 percent went infrequently, and 4.6 percent never or very seldom attended. That figure increased for sacrament meeting after their conversion to Mormonism: 81.1 percent said they went weekly. These figures dropped slightly for Sunday school—78.6 percent and 72.6 percent for Relief Society/priesthood meetings.

All three of these meetings are now held in a three-hour block on Sunday, but before 1981 meetings were scattered throughout the week. On Sunday priesthood meeting and Sunday school for all ages were typically held in the morning. The worship service—sacrament meeting—was usually in the evening. Primary (a meeting for children from three to twelve), Young Men and Young Women Mutual Improvement Associations (organizations for teenagers twelve to eighteen), and Relief Society (for women over eighteen) were weekday activities. Partly as a result of the gasoline shortage of the late 1970s, these meetings were consolidated. Church leaders hoped this would not only reduce travel on Sunday but allow families more time to worship together. Most respondents have joined since 1978, so they are only familiar with the consolidated schedule, yet a significant number do not endure the entire three-hour block.

It is more difficult to compare how often black members attend social activities, which vary in frequency depending on the ward. Thirty-eight percent of survey respondents said they went to activities "a few times" a year; 42 percent went monthly or "a few times" a month. Since each ward determines how many socials it will hold, it

---

13. C. Eric Lincoln and Lawrence H. Mamiya, *The Black Church in the African American Experience* (Durham, NC: Duke University Press, 1990), 382.

is impossible to estimate percentage of participation. However, four-fifths of black members attend at least some socials. No comparable information is available for white members.

Blacks also participate in exclusive LDS rituals. Three-quarters of survey respondents had participated in temple ordinances. Probably because of distance 43.8 percent attend only a "few times" a year. For the 30.4 percent of survey respondents who live in the deep South, the only temple is in Atlanta, Georgia. The 17.6 percent in the near South and Northeast must travel to Washington, D.C. For the 19 percent in the Midwest, the only temple is in Chicago. Only those in the Intermountain West (3.9 percent) and in the Pacific Coast states (16.4 percent) have closer temples. Just over a quarter (26.4 percent) go more frequently than a few times a year, and slightly more than half of this group attend monthly.

Although genealogy is not an exclusive LDS activity, its strong link with temple worship provides both a theological and a practical connection between the two. Almost 30 percent (29.9 percent) of survey respondents never did genealogy, while half (50.7 percent) do research a few times a year, and 14 percent work on family history more frequently. Inconvenience, not unwillingness, seems to be the main obstacle for blacks in participating in temple ordinances and researching their genealogy.

PERSONAL DEVOTION

Another important element of religious practice is an individual's personal relationship with God. While church attendance may be socially motivated and socially rewarding, prayer, scripture reading, and meditation are private functions of the believer. For example, in the 1960s Catholics were more likely to attend church than Protestants. But only 14 percent of Catholics in Stark and Glock's survey read the Bible regularly. No studies have examined changes among Catholics. With a long tradition of emphasizing Bible familiarity, 46 percent of Protestants included Bible reading in their lives. These figures vary by denomination. Only 20 percent of Congregationalists read the scriptures "frequently" in contrast to 86 percent of Southern Baptists and 89 percent of Pentecostal groups.[14] More specifically 35

---

14. Stark and Glock, *American Piety*, 109.

percent of Southern Baptists read daily, 28 percent weekly, and 23 percent "often" but not regularly.

Black Latter-day Saints who responded to the survey did not read the scriptures as frequently before their baptism as Southern Baptists. The option of daily reading was not included in the LDS African American Survey, but a few people wrote that in and almost certainly more would have marked it. A quarter (24.4 percent) read scriptures weekly before joining the LDS church; 15.4 percent read "a few times" a month. After conversion these figures rose dramatically with 81.6 percent reporting weekly reading and 9 percent reading them monthly.

Another aspect of personal devotion is prayer. In the 1960 northern California survey, 75 percent of Protestants and 83 percent of Catholics prayed at least weekly. Ninety-two percent of both Southern Baptists and Pentecostals reported praying at least once weekly. Only some Congregationalists (10 percent) and Methodists and Episcopalians (9 percent each) "rarely" or "never" prayed.[15] A decade later in Albrecht's Utah sample, 36 percent of Protestants and Catholics prayed "daily" and 42 percent prayed "often." Of the rest, 22 percent "never" prayed or prayed only for "special occasions." Utah Mormons rated higher: 63 percent of lifetime Mormons prayed daily and 25 percent often; 12 percent said "rarely" or at "special occasions." Of converts 72 percent prayed daily, 20 percent often, and 8 percent "never or only on special occasions."[16]

Although this question was not included in the LDS Afro-American Survey, prayer apparently played an important role in respondents' lives. Those interviewed were asked about their daily religious lives: "Tell me about your current daily life in terms of prayer, scripture reading, and home evening." Since the answers were open-ended, the responses varied, but many mentioned the importance of prayer. For example, Michelle Evette Wright, a student at Southern University in her early twenties, explained, "I have personal prayer in the morning and at night and sometimes throughout the day. Most of the time it's when I need Heavenly Father to help me

---

15. Ibid., 112.

16. Stan L. Albrecht, "The Consequential Dimension of Mormon Religiosity," *Brigham Young University Studies* 29 (Spring 1989): 87.

through something. I pray before some of my tests."[17] Joelle Margot Aull, also a young college student at Brigham Young University, talked about her difficulties in praying about her mother's death and her dating relationships with non-Mormon blacks at BYU. Yet when she was interviewed, she felt "I'm better [about praying] now than I was last year. . . . I've grown a lot closer [to God] since I just decided that is what I want to do. I want to be close to my Heavenly Father."[18] Tom Porter, a businessman who joined the LDS church prior to the 1978 revelation and did not attend for several years, recalled his experiences when he returned to church: "When I became active again, I set a goal to myself. First I have my morning and evening prayer. I am uncomfortable if I don't have it."[19]

FAMILY DEVOTION

The LDS church has emphasized family worship for years. This includes family scripture reading and weekly family meetings (now called family home evenings). The practice of family gatherings started in the Salt Lake Valley in 1909. Families were instructed to set aside time to study church teachings, participate in activities, sing songs, read the scriptures, play games, and enjoy refreshments.[20] Six years later in 1915 the First Presidency of the church officially endorsed the locally-organized program. They asked "presidents of stakes and bishops throughout the church [to] set aside one evening each month for a 'Home Evening'" where "fathers and mothers may gather their boys and girls about them in the home and teach them the word of the Lord." The First Presidency promised, "If the Saints obey this counsel, . . . love at home and obedience to parents will increase. Faith

---

17. Michelle Evette Wright Oral History, 9, interviewed by Alan Cherry, 1987, LDS Afro-American Oral History Project, Charles Redd Center for Western Studies, Archives and Manuscripts, Harold B. Lee Library, Brigham Young University, Provo, Utah (hereafter LDS Afro-American).

18. Joelle Margot Aull Oral History, 13, interviewed by Alan Cherry, 1987, LDS Afro-American.

19. Tom Porter Oral History, 6, interviewed by Alan Cherry, 1988, LDS Afro-American.

20. Thomas G. Alexander, *Mormonism in Transition: A History of the Latter-day Saints, 1890-1930* (Urbana: University of Illinois, 1986), 108.

will develop in the hearts of the youth of Israel, and they will gain power to combat the evil influence and temptations which beset them."[21] The program was formalized in 1965, as local leaders were encouraged to set aside Monday for the weekly family meetings. They prohibited ward or stake functions on that night and provided lesson and activity manuals.[22]

This formal emphasis on family worship has influenced LDS African Americans. Responses to a question about how often they discussed religion with their families before joining the Mormon church were 43.8 percent "never" and 29.9 percent "a few times a year." Even fewer read the scriptures as a family, 60.2 percent never did and 14.4 percent did a "few times" a year. Once they became Latter-day Saints, the figures were almost reversed; 46.8 percent discussed religion "weekly" with their families and 18.9 percent were not always consistent but discussed religion "a few times" a month.

Another Mormon practice is daily family prayer. In the Albrecht survey of Utah adults, 42 percent of lifetime Mormons had "daily" family prayer, with another 27 percent specifying "often." The comparable figures for converts were 45 percent and 23 percent respectively. Although the figures "never" or "only on special occasions" were quite high (31 percent for lifetime members and 32 percent for converts), Mormons prayed as families more often than Catholics and Protestants who collectively reported 16 percent had daily family prayer, 13 percent less frequently, and 71 percent "never" or "only for special occasions."[23] Black Latter-day Saint survey respondents showed marked behavior changes in this area. Although 53.2 percent said they "never" prayed as families before baptism, 51.7 percent prayed together at least weekly after baptism, and 10 percent were not completely regular but tried to pray together "a few times a month."

Because interviews asked about family religious practices in an open-ended format, it is impossible to compare responses accurately. However, of 93 people who discussed family prayer, 73 percent held it regularly, 18 percent sometimes, and 8 percent never. Seventy-two

---

21. "Editor's Table," *Improvement Era* 18 (June 1915): 733-34.

22. James B. Allen and Glen M. Leonard, *The Story of the Latter-day Saints* (Salt Lake City: Deseret Book Co., 1976), 602.

23. Albrecht, "Mormon Religiosity," 87.

men and women described family home evening practices. Of these, 49 percent held them faithfully, 31 percent occasionally, and 21 percent never. (The total is 101 percent because of rounded figures.) Sixty-two talked about family scripture reading, and 56 percent held scripture study regularly, 29 percent did "sometimes," and 15 percent "never" did.

Interviewees also discussed some of the problems they faced in including family devotion in their lives. For example, twenty-five-year-old Angela Brown, her husband, and their young son had been members for two years when she was interviewed in 1986. She explained, "On a scale of one to ten, I would say they [family home evenings] are going about seven right now. But in comparison to my life before joining the church it is ten. Prayer and studying is a really vital part of our family relationship. It is not as active as I would like it to be." Getting the whole family together for family home evening was difficult, but "I like the feeling that I get when we have them. . . . I remember the missionaries taught that families can be together forever." She also liked family scripture study: "I know if we study the scriptures together we learn to live them together."[24]

Charles Lancaster, a truck driver since 1986 when he became a Mormon and lost his job as an AME minister, pointed to the competition for family home evening time. When he was interviewed in 1988, he explained, "I wish I was as diligent as I should be, but the job that I have kind of throws a monkey wrench into my family home evening on Mondays." He added, "We do pray together. It's usually in the evening at bedtime." He also listened to scripture tapes and took the Bible, the Book of Mormon, and *Gospel Principles* to work. "I try to do as much reading as I can in between stops."[25]

Alva Baltimore was born in 1964 and joined the church in 1982, the summer after her mother was baptized. A single working mother when she was interviewed in 1986, she lived with her mother. "I think our family home evening is probably Sunday when we get in from church." They both worked in the Primary nursery but with different

---

24. Angela Brown Oral History, 7, interviewed by Alan Cherry, 1986, LDS Afro-American.

25. Charles Lancaster Oral History, 14, interviewed by Alan Cherry, LDS Afro-American.

age groups. After meetings they shared their Sunday experiences and discussed scriptures. Another "probably unusual" time for religious activities was in the car. "We sing a lot of spiritual hymns in the car and read a lot of scriptures to each other. . . . We've always said prayers in the car. It's a time when we're both together, and it's quiet."[26]

When a family has mixed religious affiliations, activities together are more difficult. Rosetta Moore Spencer, who grew up in Chicago, met her husband at Lamar College in Colorado and attended the Lutheran church with his family when they returned to Chicago. She was thinking of becoming a Baptist when she met the missionaries in 1981. She and her husband Charles were baptized Mormons, but his activity later lapsed. When she was interviewed in 1988, she answered a question about family religious practices realistically. "We've been in the church now six and a half years, and it seems like there has been a steady decline in family home evening. Recently within the year there has been a decline in family prayers and family scripture reading. . . . I guess it's making excuses, but I have recently felt if I had the support of my husband I would have more strength." Earlier "we enjoyed family home evening," she said, but her husband's work as a bus driver made scheduling a problem.[27]

CALLINGS

Catholic sociologist Thomas F. O'Dea in his study of Mormons observed that the church's lay ministry means "the church has provided a job for everyone to do and, perhaps more important, has provided a formal context in which it is to be done. The result is a wide distribution of activity, responsibility, and prestige."[28] O'Dea explained lay structure as historically influenced. Mormonism came into being "when lay responsibility in church government was widespread and developed in circumstances that demanded lay participation for the survival of the group and the carrying-out of the program.

---

26. Alva Baltimore Oral History, 25, interviewed by Alan Cherry, 1986, LDS Afro-American.

27. Rosetta Moore Spencer Oral History, 9-10, interviewed by Alan Cherry, 1988, LDS Afro-American.

28. Thomas F. O'Dea, *The Mormons* (Chicago: University of Chicago Press, 1957), 184.

. . . If western conditions caused older and established churches to make use of laymen, a new and struggling religious movement had all the more reason to do so, and no inhibiting traditions."[29] However, even a fully established Mormonism did not shift to a professional system. O'Dea contrasted Mormonism with "the Disciples [of Christ (Campbellites)], who also obliterated the distinction between the clergy and the laity by holding that no man be called a priest." He continued, "Mormonism accomplished the same thing by making every man a priest and giving him the titles of office."[30] Mormonism's already expansive definition of priesthood broadened over the years, becoming increasingly universal.

Church callings serve a variety of purposes for new members of the church. First, having a responsibility can give converts more reason to become and remain involved; they recognize they are needed and wanted in the church organization. Bryan Waterman, a white missionary in Newark, New Jersey, described the dynamics of an inner-city branch with a mostly black membership. Missionaries told soon-to-be-baptized members that they would be interviewed by the local leaders and asked to serve. But because of high drop-out rates, local leaders were reluctant to offer callings, thus contributing to a negative spiral. "If they had to . . . pay the bus fare just to get to this Mormon church which is located on the opposite side of the city and they don't have a calling, they don't have any responsibility, then they can just go to church on the corner," explained Waterman. "If they don't have a responsibility, then there is really nothing at face value separating our church from theirs." Local leaders' view of new converts as potential backsliders became, Waterman felt, a self-fulfilling prophecy.[31]

Mazie Gathers of Pineville, North Carolina, expressed concerns about callings that were slow in coming. She felt that she and her husband David had been inspired to purchase a home in a white neighborhood so missionaries could find them. Mazie, who had been active in the Methodist, Baptist, and Holiness churches as a child in North Carolina, moved to New York City in her late teens

---

29. Ibid., 174.

30. Ibid.

31. Bryan Waterman Oral History, 5, interviewed by Jessie L. Embry, 1991, LDS Afro-American.

to live with her sister. She married David and lived in New York until their children were in high school. They then returned to North Carolina where they met missionaries in 1981. Mazie wanted to be involved, but their first experiences were negative. They were called on to speak extemporaneously and though the leader apologized for not giving them time to prepare, they were not asked to speak again for months. Although every adult in a congregation is ideally assigned two male home teachers and two female visiting teachers who make monthly visits of instruction and service, no such teachers contacted the Gathers nor were they asked to serve in such callings themselves.

One day Mazie told David that she was not going back to church: "I like the church. I like the teachings. It is one church that I have been to that I really feel that love as I walk in the door. I know that there is where I need to be. But Heavenly Father does not want me to sit in the corner." After praying, she felt she should return. This time she was assigned to teach Primary and enjoyed it very much. "I really learned from my students," she said, because they asked questions that she had to research.[32]

Other interviewees related the connection between callings and strengthened commitment. DeNorris Clarence Bradley, formerly with Holiness and non-denominational churches, became interested in Mormonism after a roommate joined. Bradley was baptized in 1985 and was serving as the ward librarian in Winston-Salem, North Carolina, when he was interviewed a year later. He explained: "A good thing about the church is they do try to get you working as soon as you get into the church. I think that is good because you need to get involved in something to stay a member and to make you not feel like you are an outsider. . . . You have to work well with all the white members if you have a calling."[33] Emma Williams, a widow from Hickory, North Carolina, had been a member for over a year when she was interviewed in 1986: "I teach every first Tuesday in the Relief Society, home management. I am a visiting teacher. I am a Sunday school secretary. I enjoy

---

32. Mazie Gathers Oral History, 12-13, interviewed by Alan Cherry, 1986, LDS Afro-American.

33. DeNorris Clarence Bradley Oral History, 29, interviewed by Alan Cherry, 1986, LDS Afro-American.

these callings. They laid their hands on my head and gave me those callings. I appreciate them and I try to live up to their expectations."[34]

The survey included an open-ended question asking for current church calling and leaving space to list previous callings. One-fifth (19.9 percent) of respondents listed no current church position. This number correlated closely with almost one-fifth (18.9 percent) who said they did not attend sacrament meeting weekly.

Respondents with callings served throughout the organizations. Eighteen percent had stake positions (more than 60 percent of these were part-time missionaries). Seven percent of the total number were clerks or members of high priest/elders' quorum presidencies, with an additional 5.6 percent of the total serving as members of bishoprics or executive secretaries to the bishop. (Of the 75 men responding to the survey, 13.3 percent served in bishoprics.) The majority, 60.1 percent, were involved in ward auxiliaries: Relief Society, Young Men and Young Women, Primary, and other callings such as the music committee, home teaching, visiting teaching, and singles programs. More people (85.5 percent) had a previous calling, suggesting that some less active individuals may have been more involved at some point. Nearly three-quarters (73.8 percent) of these positions were in ward auxiliaries. Most people listed only one or two previous church callings. This indicates either limited experience or selective reporting of the most significant positions.

Another way to evaluate church callings is to assess the degree of responsibility involved. In a hierarchical system responsibility is often equated with status, despite frequent assertions that all callings are important. Converts are not slow to draw the same conclusions. For example, Clement Charles Biggs from Birmingham, Alabama, a member since 1978, called being a counselor in the branch presidency "one of the greatest honors I could have had. . . . With that calling came a lot of responsibility."[35]

Sherrie Honore Franklin, who joined the church with her husband and children in 1984, told an anecdote that captured the perception

---

34. Emma Williams Oral History, 28, interviewed by Alan Cherry, 1986, LDS Afro-American.

35. Clement Charles Biggs Oral History, 7, interviewed by Alan Cherry, 1987, LDS Afro-American.

of status. In one ward in New Orleans, Sherrie's husband Harvey was a member of the bishopric while Sherrie was a counselor in the Primary. When they moved to a new ward, Sherrie's mother asked, "Do you carry your positions with you?" When Sherrie said no, her mother said, "I guess you have to start from the bottom, work your way on up." Sherrie said, "It doesn't work like that" and had trouble diffusing her mother's view of "politics in it."[36]

For the purpose of analysis, we devised a rating system based on level of supervision. "Major" leadership responsibility was defined as bishopric, auxiliary president, or priesthood quorum president levels. "Medium" responsibility was assigned to counselors in priesthood quorums or auxiliaries or ward clerks. "Minor" responsibility was seen as being held by people in all other positions, including teachers. This analysis showed that 23.3 percent of black LDS respondents held major current ward or stake callings; 19.4 percent held medium leadership positions; and 57.3 percent minor ones.

Only half of those interviewed volunteered information about current church positions and less than half (about 40 percent) mentioned previous church positions. Four percent of these were currently home or visiting teachers, 19.6 percent had teaching or "minor" ward callings, 8 percent were counselors or clerks ("medium"), and 10.7 percent had "major" administrative callings. In terms of previous church positions, 11.2 percent had held "major" positions.

Black members also commented on the public image aspect of their callings. For example, Winston A. Wilkinson of the Washington, D.C., area, was an attorney for the U.S. Department of Education. He had worked in several positions, including a bishopric, and was a high councilor at the time of his interview. Having blacks in visible church positions "helped in terms of the whole mystique that blacks have about the church," he observed. "They can come in and see blacks in leadership roles, which I think is very helpful in terms of the church and the outreach."[37] Roger Grayson, who was baptized in 1981, had served as ward mission leader and was a high councilor in Monroe,

---

36. Sherrie Honore Franklin Oral History, 10, interviewed by Alan Cherry, 1987, LDS Afro-American.

37. Winston A. Wilkinson Oral History, 10, interviewed by Alan Cherry, 1986, LDS Afro-American.

Louisiana, when he was interviewed in 1989. He said: "The primary reason I was assigned was because they needed a black leader in the area. Sometimes I wonder whether I was actually qualified." Then he added, "I guess the Lord qualifies you whether you're ready to do something or not. That's a growing experience."[38]

Other interviewees also mentioned reluctance to accept callings for which they did not feel "qualified" and testified to blessings they felt they gained from them. Benjamin R. Washington, a truck driver, was one of eleven children in a multi-religion family. His mother was Methodist, his father was Baptist, and his aunt was Holiness; Washington attended all three churches. He had been a Latter-day Saint for only eight months when he was interviewed in January 1986. His first calling came quickly: "When I first became a member of the church, instantly President Keele wanted me to be his counselor. I was baptized one Sunday, and a few weeks later I was sustained as his counselor and into the priesthood, all in one operation."[39]

Vivian Collier, a divorced mother from Richmond, Virginia, who had little religious training as a child, a Baptist before her conversion in 1982, recalled being asked to speak in church after she had been a member for six months. "I was petrified. It was only for five minutes, but I didn't think I was going to breathe through it. I made it through it, and since then I'm not afraid to get up and give talks." She also served as a Primary teacher and then taught mother education lessons in Relief Society. "That was a challenge for me because I was not used to getting up before people." She also served as a stake missionary and then as Relief Society president. "The church builds you as a person and lets you know what you are capable of doing," she summarized. "It puts you in positions where you grow as a person. . . . With each calling, it's like it's always been for me because I've been the one who needed to learn something."[40]

Others expressed similar feelings. James Ashley Fennell II, a

---

38. Roger A. Grayson Oral History, 7, interviewed by Alan Cherry, 1989, LDS Afro-American.

39. Benjamin R. Washington Oral History, 17, interviewed by Alan Cherry, 1986, LDS Afro-American.

40. Vivian Collier Oral History, 3-4, interviewed by Alan Cherry, 1986, LDS Afro-American.

twenty-seven-year-old medical student in Greenville, North Carolina, had been baptized in 1980 but was inactive until he "was converted" in 1984. In the two years since then he had taught children ages four, five, and six, worked with Cub Scouts, and had been a counselor in the elders' quorum. He commented: "My spiritual development has been like a staircase. It has been going forward in so many ways. I am surprised sometimes at the choices that the Lord makes for me, but I cherish every calling that he extended to me and try to do my best in every one."[41] Maxine Wardlaw, who was born in Charlotte, had been a member for two years when she was interviewed there in 1986. She had taught Primary and was currently a counselor in the Primary presidency. Her patriarchal blessing had promised her that she would "get a lot of callings in the church and there [would] be a lot of challenges." She said she was "really looking forward to it because I feel anything the Lord calls me to do has got to be worth doing. I enjoy the callings I do have."[42] Rosetta Moore Spencer, a thirty-seven-year-old mother when she was interviewed in 1988, ticked off a long list of positions in Sunday school, Young Women, Primary, and Relief Society in the Hyde Park Ward in Chicago, adding, "Each time I've had a calling, I've learned so much and everything that I've learned has improved my life."[43]

Emma Jean Ida Dickerson, an older widow, lived in Philadelphia with her divorced daughter and grand-daughter, also Latter-day Saints. She had been a member for three years when she was interviewed in 1986. She was often ill and could not leave her home, but her ward found a way for her to help:

> Right now I am sort of the one that they use for compassion. I send out letters to the different members. I send out Relief Society books to the different members. I send out get-well cards for those who are sick. If any of the members are sick and in the hospital and they have left families behind, I call the different members and get food sent there. . . . That is

---

41. James Ashley Fennell II Oral History, 5, interviewed by Alan Cherry, 1986, LDS Afro-American.

42. Maxine Wardlaw Oral History, 23, interviewed by Alan Cherry, 1986, LDS Afro-American.

43. Rosette Moore Spencer Oral History, 16, interviewed by Alan Cherry, 1988, LDS Afro-American.

my missionary work that I do here from home. I enjoy that. I know I am working for the Lord.[44]

Another benefit for some was the opportunity to see how the church operates. Winston Wilkinson had that view: "There have been some great callings in terms of my learning about the church, not only the spiritual part, but understanding the administrative part of how the church is run."[45] Gloria Turner, who grew up a Baptist, attended the Catholic church, and then converted to Mormonism in 1984, was serving as a Relief Society president in Baton Rouge when she was interviewed. "That's when my testimony of the church began to develop," she affirmed. "I received inspiration that caused my testimony to grow and to know that this was truly the Lord's church with the organization of things and the order that things were done."[46]

Jerry Watley, the seventeenth of twenty-two children, grew up in Birmingham, Alabama, during the 1950s. In 1978, working at a convenience store, he met a white woman, an inactive Mormon, who later became his wife. When she started going back to church, he became interested and joined. In recalling his church positions, he said that as "the elders' quorum president, . . . I have to get to know each and every member. I must know their needs, their problems, and things they may come in contact with." He also talked about being a ward clerk. "It was headaches! I don't think I ever want to be a clerk again. Too much paperwork! . . . [But] by being a clerk . . . I got to know so many . . . people."[47]

Another benefit some blacks saw in callings was developing a sense of community. Lester Jefferson, elders' quorum president of the Hyde Park Ward in Chicago, had been a member since 1982. Involvement in group family home evenings, Boy and Girl Scouts, literary classes, and signing classes for the hearing impaired helped

---

44. Emma Jean Ida Dickerson Oral History, 5, interviewed by Alan Cherry, 1986, LDS Afro-American.

45. Wilkinson Oral History, 10.

46. Gloria Turner Oral History, 5, interviewed by Alan Cherry, 1987, LDS Afro-American.

47. Jerry Watley Oral History, 18-19, interviewed by Alan Cherry, 1987, LDS Afro-American.

bring the ward close together because "we've got something to do together."[48]

Having church positions was not always a positive experience. Prejudice from whites unused to working with blacks was a persistent problem. Mazie Gathers, called as second counselor in the Relief Society, admitted, "It was hard for me. I did not know what to do. I was told I had to go ahead and do the job myself if no one else would." When she told the branch president that she was having trouble in the calling, he held a meeting with the whole presidency. One of the women "was so upset that she said I owed her an apology. The president of the branch asked if I would apologize to these sisters because I said my feelings and they felt that I did not want to participate. They had it all turned around." She did apologize, but problems continued. Prepared by a premonition of her release, she was not surprised when the branch president released her because of "some confusion in the Relief Society." He asked if she would leave the church over the incident. She assured him that she knew about the release spiritually and she would not become inactive.[49]

Edwin Burwell, who lived in Greensboro, North Carolina, in 1986 where he was interviewed, had been a member for eleven months. He noticed that one member of the elders' quorum would not accept assignments from him, though he would from other members of the presidency.[50]

Sarah Kaye Gripper, who lives in Springfield, Illinois, and became a Mormon in 1985, was struggling with her feelings about the church when she was interviewed in 1988. She felt "totally alone in Relief Society. I hate it. It's just very cliquey." She enjoyed being a Primary teacher, but "then the Primary president was calling us every Saturday afternoon and talking about gossipy things to me. She was cutting people down. . . . It was just too much for me. . . . I asked the bishop to release me from that calling because it got so bad." Her next calling

---

48. Lester Jefferson Oral History, 12, interviewed by Alan Cherry, 1988, LDS Afro-American.

49. Mazie Gathers Oral History, 13-14.

50. Edwin Burwell Oral History, 9, interviewed by Alan Cherry, 1986, LDS Afro-American.

was ward chorister even though she had "no musical background whatsoever." Eventually "it just didn't gel together. I did learn something out of the calling which is what the bishop said. Again, I asked to be released." After that, she said, "I fell into a valley." She felt that she didn't fit in, not only because she was black but for other reasons she didn't fully understand.[51]

For Robert Brown, trained as an AME minister, fitting in was not a problem. He became a Mormon in 1975. After the priesthood announcement, he served a mission to Brazil and was a counselor in the bishopric when he was interviewed in 1987. As "a black man that's in the bishopric," he acknowledged, "he could become bishop" but felt that it was not an issue for the members.[52]

Home teaching and visiting teaching ideally function to keep members in contact with each other and to take care of each other. However, because they are low-visibility positions, virtually universally available to all interested adults and outside the Sunday meeting hierarchy, there is often a sense that these are not important callings and they are sometimes neglected. The oral history participants reported mixed reviews on these callings. Bryan Waterman expressed frustration that one new family received neither callings nor regular visits from home teachers. The white home teacher lived outside the branch boundaries and was one of several men assigned "imported" to the branch to provide leadership. This home teacher lived half an hour away "and he has his full work schedule." Waterman was sure "there is someone who lives close to them that could fill the role," adding, "There are a number of times the members don't even know that just on the other side of their block is another member of the church. . . . They could be responsible for each other."[53]

Crystal Gathers Clark, who attended a ward in Raleigh, North Carolina, had been a member for over a year when she was interviewed in 1986. She and her visiting teacher partner got "along great," but her husband and his home teaching partner did not. "The partner

---

51. Sarah Kaye Gripper Oral History, 3-4, interviewed by Alan Cherry, LDS Afro-American.

52. Robert Coleman Brown Oral History, 10, interviewed by Alan Cherry, 1986, LDS Afro-American.

53. Waterman Oral History, 11.

could care less about us. It is like he speaks only when we speak to him first. . . . He won't even call Matt to go home teaching. Matt will have to ask him, and he is supposed to be the senior partner."[54]

In contrast Richard Lowe had the opposite experience when he was investigating the church in the 1960s. He and his wife had moved to California from Hawaii. Someone from the telephone office came to connect their phone and invited him to church. When Lowe said his wife was LDS, the telephone representative wrote something down. "Three days later the home teachers came over. Since I have been in the church, home teachers don't ever get anything in three days." One of the home teachers was a stake missionary, so they asked Lowe if he wanted to know more about Mormonism. The home teachers helped the Lowes move. He recalled one "just picked up the stove and walked out with it."[55] He was baptized after they moved.

Catherine Stokes, who served as a Relief Society president in Chicago's Hyde Park Ward, used the visiting teaching program so that people from different cultures could get to know each other individually. She told the visiting teaching coordinator to assign "new converts with experienced members and black sisters with whites" and chuckled as she recalled one example of culture shock. A single convert innocently asked the visiting teachers to take her to the drugstore to refill her birth control pill prescription. In a more personal vein, Stokes recalled her automatic assumption of bigotry when one sister she visited had a sign on the door, "Please use the back door." Deliberately she stifled her response, went to the back door, and had an enjoyable visit with the Chinese sister who knew nothing of the significance of back doors.[56]

SUMMARY

A comparison of primarily white American Mormons with black Mormons shows blacks to be religiously committed. There are several

---

54. Crystal Gathers Clark Oral History, 10, interviewed by Alan Cherry, 1986, LDS Afro-American.

55. Richard Lowe Oral History, 11, interviewed by Alan Cherry, 1986, LDS Afro-American.

56. Catherine M. Stokes, "'Plenty Good Room' in Relief Society," *Dialogue: A Journal of Mormon Thought* 21 (Winter 1988): 85, 88.

reasons for this. First, almost all black respondents were converts and are more likely to be religiously active and theologically orthodox. (The snowball technique of finding blacks through referrals probably resulted in selectivity, as well.) Also both the LDS Afro-American survey and the general LDS church survey had higher response rates from people who consider themselves practicing Mormons. All this aside, blacks in the United States are more religious than whites. The black church is central to the lives and community of most blacks, and this centrality of religion transfers to the LDS church when blacks become Mormons. They seem to be more believing and committed than other members of the LDS church. An overwhelming majority of black Latter-day Saints are religious people who came from religious backgrounds and who continue in that tradition. They believe strongly in traditional Christian doctrines. They attend church services as much as other Mormons and more than Protestants and Catholics. They continue a personal relationship with God through private devotions and try to heed Mormon church leaders' counsel to worship in their homes as families. They are also slowly emerging in ward- and stake-level leadership positions, a further reflection of their devotion.

6.

CULTURAL INTERACTION

Whenever two individuals interact, personality differences, undefined expectations, and unexpressed motives can hinder good relationships. These obstacles are magnified when people from separate cultures meet. Human nature simplifies and generalizes experience. Stereotypes develop when attributes of one member of a cultural group are bestowed on others of that group. When generalizations are pejorative, discrimination results. When views are positive, integration is more likely.

Sociologists chart several ways cultures deal with other groups. At the extreme of nonassimilation and conflict are extermination, expulsion, and secession.[1] Less drastic responses include segregation, assimilation, and cultural pluralism. To use food as a metaphor, segregation is meat and potatoes in separate spots on a plate, cultural pluralism is stew, and assimilation is potatoes without meat. Another solution is fusion—a puree, where meat and potatoes are indistinguishable from each other.

Assimilation has nearly always been the expressed choice of dominant cultures because it requires the minority culture to adapt. The controlling group makes few adjustments.[2] Although the "melting pot" metaphor has been used to characterize the expressed intent in the United States, this goal is seldom realized for peoples of color, and

---

1. Richard T. Schaefer, *Racial and Ethnic Groups* (Boston: Little, Brown, and Co., 1979), 33-35.

2. Ibid., 37.

the United States remains a racially conscious society where fusion is rarely realized. This chapter examines whether the LDS church has been more successful in integrating black Americans.

ASSIMILATION IN THE LDS CHURCH

Assimilation describes Utah Mormon immigrants during the nineteenth century. Up to World War II, immigrants considered it a virtue to accept the dominant culture. In a 1903 open letter "to the Swedish Saints: Instructions in Regard to the Holding of Meetings, Amusements, Social Gatherings, etc.," the First Presidency emphasized, "The council of the Church to all Saints of foreign birth who come here is that they should learn to speak English as soon as possible, adopt the manners and customs of the American people, fit themselves to become good and loyal citizens of this country, and by their good works show that they are true and faithful Latter-day Saints."[3]

In this emphasis the LDS church did not differ greatly from the larger pattern of European immigration in the United States, although Andrew Rolle argued in his study of Italian Americans that the necessary interdependence among colonists in the sparsely settled West made it easier for immgrants to be absorbed there than in the urban East.[4]

Additional factors worked for assimilation in LDS society. Those already in Utah understood the desire of newcomers to be in Zion and felt a religious obligation to accept and love them as brothers and sisters in the gospel. Historians Leonard J. Arrington and Davis Bitton state, "If the reality fell short of the ideal, it seems fair to say the usual harsh lines between different nationalities and between old and new arrivals were softened by Mormon values and programs."[5] Newcomers to Logan, Utah, assigned to work on the Logan temple expressed the same idea when they inscribed in the wet plaster of an interior wall:

3. In William Mulder, *Homeward to Zion: The Mormon Migration from Scandinavia* (Minneapolis: University of Minnesota Press, 1957), 252-53.

4. Andrew F. Rolle, *The Immigrant Upraised: Italian Adventurers and Colonists in an Expanding America* (Norman: University of Oklahoma Press, 1968), 5-6, 13.

5. Leonard J. Arrington and Davis Bitton, *The Mormon Experience* (New York: Alfred Knopf, 1979), 136-37.

"We ar hear seavral nachanaletey and the beast of feleing with all men" ("We are here several nationalities and the best of feelings with all men"). Estimates of Salt Lake City's foreign born population during the 1880s ran as high as 80 percent, but there were few conflicts.[6]

LDS immigrants worked actively to adopt the English language and American lifestyle. In marked contrast to Scandinavian and German Lutherans in other parts of the country, where the native-language newspapers and denominational schools conducted in the mother tongue held communities together for generations, LDS converts accepted American culture as a part of becoming Mormon. Although non-English congregations and newspapers existed in Salt Lake City,[7] immigrants tried to learn English rapidly so their associations could be expanded to include Mormon neighbors and ward members from all countries. As a result LDS Euro-Americans were largely assimilated in one generation, whether immigrants came to Utah during the 1850s or the 1950s.

For converts Mormonism was more than religion; it was a new cultural tradition. According to historian Klaus J. Hansen, "Those who became Mormons did not merely exchange one religion for another such as exchanging Baptism for Presbyterianism, but entered into a new and all-encompassing world that, like Islam, regulated the lives of its members both spiritual and temporal."[8] Indians who join the church in Bolivia wear white shirts and ties to church, the encouraged dress of Mormon men everywhere. The church builds standard plan chapels recognizable whether they are in Orem, Utah; Independence,

---

6. John Taylor Exhibit, President Gallery, Museum of Church History and Art, Church of Jesus Christ of Latter-day Saints, Salt Lake City, Utah.

7. For a general study, see Richard L. Jensen, "Mother Tongue: Use of Non-English Languages in the Church of Jesus Christ of Latter-day Saints, 1850-1983," in *New Views of Mormon History: A Collection of Essays in Honor of Leonard J. Arrington*, eds. Davis Bitton and Maureen Ursenbach Beecher (Salt Lake City: University of Utah Press, 1987), 273-303. Some specific studies include Mulder, *Homeward to Zion*, and Jessie L. Embry, "Little Berlin: Swiss Saints of the Logan Tenth Ward," *Utah Historical Quarterly* 56 (Summer 1988):222-35.

8. Klaus J. Hansen, *Mormonism and the American Experience* (Chicago: University of Chicago Press, 1981), 120.

Missouri; Frankfurt, Germany; or Tokyo, Japan. In these small examples of outward appearance lies the assumption that being Mormon means leaving one cultural tradition and entering a new one.

The process has not been complete. According to historian Jan Shipps, "Notwithstanding the rosy picture of a world filled with Mormons which is being projected by the *Church News* and the official *Ensign*, the power of the LDS gospel to sustain communities of Saints throughout the world without requiring them to adopt peculiarly American attitudes and stereotyped life styles has not yet been fully proven."[9]

The question Shipps raises is relevant even in the United States, just as multicultural studies show that historically America has not been the melting pot that was presented in earlier history books. Contemporary Latino Americans, native Americans, Polynesian Americans, and Asian Americans as well as African Americans have resisted cultural obliteration and can all point to examples of not being fully accepted by white Latter-day Saints. Odessa Neaman, a Yakima-Shoshone, for example, told a story about Mormons protesting loudly against her cousin playing native American music in her apartment.[10] Many ethnic students at Brigham Young University explained they first felt they were a minority when they were treated differently by the predominantly white student body.[11]

Although some people from different cultures might learn to interact in the public sphere, work, school, and church meetings, they might not interact at all in their private lives. Two businessmen might speak the same professional jargon, wear the same accepted three-piece suit, and conduct committee meetings using Roberts's *Rules of Order*. Yet one might go home, pull on a t-shirt, and relax in front of the television with a Coke while the other removes his shoes, meditates

---

9. Shipps, "The Mormons: Looking Forward and Outward," *Christian Century*, 16-23 Aug. 1978, 39.

10. Odessa Neaman Oral History, 36, interviewed by Jessie Embry, 1990, LDS Native American Oral History Project, Charles Redd Center for Western Studies, Archives and Manuscripts, Harold B. Lee Library, Brigham Young University, Provo, Utah.

11. Steven Chris Vigil Oral History, 2, interviewed by Katuska Serrano, 1991, LDS Hispanic Oral History Project, Charles Redd Center for Western Studies, Archives and Manuscripts, Lee Library.

in a Zen garden, and relaxes with a highly stylized tea ceremony. LDS ethnics thus struggle to determine what part of their cultures they may maintain in the Mormon church and what of the Mormon culture they should adapt.

What are the private and public experiences of LDS African Americans in blending with Mormon culture and interacting with white members? Since LDS church meetings are usually integrated, some of the experiences blacks have at church are similar to their encounters with whites at work and school. In this study the sphere of public interaction is attendance at church meetings and church-sponsored socials. Private experiences involve friendships and participation in non-church-related social activities.

Worshipping with people who are not black is a new experience for most black Mormons. Survey respondents had considerable contact with non-blacks before joining the Mormon church, but even more after conversion. While many (54.2 percent) said they "very often" spent time with "non-blacks" before joining the church, more (71.1 percent) do now. When "very often" and "sometimes" responses are combined, the figures jump from three-quarters (75.6 percent) before joining to almost 90 percent (89.6 percent) after. Most of that contact is apparently with members. When asked how often they now spend time with non-members, responses were similar to interaction with non-blacks before they became Mormon (49.3 percent "very often"). Obviously, this increased exposure escalates the possibility of both positive and negative experiences. What in fact happens?

Bobby Darby grew up in Erie, Pennsylvania, and lived in Buffalo, New York, before moving to Charlotte to stay with an uncle. There he met his wife Darlene, also from North Carolina. The Darbys had not been active in a church before Mormon missionaries knocked on their door. When asked how white Mormons had accepted him, Bobby responded: "We were accepted pretty good, better than we would have expected. We see in some people that they really do not like being around us; but out of a love of Christ, they do it anyway. We can respect that, too. A lot of things that I do, I do not like doing; but if the Lord says it is the right way to do it, then we just do it and just expect the best."[12]

---

12. Bobby Darby Oral History, 7, interviewed by Alan Cherry, 1986,

Simultaneous perceptions of positive and negative experiences were not uncommon. As Alan Cherry conducted interviews, he concluded that black Latter-day Saints are experiencing integration in the church, while at the same time cultural differences lead to prejudice and discrimination. According to Cherry, this is not necessarily contradictory. American blacks confront negative experiences daily in the United States, and an incident that Euro-Americans might respond to negatively may well be dismissed by many African Americans as "the way things are."

EFFECTS OF 1978 PRIESTHOOD ANNOUNCEMENT

What effects has the priesthood announcement had on black Mormons' experiences? Has the lifting of priesthood restriction made a difference in how black members feel about the church, and if so in what way? Did white Mormons change their views of blacks after the announcement?

After due allowance for individual variation, the perhaps unexpected pattern that emerged from the survey showed that many who joined prior to 1978 were as positive about their feelings of acceptance as those who joined afterwards. Six of the survey questions were directed to those who joined the church prior to the announcement. Only twenty-five answered these questions, and their responses varied widely. While this number is small and the results statistically insignificant, they do show some of the concerns that black Mormons had before and after the announcement. When asked whether they agreed with the statement, "My feelings about the church have changed dramatically since the revelation," a fifth (20.8 percent) said yes; less (16.7 percent) said no. More than three-fifths (62.5 percent) said there was not much change. However, to the statement, "I feel that I am more accepted by other members of the church," 4 percent said "very often" and 8 percent said "never." The majority, 52 percent, responded "sometimes," and 32 percent said "seldom." To "I feel I am a more important part of the church experience since the revelation," 22.2 percent said "very often" and 44.4 percent said "sometimes." And to "I

LDS Afro-American Oral History Project, Charles Redd Center for Western Studies, Archives and Manuscripts, Lee Library (hereafter LDS Afro-American).

feel even less accepted by other members of the church, a third (33.3 percent) said "never," and 48.1 percent said "very seldom." So while some felt the priesthood announcement made a difference in their acceptance in the LDS church, others felt it made no difference at all.

The survey included two open-ended questions. To "the biggest differences I have noticed among black members since the revelation," the most frequent responses were priesthood ordinations and outreach to other blacks. To "the biggest difference I have noticed among non-black members with regard to black members since the revelation," the main response was more acceptance.

The interviews allowed people to elaborate on these feelings. Tom Porter, who was baptized in 1958, said he enjoyed working with white LDS servicemen in Europe. He became a Latter-day Saint after he returned and was living in Indiana, where "I was totally accepted into the church. I had not one derogatory word spoken to me about it. It was just a beautiful experience for me. I loved it." He was inactive for seven years, but when he went back, "I walked into the church and sat down, and it was as though I'd never been away. I was totally accepted. I have yet to be any place I've felt uncomfortable in the church in Alaska and Hawaii and throughout the continental United States. Any place I am on a Sunday I go to church. I'm just totally accepted as though I was a member of that ward and was there last Sunday."[13]

About the time Van Floyd joined the church in 1975, the family moved within the Los Angeles area. They were immediately welcomed into the new ward. A daughter, Gayla Renee Floyd, who had joined in 1973 when she was eleven, recalled: "Everybody was interested in the Floyd family. It was very comfortable. We were a different family than anything that they'd ever seen. We started to feel comfortable with them." When asked how she was accepted by the wards where she has lived, she replied: "I think very well. They think of me as one of them."[14]

Robert Lang commented, "One thing I found out about people: if they have a love for you, they will do anything for you. I do not know

---

13. Tom Porter Oral History, 4, 6, 10, interviewed by Alan Cherry, 1988, LDS Afro-American.

14. Gayla Renee Floyd Oral History, 4, 12, interviewed by Alan Cherry, LDS Afro-American.

of anybody in the Inglewood Ward that, if I would ask them to do anything, they would not put forth an effort to do it. They are good ward brothers."[15]

HYDE PARK WARD

Most black Latter-day Saints never dealt with priesthood restriction. The more recent issue has been acceptance in integrated congregations. The Hyde Park Ward in Chicago demonstrates how acceptance, individual personalities, and expectations play a major role in how black members perceive their lives as Latter-day Saints. The Hyde Park Ward is by no means typical. The congregation represents a number of cultures and provides an interesting case study. These LDS African Americans in the ward openly discussed their feelings of acceptance by black and white members and attempted to understand the situation. They articulate well the various cultural dilemmas that they face.

In 1988, when Alan Cherry conducted interviews there, the Hyde Park Ward blended Mormon faculty and graduate students with local residents. Most members perceived this diversity positively as an enjoyable challenge. Marie Smith, a forty-year-old black single mother who worked as a secretary at the university, liked the diversity that came from having "all nationalities."[16] Catherine Stokes, a black health care facility supervisor for the state of Illinois and a former Relief Society president, was openly delighted by the cultural diversity. She later reported: "We have Samoans, Chinese, blacks, Jamaicans (there is a difference), Caucasians of all flavors, Spanish, Mexican, and [the] deaf group. . . . On a given Sunday in Relief Society, you may see translating in French, Spanish, and Cantonese, and signing for the deaf."[17] One white member of the Hyde Park Ward loved singing Mormon hymns and NAACP songs in the same meeting.[18]

---

15. Robert Lang Oral History, 4-5, interviewed by Alan Cherry, 1985, LDS Afro-American.

16. Marie Smith Oral History, 16, interviewed by Alan Cherry, 1988, LDS Afro-American.

17. Catherine M. Stokes, "'Plenty Good Room' in Relief Society," *Dialogue: A Journal of Mormon Thought* 21 (Winter 1988): 85.

18. Catherine M. Stokes, videotape of Afro-American Symposium, 8

Despite this openness to diversity, some black members questioned the congregation's ability to accept African Americans. Those blacks who had been members longer helped calm troubled waters. Stokes had "regular contact" with newer blacks "to talk over things because they want to know what the white folks mean when they say thus, thus, and thus."[19] Natalia F. Thompson, an African American widow in her early sixties, had been crippled by an accident shortly before she was baptized in 1985. She listed black members to whom she felt close but added, "We haven't segregated ourselves."[20]

Other African Americans reported that other black members were not personal friends. Juanita H. Johnson, a Chicago policewoman who was baptized in 1985 and whose husband is not a member, saw Thompson as "family" and Stokes as her "mentor" in the church but stated: "The other ones I speak to and try to be encouraging if they're feeling down about certain things that are going on. I try to be positive, but I don't associate with them socially. It's strictly church-related for the most part."[21]

Marie Smith, who joined the church in 1985, agreed that most of her contact with other black Latter-day Saints was at church but attributed most of the situation to her status as a single mother: "I've never had any close relationships, and that's been sad for me. . . . The black women . . . in our ward when I first came . . . were all looking for husbands. When I came and I wasn't that kind of a person, they wondered what I was looking for probably. They felt like I was a very independent person. . . . [As a result] there's just not a closeness. No one says, 'Why don't we have Sister Smith come over?'"[22]

Natalia Thompson felt similarly frustrated at not being able to share her feelings about the gospel with a close friend: "I wish I did

June 1988, Charles Redd Center for Western Studies.

19. Catherine M. Stokes Oral History, 20, interviewed by Alan Cherry, 1988, LDS Afro-American.

20. Natalia F. Thompson Oral History, 13, interviewed by Alan Cherry, 1988, LDS Afro-American.

21. Juanita H. Johnson Oral History, 22, interviewed by Alan Cherry, 1988, LDS Afro-American.

22. Marie Smith Oral History, 18, interviewed by Alan Cherry, 1988, LDS Afro-American.

have a study partner. At church we have forty minutes in [Sunday school]. Before we can have a little discussion, the time is gone."[23]

Black members expressed a range of feelings about their inter-actions with white members. For Samuel Coggs, a single father and professional who became a Mormon in 1987, the experience was positive. Before he joined the LDS church, he reported, he had often felt like a token in mixed groups; but in the church, "I walked into a situation . . . where there's 5 percent blacks and [I] felt comfortable. . . . I haven't seen where they made any color-line distinctions in terms of how they treat me and in terms of the opportunity that I have to serve. Nobody's made me feel color-con-scious even though the numbers dictate that would happen in other situations."[24] Linda Williams, who joined the church as a teenager, was a twenty-two-year-old college student when she was interviewed. She said one reason she joined the church was because "the people were very friendly there. . . . I see no discrimination with the blacks and the whites in the church. I pretty much believe that we all believe that we are brothers and sisters."[25]

Rosetta Moore Spencer reported feeling that one ward member did not like her because she was black. However, when the man bore his testimony, he mentioned marching during the Civil Rights era, and she realized she had misjudged him. "I use that as a testimony to others," she commented. "As I've seen black sisters and brothers come and go in the church. I use [this experience] to let them know that if you look for something, you can find it."[26]

A number of Hyde Park Ward members commented that their only real interaction with other ward members, black or white, was on Sunday. Some recognized that belonging to a ward with a "big turnover" meant limited time for establishing relationships, and ac-cording to Natalia F. Thompson, "We had a pledge that everybody's

---

23. Thompson Oral History, 7.

24. Samuel Coggs Oral History, 10, interviewed by Alan Cherry, 1988, LDS Afro-American.

25. Linda Williams Oral History, 5, interviewed by Alan Cherry, 1988, LDS Afro-American.

26. Rosetta Moore Spencer Oral History, 13, interviewed by Alan Cherry, 1988, LDS Afro-American.

a committee of one as a welcome committee."[27] Others want more social interaction. Williams acknowledged that "black fellowshipping" was "low," adding, "We are so busy with our own schedules that we don't have the time to help someone else." Since she did not live in the Hyde Park area, she worried her daughter would not have enough contact with other Latter-day Saints: "Basically I just see them on Sundays. . . . But it seems that we have a friendlier relationship" than she did with non-Mormon acquaintances, even when she knew them longer. "Knowing that we are heavenly brothers and sisters helps a lot," she summarized.[28]

Janis E. Parker, a journalist who joined the church in 1986 and whose husband was not a member, also lived outside the Hyde Park neighborhood. She felt those associated with the University of Chicago were an unconscious clique. "It's not like they're trying to keep you out," she admitted, "but it's kind of hard to get in." She wanted to get to know the church members better but still felt close to them. She praised their concern during her convalescence from a surgery. "The love, the concern, the care is there, and it doesn't matter if we're the best of friends," she said staunchly. "They'll do more for you than your relatives or your long-time girlfriend or whoever will. They take the time; they make the time." She felt that Relief Society, especially homemaking meetings, gave her a chance to get to know the sisters and feel "the sisterhood and the love among the women."[29]

Marie Smith, disappointed at the low level of fellowship outside of Sunday services, acknowledged candidly: "I think I came with a chip on my shoulder because [I] expected open arms. . . . As Christians we're supposed to be Christ-like." She felt that white Latter-day Saints were "like foreigners; they have never been able to widen their horizons." For example, she said she had learned to relate to Peter Gillo, a deaf black African who taught in the Chicago area. "White people survive among themselves," she acknowledged, "but in other situations, they are threatened."[30]

---

27. Thompson Oral History, 10.

28. Williams Oral History, 6-8.

29. Janis E. Parker Oral History, 28-29, 20, 31-32, interviewed by Alan Cherry, 1988, LDS Afro-American.

30. Marie Smith Oral History, 13-14.

In addition to limited opportunities for socializing and inevitable racial/cultural differences, some also identified educational barriers. Johnson, a policewoman, explained that it was often intimidating to new members when "every other word is a three- or four-syllable word." She also felt that the university students did not know what it meant to be poor and did not perceive the resentment of inner-city residents toward "do-gooders."[31] When she attended singles' activities, partronized mainly by students in their twenties, Marie Smith, who was in her forties, felt: "I'm not really included in the conversation. When I am included, they get on an intellectual level that far outreaches me mentally sometimes. I wonder if it's not done purposely on subjects that they know I have no knowledge about like the ramifications of cosmology."[32] Another form of patronage was perceived by deaf members who felt "coddled."[33]

Victor Soil, who works for a school district in Chicago and has been a Mormon since 1982, was specific. Whites should be "reeducated" to let blacks be "self-sufficient." He explained: "It's like they were keeping black people as pets. But they're not pets. They're people that can be taught and can be of service to other people and to the Lord. They're not people just to be kept around to make you feel good."[34]

SUMMARY

As these examples indicate, the experiences of black Mormon interweave public and private assimilation, independence, and positive and negative experiences. Those who describe discrimination also affirm experiences of inclusion. Relationships between black and white Latter-day Saints are based on expectations, which vary among individuals. Since social needs vary, some are satisfied with their interactions with other Mormons while others wish for more contact. Though there is overlap between private and public spheres, each has its own dynamic as the next two chapters show.

---

31. Johnson Oral History, 16-17.

32. Marie Smith Oral History, 18.

33. Ibid., 20.

34. Victor Soil Oral History, 10, interviewed by Alan Cherry, 1988, LDS Afro-American.

7.

PUBLIC ACCEPTANCE

The category of "public interaction" in this chapter refers to the experiences of LDS Afro-Americans at church-related meetings and activities. Besides the three-hour block of Sunday meetings, there are ward socials for all members and special activities for children and teenagers. Mormons with callings also go to ward and stake "in-service" meetings to help them undestand their positions. As the Hyde Park examples pointed out, much of the interaction between Mormons takes place in these several meetings. This chapter examines the experiences of LDS African Americans in such public settings.

Two survey questions, essentially the reverse of each other, asked how blacks felt about their congregations. In response to the question "I feel like I am an important part of my ward/branch," 66.5 percent said "very often" and 89.8 said "very often" or "sometimes." Only 2 percent marked "never." However, in response to the question "I feel like an oddity in my ward/branch," just over half (52.9 percent) said "never" and 18.8 percent marked "seldom" or "very seldom." More than one-quarter (28.3 percent) marked "very often" or "sometimes" (10.5 percent, "very often"; 17.8 percent "sometimes"). People under thirty were more likely to feel like they were "oddities."

The survey posed several questions about relationships with white Latter-day Saints. To the statement, "I have found that the people in my ward/branch are eager to be friends with me," more than half (55.1 percent) said "very often" and almost an additional third (31.1 percent) said "sometimes." Over 80 percent, therefore, sensed active friendliness from ward members. Only 4.1 percent felt ward members were "never" friendly.

In response to the statement "I feel included in ward or branch social activities," two-thirds (67.5 percent) said "very often" and just over a fifth (21.5 percent) said "sometimes." Thus 89 percent felt a part of the activities at least part of the time. Only 3.5 percent said they "never" felt a part; 7.5 percent said "seldom" or "very seldom." The statement "ward/branch members do not hesitate to include me at church functions" did not elicit equally positive responses. More than half (51.8 percent) sensed no reluctance by ward members to involve them. However, 12.2 percent said there was "some" caution, and slightly more (13.7 percent) said they were "seldom" or "very seldom" included. Over one-fifth (22.3 percent) felt there was hesitation by church members to include them.

Geographical location, gender, education, segregated or integrated neighborhoods, and racial makeup of previous churches were not statistically significant variables. There was a slight tendency for those who attended church more often to feel included. This is hardly surprising, since it is difficult to include someone who is absent. But acceptance goes beyond simply feeling welcome. People like to feel at ease around associates. In response to the statement, "some non-blacks avoid me or are uncomfortable around me," the responses were once again equally divided. Almost one-third (31.8 percent) said "never." Slightly less (28.3 percent) said "seldom" or "very seldom." The rest 40.2 percent felt some discomfort. Even very active black members occasionally felt they were being avoided. Johnnie McKoy, a member of the stake high council in Greensboro, North Carolina, at the time he was interviewed in 1986, recalled going to one of the wards in his stake to speak on a monthly assignment. McKoy, who usually goes out of his way to greet people, was chatting to ward members as he walked towards the chapel door. He noticed the white bishop who was approaching the same door "slide around" to another door. McKoy could not help wondering if the bishop was avoiding him.

Although McKoy considered this incident unfortunate, similar experiences led his wife to stop attending meetings. Just after they joined in 1980, they were one of three active black couples. The bishop called McKoy to be the second counselor in the Sunday school and his wife to teach junior Sunday school. "We were still new in the church, and there was some tension there," McKoy recalled. "My wife was beginning to be treated one way, and I was beginning to be treated another. They respected me and admired me for coming to church, but they seemed to try to push my wife out. They were saying some nasty things to her." With startling candor the Sunday school officers had told Mrs. McKoy that "they were really giving her that calling because they were the worst kids in the church . . . [and] because she was black." She interpreted the calling as being a desperation move on their part; but the worst part was that "the [white] kids would start calling the [black] kids 'niggers,'" said McKoy. As a result Mrs. McKoy "woke up one Sunday morning and said she was not going back to church anymore. She said those people were not Christians."[1]

Matthew Clark, a student who lived in Raleigh, North Carolina, had been a member for about a year before his interview in 1986. He was also aware of members' discomfort. He and his wife, Crystal Gathers Clark, had been married in her parents' Mormon meeting-house in Southern Pine, North Carolina, and enthusiastically fellow-shipped by the members before their own conversion. Matthew recalled, "When we first became members [in Raleigh], everybody was very excited about us becoming a part of the church." However, it soon became apparent that members were mainly interested in a baptism, adding, "[But] as time progressed, it got to the point that it was rare that any of the members would speak to us. . . . They would always stand off and look at us like we were some freaks. We couldn't figure out why they acted distant towards us. We thought maybe it was us that were acting funny. . . . We tried to be friendlier, and it didn't work."[2]

Since adult Sunday school and other classes encourage open discussion, the survey asked, "How often do you ask questions or share your ideas during church meetings?" Over half (55.7 percent) said "very often"; a quarter (25.9 percent) said "sometimes," making a total of 80.6 percent who regularly made comments. Only 1.5 percent said "never." The survey also asked for a response to the statement,

---

1. Johnnie McKoy Oral History, 9-10, interviewed by Alan Cherry, 1986, LDS Afro-American Oral History Project, Charles Redd Center for Western Studies, Archives and Manuscripts, Harold B. Lee Library, Brigham Young University, Provo, Utah (hereafter LDS Afro-American).

2. Matthew Clark Oral History, 15-16, interviewed by Alan Cherry, 1986, LDS Afro-American.

"Non-black members of the church think I know less about the gospel simply because I am black." Over half (57.4 percent) said this "never" happened and an additional fifth (21.6 percent) said "seldom" or "very seldom." The remaining fifth were split between saying it happened "very often" (6.7 percent) and "sometimes" (14.4 percent).

Since the LDS church calls on members to be leaders and teachers, the survey asked for a response to the statement, "I feel that I have not been given as many opportunities for church service because of my race." Over three-fourths (77.7 percent) said "never"; 3.6 percent said "very often," and 6.1 percent said "sometimes." Because church leadership is overwhelmingly white, black Mormons who seek ecclesiastical or personal counsel must deal with white preconceptions. Three-fourths (76.5 percent) said church leaders had never "given me prejudicial counsel or advice." Although 8.6 percent said "sometimes," only 2 percent said that the counsel "very often" reflects prejudice. But whether the counsel is overtly prejudiced or not, a significant gap appeared in response to the statement, "I feel understood by my church leaders." Only about a third (36.3 percent) said "very often"; slightly less than a third said "sometimes" (31.3 percent); a fifth (20.4 percent) said "seldom"; 7.5 percent said "very seldom"; and 4.5 percent said "never."

Black American Mormons sense a similar gap in understanding on the part of fellow church members. To the statement, "I feel understood by the members in my ward or branch," only 28.9 percent said "very often," and 34.3 percent said "sometimes." Again the percentage of "seldom" responses (25.9 percent) was high. Only 4 percent said "never." In a rephrasing of the same issue, even fewer felt "white members of the church are aware of the needs and problems of black members." Only 16.5 percent responded "very often" while 37.2 percent said "sometimes." Almost one fifth (19.7 percent) said "very seldom," and slightly less (19.1 percent) said "seldom." Seven percent (7.4 percent) said white members were "never" aware of the needs and problems of black members. These said, however, that this perceived misunderstanding had not made them leave the church (63.2 percent, "never"; 21.4 percent, "seldom" or "very seldom"; 6 percent, "very often"; 9.5 percent, "sometimes").

Fleshing out the surveys' bare numbers, the interviews describe remarkable experiences of integration along with instances of prejudice and discrimination.

INTEGRATIONAL EXPERIENCES

All types of questions probably run through new members' minds as they approach the chapel door for the first time. Will members welcome them? Will they see any blacks? Darrin Davis joined the church in Summit, New Jersey, in 1977 as a teenager. Although "there were no black members in our ward," he recalls, "when I went to church, the people just really grabbed on to me. They were really, really super friendly. The biggest asset the church will ever have are its members and how they treat each other and how they treat newcomers."[3]

Joseph C. Smith grew up as a Baptist in Tennessee and Nebraska and joined the LDS church in 1982 while he was in military service in Germany. He and his wife Marilyn "walked into the church. There was not a black soul in there for one thing. But the people were just so friendly. Everybody shook our hands and greeted us. I did not feel uncomfortable around anyone."[4]

Elijah Royster, who worked with a Mormon in 1978, went across Honolulu to attend a fellow employee's ward. Arriving late, he was seated in an overflow area with parents and their restless children, whose noise easily defeated his efforts to "listen to the speakers." This "negative mood," however, changed after the meeting. "Then I noticed how all the Saints were so friendly and kind and shaking our hands. . . . Immediately I recognized it was genuine; it wasn't a put-on; it wasn't something phony."[5]

Van Floyd, who had been raised Methodist Episcopal during the 1930s and 1940s in Texas, was overwhelmed when he joined the Mormon church in southern California in 1975. "You could tell their feelings came from the heart," he remembered. "That type of acceptance I'd received so much until the one or two instances where someone was derogatory don't even matter. . . . It just rolls off because you know the majority is good."[6] Ed Scroggins commented on the

---

3. Darrin Bret Davis Oral History, 11, interviewed by Alan Cherry, 1985, LDS Afro-American.

4. Joseph C. Smith Oral History, 6, interviewed by Alan Cherry, 1985, LDS Afro-American.

5. Elijah Royster Oral History, 6, interviewed by Alan Cherry, 1986, LDS Afro-American.

6. Van E. Floyd Oral History, 11, interviewed by Alan Cherry, 1986,

absence "of this faked, canned jive. . . . They are for real." The sole awkward moment came when a Sunday school teacher was not sure how to describe him. Scroggins told her to "just say black."[7]

Dorothy Gray Jones grew up during the 1930s in Alabama and then moved to New York where she and her husband lived until they moved to Philadelphia in 1978. She went to college and trained to be a teacher. She was also interested in religion, so she and her husband accepted the missionaries' invitation to attend church. "Everywhere I looked I saw families," she recalls fondly. Her husband dampened her enthusiasm; "he said, 'Aw, don't be fooled. These are all people putting on a show for you. They probably knew they were going to have visitors.' . . . I thought about it and I said, 'You are probably right. I guess I have to go again then to find out for sure.'" Although her husband decided not to return, Dorothy called the missionaries a month later and asked for a ride to church. "I knew this wasn't planned. . . . When I walked in there, everybody was hugging me and shaking my hand." She added the experience was very different from the Catholic church of her childhood. "We came in, and we sat down quietly. We didn't even look back to see who was behind us. . . . When the service was over, we got up and went. There was no warmth."[8] She became a Mormon in 1980. Even though her husband never joined, ward members were "so loving, warm, and helpful" during the two years he suffered from cancer and at the time of his death; they also continued to offer her support during her widowhood.[9]

When the Wright family from Baker, Louisiana, joined the Mormon church, they heard that some white members stopped attending church services. But the rest willingly accepted the Wrights. Betty Wright Baunchand, formerly a Baptist and a member of the Church of God in Christ before joining the Mormon church at age thirty in 1978, recalled, "I think we have been accepted graciously with open

LDS Afro-American.

7. Ed Scroggins Oral History, 13, interviewed by Alan Cherry, 1985, LDS Afro-American.

8. Dorothy Gray Jones Oral History, 12-13, interviewed by Alan Cherry, 1986, LDS Afro-American.

9. Ibid., 15-16.

arms." She added, "Some of them, of course, are withdrawn, but in general they know that this is the Savior's church and this is the way it has to be. It's not a white church or a black church. It's His church."[10] Her niece, Michelle Evette Wright, who was also baptized in 1978 at age twelve, said many of the members were "excited" to see black members. Some who are now "our closest friends" confessed that they had initially "opposed . . . letting blacks come in."[11]

Johnnie McKoy attended a crowded investigator's Sunday school class in Greensboro, North Carolina, as a new member in 1980. The next week few returned. "I recognized then that I was the only black in the church. I felt like the people were not coming in the class because I had joined the church and I had already run the people out of the church. I had a guilty conscience about it." However, when he checked this perception with the members, they told him that a high turn-over among unbaptized investigators was perfectly normal. "I gave a sigh of relief to know that I was not really experiencing what I thought it was."[12]

William Thompson, who lived in Decatur, Georgia, when he was interviewed in 1987, was apprehensive when the missionaries invited him to a stake conference in Jackson, Mississippi, where he first contacted the church. He knew the meetinghouse was in a white neighborhood, yet "I was stunned" by the warm welcome. "The people were so receptive. I couldn't believe it."[13] As a result Thompson continued to investigate the church and was baptized in 1980.

Clement Biggs, who grew up in segregated Alabama, related a heartwarming story of Christian acceptance. His ward accepted an invitation to participate in a Christian fellowship bowling league. At the bowling alley a woman from another team informed him blacks were not allowed in the league: "I'm sorry you can't bowl with us today,

10. Betty Wright Bauchand Oral History, 8, interviewed by Alan Cherry, 1987, LDS Afro-American; Katherine Warren Oral History, 15, interviewed by Alan Cherry, 1987, LDS Afro-American.

11. Michelle Evette Wright Oral History, 6, interviewed by Alan Cherry, 1987, LDS Afro-American.

12. McKoy Oral History, 8.

13. William Thompson Oral History, 11-12, interviewed by Alan Cherry, 1987, LDS Afro-American.

but one day we're all going to be together. There's not going to be any black and white. It's going to be all one people." Rather than make a scene though, Biggs "just told her, 'Yes, ma'am,' and walked on out." The ward members, however, did not offer platitudes. Instead they withdrew en masse. "Everybody from our branch came on out. . . . If we couldn't bowl they weren't going to bowl," he recalled emotionally. "We all stood outside. We hugged, and we had tears." The incident was especially hard on his fifteen-year-old daughter who kept asking why they were not bowling. Biggs "waited until later when I felt better about it" to explain. He added, "I can truly state that all of the experiences . . . that I have had in this church have been positive experiences. I looked for fault when I first became a member. I couldn't find any."[14]

FACTORS INFLUENCING ACCEPTANCE

Several variables influenced black perceptions of white acceptance. Blacks who had frequent interactions with whites in other institutions found relationships at church to be more comfortable. Over half (57.4 percent) of survey respondents said they had frequent contact with whites prior to joining the Mormon church. An additional one-fifth (22.6 percent) said they "sometimes" had contact with whites before they were Mormons. Those interviewed talked about how previous contact helped relationships. Joseph Faulkner, who was instrumental in integrating Republic Steel of Gadsden, Alabama, praised Gadsden Ward members: "So many people there . . . just don't show any prejudice because they are in business and they work with both black and white."[15]

Rhoda Shelby grew up in Moses Lake, Washington, where there were few blacks. She joined the LDS church in 1981 in high school and then attended BYU. "I guess I am lucky," she commented, "because it was not that much different for me to come from Moses Lake to BYU because it was basically the same kind of atmosphere." She had no "culture shock" because she "never had [barriers] in the

14. Clement Charles Biggs Oral History, 7-8, interviewed by Alan Cherry, 1987, LDS Afro-American.

15. J. Joseph Faulkner Oral History, 15, interviewed by Alan Cherry, 1987, LDS Afro-American.

first place."[16] David Diamond Gathers, who grew up in New York City and then moved to a white neighborhood in North Carolina with his family as a teenager, always associated with whites. When he first went to church in Raleigh, when he was in college, "I was the only black there. I did feel a little uncomfortable at first, but I figured I had always grown up around [whites] and I should not feel uncomfortable."[17]

A number of blacks attributed comfortable relations to their own attitudes. Burgess Owens grew up in Tallahassee where his father taught at Florida A & M. He played football for the University of Miami because he wanted to be in a racially mixed area. He later started a business in New York City, where he found his ward accepting. "Obviously there are going to be some folks that haven't understood that love yet," he acknowledged,

> but you should be able to get into an environment where that isn't an issue. You should not come and feel that you are the only black, the only white, or the only Hispanic. You come into an environment where people accept you because you are there and because you are their brother or sister. Now to a lot of people this sounds very dreamy. But one thing about this church is that is exactly the way I feel. I have friends of mine in this church that I don't look at the color.[18]

Ed Scroggins, an inactive Southern Baptist, married an inactive white Mormon woman. He joined the church in 1980, and then his wife and children died in a house fire. When he was interviewed in 1985 in Phoenix, Scroggins was married to a Hispanic Latter-day Saint. He recognized "that nice, warm glow" which he identified as common among Mormons because "we all came from the same Savior, and we all have his sweet spirit. That is what draws us to one another. As long as that sweet spirit is there, there is no interference."[19]

---

16. Rhoda Shelby Oral History, 22, interviewed by Alan Cherry, 1985, LDS Afro-American.

17. David Diamond Gathers Oral History, 11, interviewed by Alan Cherry, 1985, LDS Afro-American.

18. Burgess Owens Oral History, 18, interviewed by Alan Cherry, 1986, LDS Afro-American.

19. Ed Scroggins Oral History, 14, interviewed by Alan Cherry, 1985, LDS Afro-American.

Virginia Johnson, who works with contestants on television game shows, converted in 1981. Although she stated that some comments at church would have angered her in her "black power" days, she is now assertive about acceptance: "I do not go in expecting not to be accepted. I will put my hand out especially to somebody who I think will not want to shake my hand." Members comment that it seems as if she has always been a member. She corroborated, "I just feel natural there. I feel like I have been there forever."[20]

Lois W. Poret from New Orleans had attended Catholic and Baptist services before becoming a Mormon in 1982. "I sense prejudice," she acknowledged, "but I just overlook it in most cases because I treat people the way I want to be treated whether they dislike me or not. I kill them with kindness. I really don't have any problems . . . because I don't let it bother me."[21]

Mary Jean Harris from the St. Louis area had been a member for three years before her interview in 1988. She had joined mainly because her husband Edward did and found Mormon friendliness in direct proportion to her own. "If you want to act snobbish around me, I can do the same. If you act like when you speak to me your nose will stop up, I will speak to you and I try to make my nose stop up." One woman spoke to her only when she could not avoid it, but Harris recognized "that's just her way. She really doesn't mean any harm. . . . She's old and this is the way that she was brought up. When she's around me, she's nice just like anybody else. She has a kind of way of saying, 'I know you're black.' As Sundays go by every time we see each other, she has a little more to say."[22]

Several other blacks expressed the same feelings. Gehrig Harris, who had been active in sports in college and was a high school principal in White Castle, Louisiana, when he was interviewed in 1987, said: "Some people may be a little cold; but if you're cold, then you have got two people cold. I have warmed up a lot of

---

20. Virginia Johnson Oral History, 19-20, interviewed by Alan Cherry, 1985, LDS Afro-American.

21. Lois W. Poret Oral History, 7-8, interviewed by Alan Cherry, 1987, LDS Afro-American.

22. Mary Jean Harris Oral History, 9-10, interviewed by Alan Cherry, 1988, LDS Afro-American.

people."[23] Vivian Collier, who had actively sought a religion at age twenty-three in Richmond, Virginia, found that some people were "stand-offish" because they felt uncertain how to relate to people from other cultures. "I feel like I can help their outlook and perspective of blacks and of others. A lot of them have really opened up to me, I guess, because I'm willing to open up to them."[24]

Betty Jean Hill of Jamaica came to the United States when she was eighteen during the 1940s, married, divorced, met Mormon missionaries in Colorado Springs, and was baptized in 1981. She married a white Mormon that same year. She articulated a common ideal: "In Christ's church there is no black and white," adding more realistically: "I never let race enter my mind too much if at all."[25] Melonie Quick felt that the members in Charlotte "accept me as just a person, not a black person or weird person, but just a person. That is how I accept them."[26] Calvaline Burnett joined the church at age fifty-one and had been a member for a year when she was interviewed in 1986. She attended a Birmingham ward that was "99 percent white" and explained: "Even though they were all white, I did not look at them as all white. I looked at them as individuals. They took me in as an individual, as a person."[27]

For many the key to acceptance was not overreacting. David Diamond Gathers served a mission in Utah. In describing his interactions with Latter-day Saints, he observed, "I look at it as if they cannot accept me just because of what the color of my skin is, then they have the problem and I don't. If that is their hangup, they will have to answer for it when it comes judgment time." Rudeness, he felt, was not an invitation to invoke the law of Moses, "an eye for an eye," but to follow Jesus' admonition to "turn the other

---

23. Gehrig Leonard Harris Oral History, 24, interviewed by Alan Cherry, 1987, LDS Afro-American.

24. Vivian Collier Oral History, 11, interviewed by Alan Cherry, 1986, LDS Afro-American.

25. Betty Jean Hill Oral History, 11, 28, interviewed by Alan Cherry, 1985, LDS Afro-American.

26. Melonie Quick Oral History, 15, interviewed by Alan Cherry, 1986, LDS Afro-American.

27. Calvaline Burnett Oral History, 7, interviewed by Alan Cherry, 1987, LDS Afro-American.

cheek." "If somebody says something to me that is not quite right," he explained, "I feel that it is not my responsibility to say anything rude to them. I just say something nice to them and keep going."[28] Nathaniel Womble, who joined the church in 1978 in Atlanta and lived in Salt Lake City before returning to his home state, said: "I've heard people make off-color remarks, but I understand . . . that these are things people have grown up with and that's something they have to overcome."[29]

Some explained that a minority of white Latter-day Saints had problems accepting them. Nathleen Albright, who joined the church in 1971 and has lived in Virginia, Pennsylvania, Utah, and California, said "99.9 percent" of her ward members have almost forgotten that she was black.[30] Donald L. Harwell learned about the Mormon church in a bar from a Latter-day Saint woman he married and then later divorced. He commented since that he joined the church in 1983, "most Latter-day Saints do not care about race. [But] there are always that 10 percent. Once in awhile you can feel it."[31]

Black Saints often find they have to go out of their way to dispell stereotypes. Norman Lee Brown, who grew up in a black neighborhood of Baltimore and was living in Greensboro, North Carolina, when he was interviewed in 1986, asserted: "I have had no problem communicating with white people because I can talk with any white person on his level, whether he be a college president, the president himself, or the lowest of hillbillies." A two-year member, he singled out working on church welfare assignments as an integrating experience: "I know that friendship[s] have developed because they can't help but know that this is one black that works. A lot of white people have ideas that blacks don't like to work and that we are lazy."[32]

---

28. David Diamond Gathers Oral History, 23.

29. Nathaniel Womble Oral History, 20-21, interviewed by Alan Cherry, 1987, LDS Afro-American.

30. Nathleen Albright Oral History, 18, interviewed by Alan Cherry, 1985, LDS Afro-American.

31. Donald W. Harwell Oral History, 25, interviewed by Alan Cherry, 1985, LDS Afro-American.

32. Norman Lee Brown Oral History, 8-9, interviewed by Alan Cherry, 1986, LDS Afro-American.

Elizabeth Baltimore hoped to complete a Ph.D., a goal which seemed to catch many white Latter-day Saints off-guard. They "don't know what to do with me," she remarked. "A number of them are shocked that I'm bright, intelligent, and academically inclined."[33] Dan Mosley, a former employee of the NAACP, praised the Camelback Sixth Ward in Phoenix, Arizona, for being both "a highly intellectual group who have a better capability" and not "feel[ing] threatened by a black of their equal presenting an equal petition for activity within the confines of their service group."[34] Melvin Mitchell, who was born in 1937 and served in the marines, felt that he was accepted in Columbus, Ohio, where he joined the church in 1985 because he wasn't "the average black person. . . . I don't go in there flashing my credentials [but] . . . I showed them what I could do. . . . I think it startled some people . . . because they thought, 'He's not as dumb as he looks.'"[35]

Twenty-eight-year-old Darlene Bowden, from Charlotte, North Carolina, and a Baptist before her conversion in 1984, had to readjust some of her own economic stereotypes: "They surprised me at first because they were rich and white and still . . . don't mind being around blacks. If they are rich, most white people look for blacks only to scrub their floors or do some cooking in the kitchen. They hire maids." She added, however, the members were "mostly home type people" who did not maintain class distinctions.[36]

A religious doctrine that provides a bridge between cultures is the Mormon belief that all people are spirit children of the same heavenly parents. Bobby Darby from Charlotte, North Carolina, had no religious affiliation before he was baptized Mormon. "Deep in my heart I feel by the way LDS people associate and congregate with black Americans they are showing and proving to the whole world that the

---

33. Elizabeth Taylor Baltimore Oral History, 25, interviewed by Alan Cherry, 1986, LDS Afro-American.

34. Dan Mosley Oral History, 16, interviewed by Alan Cherry, 1985, LDS Afro-American.

35. Melvin D. Mitchell Oral History, 10, interviewed by Alan Cherry, 1988, LDS Afro-American.

36. Darlene Bowden Oral History, 11, interviewed by Alan Cherry, 1986, LDS Afro-American.

days and times of black Americans being treated as flunkies and second class citizens are over. We are all Heavenly Father's children."[37] Audrey Marie Pinnock, who was born in Jamaica and then raised in New York City, had been a Catholic and a Methodist before becoming Mormon. She was often the only black member in her wards and had braced herself "for times when they would treat me bad, but I only saw that we were all children of God."[38]

PREJUDICE AND DISCRIMINATION

In addition to relating positive experiences, people interviewed noted a variety of negative encounters. Some initial reactions were socially rather than racially motivated. For example, Susan Walker, a widow born in Selma, Alabama, in 1918 who was working as a volunteer in a senior citizen center in Chicago when she was interviewed, said it was some time before anyone "spoke to me" when she began attending church in 1984. With time her relationships had improved and "now [I'm] just at home."[39]

Donna Chisolm, who joined the Mormon church in 1980, had previously worshipped with blacks. While in college, she attended a Greensboro, North Carolina, ward and felt everyone was "sugary sweet" not only to her but to each other. Her reaction was "this is really fake. They are not really that nice. I didn't think everybody could be this good all the time. I saw the little kids coming up to their mothers just asking permission to do something simple. . . . I just wasn't used to children being that respectful to their parents. Everybody was smiling; everybody wanted to shake my hand. At my Presbyterian church they just liked to gossip."[40]

Vincent Lewis, who lived in Pittsburg, California, with his Pentecostal grandmother, had been a member for eight months when he

---

37. Bobby Darby Oral History, 7, interviewed by Alan Cherry, 1986, LDS Afro-American.

38. Audrey Marie Pinnock Oral History, 19, interviewed by Alan Cherry, 1985, LDS Afro-American.

39. Susan Walker Oral History, 11, interviewed by Alan Cherry, 1988, LDS Afro-American.

40. Donna Chisolm Oral History, 6, interviewed by Alan Cherry, 1986, LDS Afro-American.

was interviewed in 1985. He admits he went to church to "shock them," deliberately wearing "braids in my hair and things like that" to this "all-white church. . . . I guess at first they probably thought I was kind of strange." After the initial shock, he admits, "They have become really friendly."[41]

Most of the survey respondents did not identify "outright" prejudice from white members. Only 4 percent said they experienced prejudice "very often," 17.7 percent said "sometimes," 13.1 percent said "seldom," 21.2 percent said "very seldom," and 43.9 percent said "never." Perhaps the most painful experience was reported by Mary Angel Wilbur, a high school student in New Kensington, Pennsylvania. She joined the church in 1983 six months after her mother. She recalled a bus excursion to the Washington, D.C., temple with the stake's teenagers. A boy sitting behind her "talked a lot about 'niggers,'" and "poured pop over the back of my chair so it went over my hair and on my dress." She was completely "humiliated" and so confused at such unkindness on the way to the temple that "I think I cried the whole time." A girlfriend, the branch president's daughter, tried to console her, but "it didn't really help because it was done." Adult leaders were unaware of the incident. She recalled: "They could see that I was really upset the whole time," but they did not ask her why, and, feeling alienated, she would not approach them. She returned from the excursion, resolving never to go back to church. The branch president's wife called and "made me feel a lot better because she told me that he was just one person. The church was true, and it wasn't the church's fault that some people were rude and ignorant. That really kept me going through all that."[42]

Elizabeth Pulley, who grew up in the Church of God in Christ and joined the LDS church in 1977 after marrying a Latter-day Saint, felt she was often "overlooked or left out" in Relief Society when she first joined the church. "It was always, 'Oh, I didn't see you' or 'I didn't mean to slight you in any way.'" Excessive cordiality made her uncomfortable. One woman hugged and kissed her and then went into the

---

41. Vincent Lewis Oral History, 9, interviewed by Alan Cherry, 1985, LDS Afro-American.

42. Mary Angel Wilbur Oral History, 4, interviewed by Alan Cherry, 1986, LDS Afro-American.

restroom. Pulley went too and found the woman at the sink "scrubbing her lips." Pulley concluded, "She is really not sincere." Yet she interpreted such experiences as "trials and tribulations" to help her "grow" and learn "patience or love or understanding."[43]

West Virginia native Arthur Preston, who had lived in Chicago since age eighteen and was looking for a religion when the missionaries came, said, "You have to have a strong spirit to be in that church. I am quite sure that there are some earnest people within the church that are good, but overall some of the people's hearts are not right." His son had been attending church regularly when a white youth came up and told him: "Hey, black boy, what are you doing in here?"[44] James Mallory from Stone Mountain, Georgia, baptized in 1982, recalled that his patriarchal blessing contained a warning: "I would have callings in the church and I would have to approach some of the brethren. [The patriarch] said some of them would be resentful with me. I have sensed that on some occasions. I guess you could call it prejudice."[45] Forewarned he dealt with such reactions calmly.

The survey also asked how blacks perceived the experiences of all LDS African Americans. Answers to the statement, "I don't think prejudice is a serious problem among church members," were split: 16.8 percent felt that prejudice was a problem "very often," 27.6 percent said it was "sometimes," 23.5 percent "seldom," 17.3 percent "very seldom," and 14.8 percent "never." Interpreting motive is inexact, but survey respondents, when asked if other Latter-day Saints said "offensive things to black members on purpose," also gave ambivalent responses. A quarter (26.1 percent) were "not sure," but 1.5 percent "strongly agreed" and 8.5 percent "agreed" that offensive comments were made "on purpose." But 63.9 percent "disagreed" or "strongly disagreed." The difference in responses might be related to a number of factors. After reading some of the interviews, sociologist Armand Mauss felt that people seemed reluctant when asked to discuss their

---

43. Elizabeth Pulley Oral History, 10-11, 17, interviewed by Alan Cherry, 1985, LDS Afro-American.

44. Arthur Preston Oral History, 5, interviewed by Alan Cherry, 1988, LDS Afro-American.

45. James Mallory Oral History, 13, interviewed by Alan Cherry, 1987, LDS Afro-American.

own examples of discrimination. This may be due to embarrassment, fear of sounding petty or weak, or appearing to denigrate their church. They were sometimes more able to discuss other blacks' experiences, which were often hearsay but reinforced perceptions of discrimination.

A more serious problem than deliberate malice was ignorance, insensitivity, and a general lack of experience with cultural and racial diversity. When asked if "non-black members often ignorantly say things which are offensive to black members," 37.0 percent "agreed" or "strongly agreed." Nearly half (49.5 percent) "disagreed" or "strongly disagreed," and 13.5 percent were "unsure." Samuella Brown, who was born in Knoxville, Tennessee in 1948 and lived in Columbus, Ohio, where she had been a member since 1983, talked about the distinctions based on intent: "I've seen more ignorance than prejudice because Mormons, from what I've picked up and from what I learned, . . . were always kind, caring, [and] considerate. . . . I perceive them as being a caring people, but just ignorant to certain things."[46]

Ardelia Stokes, who joined the Mormon church in Chicago, recalled no acceptance problems until she began attending BYU in 1980. "People were not out and out hostile racists per se," she observed. "They were ignorant. They did not know how to deal with me—or me with them, for that matter. I guess I would have to say we were ignorant of each other."[47]

Emanuel Reid, a former Baptist, praised the Saints of Roopville, Georgia: "Even though they had their problems and they were growing too, they were real people. They showed me love, understanding, and it was a true friendship. Some of them didn't quite know how to approach me or what to say, but I knew they were sincere and they were good people." He acknowledged: "A lot of them still don't quite understand black people. A lot of them ask—I don't want to say stupid—questions, but if they thought about what they were saying when they said it, I don't think they would ask

---

46. Samuella Brown Oral History, 7, interviewed by Alan Cherry, 1988, LDS Afro-American.

47. Ardelia Stokes Oral History, 8, interviewed by Alan Cherry, 1985, LDS Afro-American.

the questions that they do from time to time."[48]

Donald L. Harwell, a Utah businessman, corroborated the racial naivete of Utah Mormons. It "amazes me. This is 1985, and people still do not know that we are no different than they are.... I ... make jokes about it. I ... tell them my skin will not rub off on them." But he added he often wishes there was more than humor to his comments. "Sometimes I think maybe the skin should rub off and they would have less to worry about. It might be something they could deal with."[49]

Robert Lang, who owned an insurance business and had worked as an appliance repairman, regards "off-the-wall" comments as "teaching moments." He added charitably, "Anything like that comes through ignorance, not knowing and curiosity."[50]

One manifestation of ignorance was oblivion to the pervasiveness of racism in America. William B. Jenkins's bishop asked if he had had any "unpleasantness with some members." Jenkins, who had joined the church in 1982 at age sixty-eight, told the bishop gently: "There's nothing for me to tell you about that because the one that does it may be a good friend of yours." Taken aback the bishop said he had not thought of that. Jenkins said, "Bishop, there are a lot of things you all overlook."[51]

When someone asked DeNorris Bradley if he had experienced prejudice in his ward in Winston-Salem, North Carolina, he said yes. The person was surprised. "He honestly thought that I had been in the church this long and hadn't experienced any type of prejudice, any type of slanders, any type of remarks. He thought their church was just that good and there were no problems." Problems included difficulty in finding someone to give him a ride to church, an older sister who dubiously said she hoped he would "stick" with the church, and people leaving when he entered a room and avoiding eye contact. "I don't think I was being overly sensitive," said Bradley. "You have to

48. Emanuel Reid Oral History, 9, 19, interviewed by Alan Cherry, 1985, LDS Afro-American.

49. Harwell Oral History, 25.

50. Robert Lang Oral History, 13, interviewed by Alan Cherry, 1985, LDS Afro-American.

51. William B. Jenkins Oral History, 5, interviewed by Alan Cherry, 1988, LDS Afro-American.

realize that being black in the South, you develop somewhat of a sense about prejudice. Whites don't realize . . . their body language, their handshake, or their eye contact could give it away."[52]

John Phoenix observed such unconscious behavior. He was born in the Washington, D.C., area, graduated from high school in 1937, and fought in World War II before graduating from Howard School of Pharmacy in 1953. Some whites "feel that their educational level and their social level is above most blacks," he observed. "Even though they have their scriptures and they know that their black brother is equal and there's supposed to be a feeling of equality, subconsciously they don't always get this feeling. Their true feeling is manifested in their actions. Now they do a pretty good job of covering up, [but] being a black, I can make this determination pretty easily."[53] Phoenix attended the LDS church during the 1970s but did not join until 1980 because of the priesthood restriction. His wife had attended meetings with him and was also disturbed by the priesthood ban. They separated in 1981, partly because of Phoenix's activity in the church.

Another manifestation of cultural ignorance was over-enthusiasm. Vanessa A. Carter attended Baptist and Pentecostal Holiness churches as a youngster in Sacramento. At the time she was interviewed in 1985, she had been a Mormon for five or six years and was studying to be a nurse. It was the conspicuousness of her situation that she disliked. Some stared. She was flooded with invitations to speak at meetings from Latter-day Saints who, with unconscious patronage, assured her, "I just know you will have a good talk."[54] When Donna Chisolm moved to Greensboro to attend college, she "felt people looking at me. I even heard people say, 'It is nice that black people are beginning to accept the gospel.' That made me mad. I don't even know why. It was like they were really making a big deal out of it, and we were people just like everybody else."[55] George Garwood, Jr., who joined the church in

---

52. DeNorris Clarence Bradley Oral History, 17-18, interviewed by Alan Cherry, 196, LDS Afro-American.

53. John W. Phoenix Oral History, 11, interviewed by Alan Cherry, 1986, LDS Afro-American.

54. Vanessa A. Carter Oral History, 14, interviewed by Alan Cherry, LDS Afro-American.

55. Donna Chisolm Oral History, 6.

1972 in Tooele, Utah, also felt people were "overly friendly" and believed that he was "always on display."[56] Audrey Marie Pinnock of New York City, who was serving a mission in Utah in 1985, explained that Utah Mormons "feel it is their fault that blacks did not have the priesthood. They try to overdo. . . . One of the best things I am doing on a mission is to show them that I am a person and a child of God. They do not have to roll out the red carpet. They can ignore me or treat me as a regular person."[57]

Linda Reid, who had attended Unitarian, Baptist, and Methodist churches before becoming a Mormon in 1977, said wistfully, "If [only] the members of the church would just get to know Linda for Linda, instead of, 'Oh, yes, she's that cute little black gal.' I would honestly hope that when I die that my headstone doesn't read, 'Oh, yes, she's that cute little black gal.'"[58]

Survey respondents did not see this as a major problem. To the statement "non-black members of the church give me overexaggerated flattery just because I am non-white," 55.4 percent said it never happened, 28.2 percent said it happened but did not "bother" them, and 16.4 percent said it happened and they were "bothered" by it.

Katherine Warren, who joined the church in the 1970s, resented her bishop in New Orleans stereotyping her—even though it was positive. "You're a good person," he said. "I'm thinking about making you a missionary. Sister Freida [the only other black member in the ward] is all right." Warren added with astonishment: "He was thinking all blacks were the same."[59]

Survey respondents found conspicuousness less of a problem than those interviewed. When asked if feeling stared at in church was irritating, 9.5 percent acknowledged that it "bothered" them, but 50.7 percent said that it "never" happened. The rest said it "happened" but it did not "bother" them. When asked if people assumed they were not members when they visited another ward, only 12.1 percent said it

---

56. George Garwood, Jr., Oral History, 18, interviewed by Alan Cherry, 1985, LDS Afro-American.

57. Pinnock Oral History, 17.

58. Linda Reid Oral History, 9, interviewed by Alan Cherry, 1987, LDS Afro-American.

59. Warren Oral History, 15.

"bothered" them; 42.6 percent said that it "happened" but didn't "bother" them; and 45.3 percent said that it "never happened." Only 16.5 percent reported discomfort about attention that "had more to do with color of skin than the individual." Over a third (35.6 percent) said it "happened" but didn't "bother" them, and 47.9 had "never" experienced it.

Finally we asked if other Mormons referred to the "curse of Cain" and blacks' experience in a pre-earth life. Nearly 70 percent said that other members of the church "never" attempted to "explain why they were black." Only 13.6 percent said that it "happened" and "bothered" them, and 16.6 percent said it did "happen" but was not a problem.

Sharon Davis, a Jamaican who moved to the United States with her mother after her father's death, turned down several invitations from her boyfriend, Darrin Davis, before she visited his ward. Although she knew Shorthills, New Jersey, was a "very exclusive" and "all-white town," she expected to find other people of color. She explained she was "very uncomfortable. I thought, 'If people really cared, they wouldn't be staring.'" She told Darrin she would never return "because it was the most embarrassing situation."[60] She later changed her mind and Darrin baptized her in 1978.

Sylvia V. Arnold, a student and a single mother who was baptized in 1986, lived in Richmond, Virginia. She felt "loved" in the ward but was bitterly hurt when she needed a ride home from church one Sunday and the sister she wanted to approach "didn't want to give me a ride." She stated: "It might be something small. . . . I just felt like dying that day right in church, but I held it in. The woman was trying to avoid me asking for a ride home. . . . I think I should have been a little stronger and understanding about that," she added tolerantly, "and to look at it that nobody's perfect."[61]

Janet Brooks from the St. Louis, Missouri, area who joined the church in 1982, drew on her own wellsprings of Christianity to deal with prejudice. She said, "You know when a person's real within his heart and sincere, and you know a phony when you see one." Yet she

---

60. Sharon Davis Oral History, 6, interviewed by Alan Cherry, 1985, LDS Afro-American.

61. Sylvia V. Arnold Oral History, 5, interviewed by Alan Cherry, 1986, LDS Afro-American.

realized she could not change the phony people. "I just smile, say, 'Lord, have mercy,' and keep going."[62]

When Emma Williams's married son asked, "Do they treat blacks right?" she answered, "As long as you have got a Heavenly Father who loves you, you do not have to worry about who is going to treat you right or who is going to treat you wrong. The Heavenly Father is able to see you through any situation."[63]

Mary Angel Wilbur found people more accepting in Provo than her hometown ward in New Kensington, Pennsylvania. "In Utah . . . even though we were the only black people there, I remember I felt so welcome. I didn't feel like I was different at all. But [in New Kensington] . . . I had been a member for three years and sometimes still feeling like an outsider has been really hard."[64] Sharon McCoy, who joined the church in Kentucky in 1979 and served a mission to the Dominican Republic, also felt that location made a difference. "In Kentucky I felt a lot of love and I felt like they were my family. . . . When I moved [to Barberton, Ohio], I hated it." She found the people "snobs," adding that they had "warmed up since I've gotten to know them and I've made an effort, too." But she concluded: "If I had to join the church up here, I probably wouldn't be active because they're just not too friendly."[65]

A contrasting experience was Barbara Ann Pixton's multi-ward membership. A career navy person, she joined the Mormon church in Italy in 1979 with her son. "All the love and affection that we were shown in that little branch made me very anxious to go to Utah." Another member warned, "People in Utah are in cliques. They usually are born, raised, work, and grow up around the same people. . . . Don't go in there and get your heart broken." Pixton noticed some reserved reactions in Brigham City, Utah, including some coolness from members of her white husband's family. But after she bore her testimony

---

62. Janet Brooks Oral History, 11, interviewed by Alan Cherry, 1988, LDS Afro-American.

63. Emma Williams Oral History, 12, interviewed by Alan Cherry, 1986, LDS Afro-American.

64. Mary Angel Wilbur Oral History, 5.

65. Sharon Cornette McCoy Oral History, 9, interviewed by Alan Cherry, 1988, LDS Afro-American.

in fast and testimony meeting when her baby was blessed, "this little old lady who was sitting way in the back pushed her way through the crowd. . . . She said she enjoyed my testimony so much she just wanted to come up and hug my neck. We both stood there hugging each other in tears. It was great. She didn't know me. . . . She only knew who I was from me bearing my testimony."[66]

Other military assignments took Barbara and her husband to wards and branches in Japan, Korea, the Philippines, and San Diego. In all of them Barbara reported positive experiences. When she was interviewed in 1986, she was living in Hawaii where she attended a ward with other military families. "The members in our ward are very loving," she said. Despite the mobility, "We're pretty close. . . . A few of the Samoan sisters are more comfortable if they are around Samoan sisters which I can understand. Some of their English isn't very good." But at an enjoyable homemaking meeting "we learned how to make leis and weave straw baskets . . . like the Samoans do."[67]

Other blacks saw regional differences as personality differences among wards. Jerry Watley, the seventeenth of twenty-two children, said his initial experience in the Birmingham First Ward was warm. "Everybody was just one." When the ward was split, "I got my feelings hurt for awhile, and I kind of stopped going. I kind of felt empty, but . . . I said, 'If a person doesn't like me, I'm not going to be around him.'"[68] Although his wife did not like his decision, she did not pressure him. After some time he started attending the new branch where he became elders' quorum president. He was serving in that position when he was interviewed in 1987.

Pauline Alice Jenkins, born in 1922, had retired from her federal job when she joined the LDS church in 1982. After being in "two wards that . . . were really great," she described a third ward as "okay" but added: "We're not really that happy with it."[69] Her husband William

---

66. Barbara Ann Pixton Oral History, 13, interviewed by Alan Cherry, 1986, LDS Afro-American.

67. Ibid., 9.

68. Jerry Watley Oral History, 5, interviewed by Alan Cherry, 1987, LDS Afro-American.

69. Pauline Alice Jenkins Oral History, 9, interviewed by Alan Cherry, 1988, LDS Afro-American.

also noticed a little less spirituality, a little less "closeness" in the new ward. He attributed the difference to economic inequalities in the ward. Some new ward members were from a wealthy neighborhood "out where the money class is."[70]

Rose Shepperson Taylor from Chesterfield, Virginia, who joined the church in 1980, found that her first two wards "pulled together as a team and everything went off like clockwork." When she was sick "my house [was] clean[ed]." She was also encouraged because the bishop printed his office hours "in the program" each Sunday for when he was available to talk to ward members. In contrast she felt less concern from current ward members and her husband Thomas could not "relate to [the] bishop. . . . I just think he doesn't know enough people over in this ward, and he's still trying to get his feet wet."[71]

A few problems are identifiably regional. Many Mormons in New York were originally from Utah. Reginald Allen, who joined the church in 1978, observed that these Utah transports "are a little more clannish." He added: "This is not the feelings of blacks but [also] many of the whites who are from the east."[72]

Some members sought explanations for prejudice in economics and education. Victor Soil, who joined the LDS church when he was forty years old in 1982, was school district truant officer when he was interviewed in 1988. He said: "I noticed a little feeling of intellectual superiority there for awhile" from white members in the Hyde Park Ward. He commented gently: "I've felt many times that they felt they were so intelligent that you couldn't understand what they were talking about."[73] This perception might be shared by whites who were not in graduate school. Vivian Troutman, who grew up in Mississippi and lived in Chicago before joining the military, observed class differences among Mormon women in Piedmont, California, who were in

70. William B. Jenkins Oral History, 9, 4.

71. Rose Shepperson Taylor Oral History, 29-30, interviewed by Alan Cherry, 1986, LDS Afro-American.

72. Reginald Allen Oral History, 19-20, interviewed by Alan Cherry, 1986, LDS Afro-American.

73. Victor Soil Oral History, 10, interviewed by Alan Cherry, 1988, LDS Afro-American.

her Oakland Ward when she joined the church in 1984. She referred to them as "snobs with their noses in the air."[74]

In one example of a lack of class insensitivity, Arthur Preston, who attended a Chicago ward, was ordained to the Aaronic priesthood in the bishop's office. He assumed whites were ordained in the chapel. "To this day, I don't know why," he lamented. "Why wasn't that in the chapel?" Because he was not paying tithing, the bishop would not give him a ticket for the Chicago temple dedication. Preston felt the reason was because there were a limited number of tickets and was hurt when he found out that was not true. "The God that I worship tells me that when you have things within your heart, you pray them out. . . . I have tried my best to see things with a right spirit. I'm trying to overcome those things, [but] to me things are not the way they could be."[75]

Eva Willis identified gender problems in acceptance. Her husband Jerry felt well accepted, but she added: "I have sisters today that won't speak to me as I go down the hall. I have sisters who teach the classes on Sunday in Relief Society that will not call on me if I raise my hand. I have sisters that if I walk up to them and start talking to them, they will completely ignore me." She said at first she was upset, but she has been able to handle the problem spiritually: "I have prayed about it and put those feelings behind me."[76]

Martha Poston, who grew up in North Carolina and was living in Georgia when she was interviewed, was a member of the Peace Corps when she investigated the church in 1983. When she asked missionaries about potential problems in attending a white congregation, they assured her: "Those people will love you." On her first Sunday "the brothers really welcomed me there, but the sisters gave me that cold shoulder."[77] Drinda Preston of Chicago also observed that Relief

74. Vivian Troutman Oral History, 16, interviewed by Alan Cherry, 1985, LDS Afro-American.

75. Arthur Preston Oral History, 5-6, interviewed by Alan Cherry, 1988, LDS Afro-American.

76. Eva Willis Oral History, 7-8, interviewed by Alan Cherry, 1988, LDS Afro-American.

77. Martha Poston Oral History, 15-16, interviewed by Alan Cherry, 1987, LDS Afro-American.

Society was emotionally trying. Except for a few sisters, the women, she explained, "are not nice. They are not friendly. . . . Only a few . . . have anything to say to me or try to get to know me."[78] Vivian Troutman agreed. The men at church were welcoming, but "it is the women that have hangups."[79] Sarah Kaye Gripper, a single working mother and part-time student in Springfield, Illinois, also noticed: "I have been very well accepted among the men in the church, more than the women of the church." She decided that "some of the wives have never come in contact with a black person and don't know how to approach a black person."[80]

Others felt generational differences, realizing that older Mormons were both less likely to have grown up around blacks and were more likely to have internalized the priesthood restriction. Charles Smith, Jr., described himself as having "key friendships especially [with] some of the younger people. We took a liking to them, and they took a liking to us." Even though he was in his sixties, he played softball and basketball with them.[81]

Keith Norman Hamilton, a law student at Brigham Young University when he was interviewed, was the first black baptized in his ward in North Carolina when he joined the LDS church in 1980. He explained: "The people were really warm." Although "some of them did not know how to approach me," he recalled with great affection a sister in her eighties who "hobbled up to me and said that she had waited for the day for this to happen and she knew that before her life ended she would see blacks come into the church in Raleigh." He added: "You have to remember that these older people still had some traces of the Civil War mentality back in North Carolina."[82]

---

78. Drinda Preston Oral History, 11, interviewed by Alan Cherry, 1988, LDS Afro-American.

79. Vivian Troutman Oral History, 16-17.

80. Sarah Kaye Gripper Oral History, 9, interviewed by Alan Cherry, 1988, LDS Afro-American.

81. Charles W. Smith, Jr., Oral History, 4, interviewed by Jessie Embry, 1988, LDS Afro-American.

82. Keith Hamilton Oral History, 4, interviewed by Alan Cherry, 1985, LDS Afro-American.

Thomas Harrison Johnson, who was seventy-nine when he was interviewed in 1986, looked back on his seven years in the church and agreed: "The Latter-day Saints my age don't know how to accept me. Most of the Latter-day Saints my age are this pioneer stock and many of them haven't had the opportunity to have the education that I have had or the experiences I have had." Meanwhile, he said, "Some of the Latter-day Saints who are in their middle fifties or early sixties . . . are hesitant because they have been brought up a certain way and my experiences are so much different from theirs. . . . The younger people accept me as an elder person. I have closer friends among the younger people than I do [those] . . . who are in their fifties and sixties. . . . I get along with the kids very well. The kids don't see any color line anyway."[83]

SUMMARY

Of all the people interviewed, Bobby Darby best summed up the feelings of black Latter-day Saints: "You prepare for the worst, but you always expect the best."[84] Most white Mormons seem well-intentioned—some overly so—or are at least willing to be reeducated. Most of those do not at least try to conceal their ambivalence or hostility. So most black Mormons find that they are accepted as equals, though aware of a subtle undercurrent of discrimination that usually disappears with time.

---

83. Thomas Harrison Johnson Oral History, 20, interviewed by Alan Cherry, 1986, LDS Afro-American.

84. Darby Oral History, 7-8.

8.

SOCIAL ACCEPTANCE

Although survey respondents socialized frequently with non-blacks at LDS church-sponsored activities, fewer felt that contact extended beyond the church house (see Table 1). There are several possible explanations for the difference in acceptance "at church" and socially. Going to church together does not imply friendship, nor does it necessarily imply prejudice if church members do not socialize together outside of church (see Table 2). Yet blacks feel that they are more likely to include whites socially (38.8 percent to 32.3 percent) than whites are to include them.

TABLE 8.1

INTERACTION BETWEEN BLACK AND WHITE LATTER-DAY SAINTS

"How often do you spend time with non-blacks at church activities?"

Very often	66.7%
Sometimes	15.9%
Seldom/very seldom	13.5%

"How often do you go to the homes of non-black Latter-day Saints?"

Very often	37.8%
Sometimes	35.8%
Seldom/very seldom	22.4%
Never	4.0%

"How often do you invite non-black church members to your home?"

Very often	33.3%
Sometimes	41.3%
Seldom/very seldom	22.4%
Never	3.0%

TABLE 8.2

LDS AFRICAN AMERICANS AND DESIRE FOR
INTERACTION WITH LATTER-DAY SAINTS

"I hesitate to include church members in activities outside of church functions."

Very Often	14.9%
Sometimes	17.4%
Seldom/very seldom	27.7%
Never	40.0%

"Ward and branch members do not hesitate to include me in activities outside of church functions."

Very often	32.7%
Sometimes	27.7%
Seldom/very seldom	25.2%
Never	22.1%

TABLE 8.3

LDS AFRICAN AMERICANS AND RELATIONSHIPS WITH
AFRICAN AMERICANS AND LATTER-DAY SAINTS

"In general, I feel closer to blacks than I do most members of the Church."

Very often	9.6%
Sometimes	24.4%
Seldom/very seldom	34.1%
Never	32.0%

"Most of my close friends are now non-blacks."

Very often	34.9%
Sometimes	24.7%
Seldom/very seldom	29.1%
Never	11.3%

Does this mean that church ties are stronger than cultural ties? Two survey statements asking for strength of agreement dealt with camaraderie: "In general, I feel closer to blacks than I do to most members of the church" and "Most of my close friends are non-blacks." The responses were equally split. (See Table 3 above.) Surprisingly, middle-class members were more likely than working-class members to say they felt closer to other blacks than to white church members. Middle-class blacks may have felt more confident in giving these kinds of responses, which working-class members may privately hold but consider inappropirate—though this is speculative.

SOCIAL ACTIVITIES

The survey figures show neither full integration nor segregation between black and white Latter-day Saints. Interviews reflect the same ambivalence about interracial friendships. Albert Wilson, a retired businessman from Williamsport, Pennsylvania, who joined the Mormon church in 1981, commented, "We don't do much socializing with [white Latter-day Saints], and primarily it is because they don't have much of a social life themselves. They are home with their families. The wife and I do stir up social activity. We will invite them to the house and to church functions when the church have things like that."[1] When one considers the time demands of a lay ministry, it makes sense that when members are involved with each other it is usually in a church setting.

Matthew Clark, a graduate student, and Crystal Gathers Clark, who worked in the engineering department of a television station, had been Mormons for just over a year when they were interviewed in 1986. They reported little interaction outside church meetings. According to Crystal, "We have invited several of our friends from the church over for dinner and just to socialize. We haven't been invited very many places in return." She admitted to feeling that such one-sided hospitality was partly racially motivated but added: "I think that they really feel, 'We're not going to invite them over here because

1. Albert L. Wilson Oral History, 14, interviewed by Alan Cherry, 1986, LDS Afro-American Oral History Project, Charles Redd Center for Western Studies, Archives and Manuscripts, Harold B. Lee Library, Brigham Young University, Provo, Utah (hereafter LDS Afro-American).

they'll look down on us.' But we are not like that. We're genuine people. We have feelings, too. We don't flaunt the things we have. . . . We had a few tell us, 'We haven't had you over to dinner because our place isn't as nice as yours.' We said, 'We're not interested in that. We couldn't care less about where you live or where we live. We just like the fellowship and like to be friends.'"[2]

"Socially I don't have a problem," said James Mallory, "because in my walking up and talking I will invite somebody over for dinner just as soon as they will look at me. I have done that on a lot of occasions and haven't been invited back." Was there an element of racial discrimination in those missing invitations? "I don't look at it from that point of view as to whether it's my color or not." But after thinking about it, he admitted, "It's a possibility."[3] Willie Perry Perkins, born in 1909, was twice widowed before she was baptized in Greensville, North Carolina, in 1983. She asserts that she does not have problems because she maintains an even-handed attitude. "If [white people] want to be standoffish, they have got the right. If they want to be mean or stiff and act low and uppity, they have the right. I still love them. If they want to be lovely, they have still got a right."[4]

As with public interaction, the interviews contain specific examples of both positive and negative experiences. For many, members of the LDS church became like family members. Anita Durphey, one of the first black Mormons in the St. Louis area, managed a store. She said her bishop, now her stake president, said if she had problems she should bring them to his attention. But she never had to do that because, she said, "I was welcomed with open arms. The church has been my family. It's my extended family."[5] Nathleen Albright, who joined the church in Virginia in 1971, said she had never felt such acceptance as that which she experienced from church members. "I

---

2. Crystal Gathers Clark Oral History, 15, interviewed by Alan Cherry, 1986, LDS Afro-American.

3. James Mallory Oral History, 13, interviewed by Alan Cherry, 1987, LDS Afro-American.

4. Willie Perry Perkins Oral History, 5, interviewed by Alan Cherry, 1986, LDS Afro-American.

5. Anita Durphey Oral History, 8, interviewed by Alan Cherry, 1988, LDS Afro-American.

finally found home, so to speak, when I joined the church."[6]

Delphrine Young grew up in Oklahoma and Kansas in a racially-conscious environment. His father was killed by a white police officer for allegedly "resisting arrest." Throughout his youth and young adulthood, he had no integregational experiences. He moved to Los Angeles in 1963, where he worked for a hospital and joined the LDS church in 1981. Although he had cause to be bitter towards whites, he commented that being around "a white Latter-day Saint is just like going around your brothers and sisters. . . . They are not bigoted people where they will speak to you here and will not speak to you there. Every time they see you, you are Brother Young. . . . Whether you are in the street, whether you are in your home, whether you are in their home, you are Brother Young. They do not have any prejudice. At least I have not met a prejudiced Latter-day Saint yet. I have not met any that berate you; I have not met any that call names; I have not met any who used racial discrimination; I have not met any that bring slanderous remarks towards you. I have not met any that are backstabbing where they say awful things about you."[7]

Mason Anderson, who was born in 1945 and grew up in a single-parent home in Charlotte, North Carolina, felt like a family member at church. "I have been accepted as a brother. . . . They accepted me as a Christian. They have worked with me to bring about a change in my life and an understanding towards the ministry and toward the word [of God]. They have worked with me as a brother. The sisters and the brothers have made me feel welcome in their homes as a part of the family . . . without seeing any color barriers."[8]

Benjamin Washington concurred. A truck driver who had served as a counselor to a missionary branch president in North Carolina, he was the employment specialist in his ward when he was interviewed in 1986. A member for eight months, he felt: "There is no color as far as I am concerned. . . . All the ones that I have come in contact with treat

---

6. Nathleen Albright Oral History, 18, interviewed by Alan Cherry, 1985, LDS Afro-American.

7. Delphrine Gracia Young Oral History, 24, interviewed by Alan Cherry, 1985, LDS Afro-American.

8. Mason Anderson Oral History, 18, interviewed by Alan Cherry, 1986, LDS Afro-American.

you just as they are your brothers or sisters. . . . They are just wonderful people."[9]

Many found the Mormons they met followed Jesus' advice to "do unto others as ye would have them do unto you." Natalia Thompson, who was born in 1925 and was older than many of the members in the Hyde Park Ward, said: "These young people are living what they preach. They don't preach brotherly love and sisterly love; they live it. That's the thing that I love about them."[10]

Leo Arrington returned to Hawaii after his discharge from the military and was working as a paramedic when he converted. He called white Mormons "my best friends" and commented on going to the temple with them: "I don't look at color, and I think when they look at me they don't see a color but they see another brother in the Lord. You can look at it in a negative way and you have feelings. But why do that? There's no reason for it. You accept people as you see them, and they accept you as they see you."[11]

Jerry Willis, a former AME minister, was working for the U.S. Post Office in St. Louis when he was interviewed. He conceded that his report sounded too good to be true. "But from Utah, California, to here, I've had no problems, ill feelings, or discrimination that I can identify with like I've had in the Protestant churches. I was in the integrated churches there. Here people really treated me swell. I felt from day one that I belonged. I never felt ostracized or that I was separated as a whole."[12]

Margie Ray White, fourth of nine children, was born in North Carolina to an inactive Baptist mother. White joined the Presbyterian church in 1971 and Mormonism in 1984. Trying to describe Mormons in her ward in Monroe, North Carolina, she groped to express her feelings: "I really don't know the words to put it in but [I have been

---

9. Benjamin R. Washington Oral History, 14, interviewed by Alan Cherry, 1985, LDS Afro-American.

10. Natalia F. Thompson Oral History, 13, interviewed by Alan Cherry, 1988, LDS Afro-American.

11. Leo Arrington Oral History, 8-9, interviewed by Alan Cherry, 1986, LDS Afro-American.

12. Jerry Willis Oral History, 9, interviewed by Alan Cherry, 1988, LDS Afro-American.

accepted] just great. I have never felt and I have never been shown so much love. To tell the truth, I really didn't know there was that much love in the world to see the way the white Latter-day Saints treat the blacks. I would have never dreamed this would have been here in this life. It is beautiful; it is great."[13] Norman Brown, a blue collar worker who grew up Catholic in a black neighborhood in Baltimore, commented simply: "I didn't know I could love white people so much."[14]

James Johnson from Monroe, North Carolina, who had been a member for less than a year when he was interviewed in 1986, spontaneously described the members of his ward in glowing terms. "I love everybody in the church. The people are just so nice. The white sisters hug and kiss me; the black sisters hug and kiss me. . . . They show me that I am somebody, they are somebody, and what type of church we are in."[15]

Emma Williams, a widow from Hickory, North Carolina, who joined the church after she retired, had been a member for over a year by 1986. Asked how she was accepted, she responded: "One hundred percent. They have shown all kinds of love, all kinds of compassion. They have shown their real feelings. When I walk into that church, I can feel the warmth. When I walk into their homes, I can feel that." She remembered appreciatively one incident. When missionaries learned she was ill, she remembered they "came over and gave me a blessing. I did not feel like cooking. Here came the Relief Society with all of that food. I said, 'I am sick. I do not feel like eating.' But they brought it anyway. I said, 'Bless your hearts.' That was an act of love."[16]

Others identified esteem that grew from a shared belief system. Joseph Faulkner was still a leader in the NAACP, yet his LDS friendships were stronger than those associations. "Because of my long-standing Civil Rights involvement, I have many whites, professionals,

---

13. Margie Ray White Oral History, 11, interviewed by Alan Cherry, 1986, LDS Afro-American.

14. Norman Lee Brown Oral History, 16, interviewed by Alan Cherry, 1986, LDS Afro-American.

15. James Johnson Oral History, 12, interviewed by Alan Cherry, 1986, LDS Afro-American.

16. Emma Williams Oral History, 20, interviewed by Alan Cherry, 1986, LDS Afro-American.

teachers, and just common workers who like to call me up, talk to me, and congratulate me." A Mormon since 1983, he commented: "Quite naturally my LDS friends treat me more cordially because they understand me better and I'm closer."[17]

Other members reported more ambiguous experiences. Lula Biggs, who grew up in Selma, Alabama, during the 1960s, was living in Birmingham, Alabama, when she was interviewed eight years after her baptism. The reactions of white members she knew varied, she explained, depending on the setting. "We'll be in church together. Just some of them. Not all of them. They're fine, and they're shaking your hand. When you go downtown and you get around the other whites, you don't know what that person might say to you in just a regular conversation. Some of them might tend not to say as much."[18]

Alan Cherry contributed a personal story from the 1970s when, as a member of "The Sons of Mosiah," a Mormon musical group, he stayed at the home of a white Latter-day Saint in Atlanta, who sincerely "[told] me that he was prejudiced. I sat there listening to him, realizing that I had eaten his meal that his wife had prepared for me. He and his wife had given up their bed for me to sleep in. I and my group were invited there by his beautiful eighteen-year-old daughter to perform for his fellow church members. When he said that, I realized, 'If this is prejudice, it certainly isn't what I always thought it would be like.'" Cherry continued: "I realized something very poignant. He had bared his soul to show that he was confused." While this white Latter-day Saint could share time with Cherry in his home, "he felt a strong attraction for and commitment to a code that as a Latter-day Saint he couldn't really accept, but yet these values had their sway with him. . . . This prejudice might flare the next day if we were seen in downtown Atlanta together, and he might treat me totally differently than he was at that moment." Acknowledging this apparent double standard "hurt him" because "he couldn't predict his behavior. He saw it as a regrettable weakness." Cherry concluded: "I saw it as a regret-

---

17. Joseph Faulkner Oral History, 18, interviewed by Alan Cherry, 1986, LDS Afro-American.

18. Lula M. Biggs Oral History, 12-13, interviewed by Alan Cherry, 1987, LDS Afro-American.

table weakness, but . . . I had other weaknesses, and all . . . I [did] was
. . . feel brotherly sorrow for him."

As a teenager growing up in New York City in the 1960s, Cherry
had determined never to cross the Mason-Dixon line because of horror
stories about Southern segregation and lynchings. And before his
conversion, he would have probably thrown the man's admission of
prejudice back into the man's face. But now he had no desire to do
so.[19]

Some blacks do not see cultural diversity as a possibility because
differences are so marked. Natalie Palmer-Taylor, raised by her single
mother in Ohio, married at eighteen, divorced, joined the Mormon
church in 1982, and decided to move to Utah. She admitted she did
not "allow" whites to feel "comfortable" enough with her to develop
close relationships: "It is not something that I even do consciously, but
I notice a lot that there is this thing about me that says, 'Do not ask
anything too personal because it is none of your business.'"[20] Nor does
she share freely her own inner thoughts, finding a certain security in
aloofness. She added that only one white Latter-day Saint, a visiting
teacher companion who had lived in multi-racial Hawaii, had asked
her about being black. "I know that she is not asking as a condemna-
tion to me but [for] knowledge for herself. . . . It is not a phony thing.
It is a very relaxed thing on her part. I like that. Other than her I have
never had anybody ask me anything on the basis of color."[21]

Other blacks withheld information from white LDS friends, feeling they would not understand. Vincent Lewis, a student who grew up
in mainly black California communities, had been a member of the
church for only eight months when he was interviewed in 1985. He
had talked to a white friend "about being black" but added: "I do not
really think he can conceive what it is like because he has never gone
through anything like that. It is hard for him to understand being black
or being brought up without the gospel."[22] Deborah Spearman from

---

19. Alan Cherry Oral History (in process), interviewed by Jessie L.
Embry, Apr. 1985, LDS Afro-American.

20. Natalie Palmer-Taylor Oral History, 29-30, interviewed by Alan
Cherry, 1985, LDS Afro-American.

21. Ibid.

22. Vincent Lewis Oral History, 10, interviewed by Alan Cherry,

Philadelph said matter-of-factly: "I don't care how nice white folks are to you. They can't relate to the problems that black people have."[23]

Betty Ann Bridgeforth grew up Catholic in Chicago, where she was active in the Civil Rights movements and knew Martin Luther King and Jesse Jackson. After she joined the LDS church in 1979, she moved to Utah. She agreed that whites have problems understanding the black experience but added sympathetically: "I think they have understood as best as they can. After all, they are kind of just going on nothing at all and then here you are. . . . They try to see [me] as a person [even if] they do not always understand what I am going through."[24]

William Johnson, a businessman who had been in the navy, had graduated from college in 1974 and had been a member since 1978, felt some blacks were overly sensitive. "I think we [blacks] are automatically programmed and we're too quick to perceive racism where it really doesn't exist. Whenever a problem comes up, we're too quick to point to the problem and say, 'The problem is racism.' That is not necessarily the case. It's not only true in the church, but it's true in life in general."[25]

DATING AND MARRIAGE

Contradictions in culture are especially wrenching in more personal interactions with the opposite sex, where race and religion are poised to collide. Black converts worry about whom their children will date and marry. Single members face the same dilemma about their prospects of dating and marriage. The contradiction stems from the LDS church's mixed messages. On the one hand church leaders insist that blacks—like all single members—date and marry only "temple-worthy" members and marry only in temples. Simultaneously, they discourage interracial and intercultural marriages. The concern about

---

1985, LDS Afro-American.

23. Deborah Spearman Oral History, 11, interviewed by Alan Cherry, 1987, LDS Afro-American.

24. Betty Ann Bridgeforth Oral History, 31-32, interviewed by Alan Cherry, 1985, LDS Afro-American.

25. William T. Johnson Oral History, 17, interviewed by Alan Cherry, 1987, LDS Afro-American.

interracial marriage was so intense that the same *Church News* announcing the 1978 lifting of the priesthood ban also carried a statement entitled "Interracial marriage discouraged." The article stated, "For a number of years, President Spencer W. Kimball has counseled young members of the church to not cross racial lines in dating and marrying." It continued by quoting a 7 September 1976 BYU devotional address by Kimball: "We recommend that people marry those who are of the same racial background generally . . . , and above all, the same religious background, without question."[26] Although no more recent statements have appeared about interracial marriages in church publications, black and white members report similar informal instructions from local church leaders.

James Ashley Fennell II, a single medical student in Greenville, North Carolina, in 1986, summarized the dilemma presented by "so many contradictions in counsel": "Naturally we have counsel not to date outside of the church because that can cause problems. . . . But then there is the counsel to avoid dating or marriage outside of your race. If you follow that counsel, then you are put in another paradox because you just don't run into that many black Latter-day Saints. Then I got some counsel that maybe I am supposed to go and find somebody that I really like who is black and bring her into the church, but that is contradictory to the counsel of not going out of the church to date. You see the paradoxes that result."[27]

Of the 80 who completed questions about their own dating and marriage possibilities on the survey, 70 percent responded "never" to "I have been told by a member of the church that I couldn't date him or her or that we would have to stop dating because we are of different races," but 15 percent said it happened "very often." The remaining 15 percent was split between sometimes, 7.5 percent; seldom, 1.2 percent; and very seldom, 6.3 percent. Slightly less (63.4 percent) responded "never" to "I have been told by another church member not to date someone because we are of different races." Survey respondents were also queried about "Trying to find a suitable mate." Almost 11 percent (10.9 percent) did not respond, perhaps because they did

---

26. "Interracial Marriage Discouraged," *Church News*, 17 June 1978, 4.

27. James Ashley Fennell II Oral History, 4, interviewed by Alan Cherry, 1986, LDS Afro-American.

not feel well informed or have an opinion. Of those answering the question about difficulty in finding a mate, 45.5 percent said it was "very often" difficult to find such a mate, 17.9 percent said "sometimes," 8.4 percent responded "seldom," and 12.3 percent expressed "very seldom."

Interviews provided anecdotal information about the problems of single black adults. The most frequently mentioned problem is scarcity of black singles, a problem especially severe prior to the priesthood announcement of 1978. Robert Stevenson, who joined the church in 1971, married a white Mormon, Susan Bevan, on 21 April 1978. They had met at Brigham Young University as students, but her Mormon family questioned the viability of the relationship. When Stevenson left for a military assignment, he thought it might be a convenient time to terminate the friendship. "Everybody from the garbage man to the stake president had told her that marrying me would be to her eternal detriment."

But they had such strong feelings for each other that they sought an interview with a general authority, Boyd K. Packer. Packer called in Marion D. Hanks. According to Stevenson, "Elder Packer squared off on one side, and Elder Hanks squared off on the other." Packer argued that Stevenson "could accomplish [his] mission in life and be more effective without being married to a white woman." Hanks said, "I think it's the best thing in the world that you marry Susan. I think that you'll be more effective and you'll be able to break down racial barriers easier." When they left that discussion, says Robert, "There was no doubt in my mind and Susan's mind that the choice that we had to make was left squarely up to us." They decided to marry and have since been sealed together for eternity in the temple.[28]

Nathleen Albright also tried to reconcile conflicting counsel. When she first joined the church, she and some close LDS woman friends "would just sit around on New Year's Eve and cry into our hot apple cider and lament over the fact that we were not married." When she moved to Erie, Pennsylvania, she spent considerable time with a white male friend, "but I did not consider it dating. . . . I didn't want to get involved with a white guy." She repeatedly inquired about single

---

28. Robert Lee Stevenson Oral History, 11, interviewed by Alan Cherry, 1987, LDS Afro-American.

black men in the church and "tried to meet them the best I could through letters and maybe even by visiting them if they were close by." None of these relationships was promising. In Utah she met a black man she liked and wanted to marry, but he saw her only as a friend. When she finally met a black man who proposed, she promptly agreed, but the relationship deteriorated sharply. After five months when she was pregnant, her bishop advised her to get a divorce.

Her efforts to have a career and raise her daughter made dating a low priority. Because of the priesthood ban, she had a "comfortable niche" not worrying about marriage. But she eventually started dating a white colleague with whom she worked in the church's singles program, and the relationship had become serious by June 1978 when they heard the double message of both the priesthood announcement and the statement opposing interracial marriage. Albright recalled reading "in the *Church News* . . ., 'We like to discourage interracial marriages.'" She thought, "Now what do I do?" Despite her concerns she felt that her answer was to marry him. She recalled, "When I finally decided to ask the Lord, 'Is it okay, Lord?', . . . He answered, 'Yes.' I could not even finish the question. . . . I [was] saying, 'Are you sure? . . . You know what the leaders of the church have said.' . . . He answered again, 'Yes.'"[29]

Melvin D. Mitchell was fifty-one years old when he was interviewed in 1988. Never married, he had adopted a son and explained: "Race doesn't have anything to do with it, but there aren't enough single black women in the Latter-day Saint church to meet up to my expectations and what we're taught as far as Latter-day Saints." He added: "I do have a couple of black female friends. They're a lot younger than I am. That's neither here nor there. It's very hard for black men to date in the church. From what I understand, it's very hard for black women also."[30]

Fifty-two-year-old Calvaline Burnett of Birmingham, Alabama, was dating a Baptist deacon in 1986. Although he was not Mormon, he was Christian and she hoped to marry him. She explained: "I prayed for a husband, a good husband. Now I'm not praying for a husband.

---

29. Albright Oral History, 7-10.

30. Melvin D. Mitchell Oral History, 4, interviewed by Alan Cherry, 1988, LDS Afro-American.

I'm praying for [this man I am dating] to be my husband."[31]

Cherrie Lee Maples joined the church in Kansas and served a mission in California before moving to the Washington, D.C., area where she was interviewed in 1987. She said her dating dropped to "zero" after she became Mormon. She wanted to date a black Latter-day Saint whom she could marry but made race a higher priority than religion. "I have had some experience with dating men outside of my race," she observed, "but I am more comfortable in dating black Americans because they are from the same culture. It is by choice."[32]

Anita L. Durphey, a store manager in St. Louis, Missouri, was the divorced mother of grown children when she was interviewed in 1988. "My only philosophy is that if Heavenly Father wants me to have a mate in this life he'll make it possible," she said.[33] Brenda Sanderlin, a former nun in her late twenties from San Jose, California, faced her options realistically, "I am female. I am black. I have entered a religion where it may not be possible for me to get a spouse, much less have a family even though we advocate families. Due to my age when I accepted the gospel, there is a very strong possibility I will never marry or have children."[34]

White Latter-day Saints sometimes try to help by match-making black LDS women and men. Rhoda Shelby, a cheerleader at BYU, accepted these efforts by "good LDS people [with] so much love in their heart and so much compassion." She acknowledged, "Sometimes they fail because they don't have the right way to do it."[35] Jerri Allene Thornton Hale from Detroit wryly pointed out that joining the church in 1977 made a "dramatic difference" in her social life. Her dating dropped "to none because they were so few blacks in the church." She recalled two black male members in her area. One "had dropped out

---

31. Calvaline Burnett Oral History, 13-14, interviewed by Alan Cherry, 1987, LDS Afro-American.

32. Cherrie Lee Maples Oral History, 6, interviewed by Alan Cherry, 1986, LDS Afro-American.

33. Durphey Oral History, 21.

34. Brenda Sanderlin Oral History, 27, interviewed by Alan Cherry, 1985, LDS Afro-American.

35. Rhoda Shelby Oral History, 28, interviewed by Alan Cherry, 1985, LDS Afro-American.

of school in the sixth grade to work." As a college student, Hale felt "there were just too many differences there." She "just didn't get along" with another black member: "We argued more than anything."[36] When whites tried to match-make, she resisted simplistic approaches of: "He is black; isn't that enough?" To such attempts she would retort: "Would you marry any white guy?"[37]

William L. Cox lived in eastern North Carolina and knew few single black Mormon women. A regional representative told him: "I know of a young lady that I think you need to meet, a member of the church, a young black woman, and a very righteous lady." Cox took the woman's name and arranged to meet her. According to Cox, she "was in the process of praying about . . . meeting someone. We started talking as if we had known each other for twenty years." However, problems developed: "She wanted to get married real quick. . . . I did not have that prompting from the spirit." "A city girl," she was "offended" by Cox's "rural life, this farming situation." She wanted to be married in the chapel first "where all of her family could be involved and then get married in the temple later. I told her, 'Absolutely not.' That is the one thing I stood firm on. I just insisted that we would get married in the temple or we would not get married." They broke off their relationship, and Cox admits ambiguous feelings: "I miss her. I think I have missed the opportunity to get married to a very good lady, a very religious lady because I felt that was the right principle to stand on."[38]

Not only whites but some African Americans felt being black should be reason enough for a relationship. Boris Spencer grew up in North Carolina as a Baptist. He recalled in one area where he lived were "one black Mormon girl, and one black Mormon guy. I don't know why they never dated. . . . They should have clung to each other just for that one thing."[39]

---

36. Jerri Allene Thornton Hale Oral History, 25, interviewed by Alan Cherry, 1985, LDS Afro-American.

37. Ibid., 25-26.

38. William L. Cox Oral History, 13-15, interviewed by Alan Cherry, 1986, LDS Afro-American.

39. Boris Spencer Oral History, 8, interviewed by Alan Cherry, 1985, LDS Afro-American.

Some attempts at match-making were successful. Annette Reid from the Bay area in California joined the LDS church in 1980 when she was twenty-four. She dated a white Mormon before and after her mission to Salt Lake City, but "there was so much opposition to this friendship." After considerable thought, Reid decided to postpone marriage plans and made her views public in a Mother's Day talk, stating single women "shouldn't sit around waiting to get married." She listed things she would like to do.

She was "actually doing those things" on her list when a mutual acquaintance introduced her to Emanuel Reid, a black member. She was good natured but skeptical about the introduction: "A member of the church figured, 'Black woman, black man. Ah, they must meet'—a match made in heaven just because we are the same shade and color. To me it was just, 'Okay, here comes another one.'" To her surprise she and Reid experienced immediate rapport. She said, "It was like old home week." Part of it was because of race. "We spoke the same language." It was not just a cultural language though. "Spiritually we were on the same wavelength," she said.[40]

Melvin Valeante McCoy from Ohio and Sharon Cornett from Kentucky were also introduced by white Latter-day Saints. Melvin was born in 1958 in Tennessee, raised Lutheran, attended the Baptist church, and then became Bahai. He was working temporarily at a mall booth during the 1984 Christmas rush, met some Mormons working in the booth next to him, and was baptized in 1985. The mother of a woman McCoy visited as a home teacher told him about Cornett, a native-born Kentuckian who had served an LDS mission. When McCoy received Cornett's "address and phone number on the piece of paper, . . . I knew that this was who Heavenly Father had in mind as my eternal companion."[41] He wrote, and Cornett telephoned in response.

After a three-month "long-distance relationship," they began seeing each other about once a month.[42] Cornett had uneasy feelings

---

40. Annette Reid Oral History, 16-18, interviewed by Alan Cherry, 1985, LDS Afro-American.

41. Melvin McCoy Oral History, 17, interviewed by Alan Cherry, 1988, LDS Afro-American.

42. Ibid., 17-18.

when they became engaged but stated: "I'd go to the temple and feel really good about it. We knew that it was the right thing to do. . . . We agreed that when we started dating that it would be a temple marriage or nothing. We both had that goal, and we worked for that."[43] The McCoys were married in 1987.

Successful interracial marriages like that of Nathleen Albright show a promising alternative to always looking for the "right" Mormon black partner. But racial barriers can fall hard for in-laws. Boris Spencer, a student at Utah State University when he was interviewed in 1985, observed: "In this little Mormon community of Logan that is 90 percent Mormon the blacks have made a bad name for themselves because of the one or two 'bros' at the college that mess around with their little Mormon girls and get them pregnant." Spencer was briefly engaged to a white girl: "Her brothers and sisters accept[ed] me. . . . Her mom just simply [wouldn't] take me in. But . . . her grandmother accept[ed] me."[44]

Kenneth K. Mack, a former football player at Utah State University and a member for four years when he was interviewed in 1985, had to deal with being idolized by sports fans but mistrusted in social settings. He married Ruby even though her "whole family classified blacks as crime oriented, abusive, loud, no manners, and no sense of direction. . . . As a matter of fact, . . . her mom said I was going to be a nobody."[45] The chill remained until the Macks' first child was born. Then Mack explained his mother-in-law "actually started communicating with me."[46]

Ruby Mack added: "Most of our neighbors are LDS. No one would speak to us until he joined the church. . . . Then they were mostly intimidated by him, I think, because he is a football player and he is big." She also reported that when they visit other wards, people would stare. But "once they listen to him speak or they listen to us speak, then they lighten up a little bit."[47]

---

43. Sharon McCoy Oral History, 4-5, interviewed by Alan Cherry, 1988, LDS Afro-American.

44. Spencer Oral History, 16-17.

45. Kenneth K. Mack Oral History, 17, interviewed by Alan Cherry, 1985, LDS Afro-American.

46. Ibid., 31.

47. Ibid., 30.

It seems logical that the problems of mixed-race dating would be even more severe for teenagers. However, survey respondents with teenage children saw fewer problems than expected. Of 57 who responded to questions about teenage dating, 83.1 percent said "never" in response to "My teenage children have been told by another church member not to date someone because we are of different races"; 13.6 percent said "sometimes" and only 3.4 percent said it happened "very often." Parents felt that their children did not get that reaction from the people in the ward. In response to the statement "My teenage children have been told by members of the church that they shouldn't date church members or would have to stop dating because we are of different races," 80.7 percent said they had "never" been told that; 12.3 percent said "sometimes"; and 3.5 percent, "seldom." When survey respondents were asked if black teens defined non-member blacks as their "only chance to date," 35.4 percent said "very often" it was true and 31 percent said "sometimes." The rest of the answers were divided among "seldom" (8.9 percent), "very seldom" (10.8 percent), and "never" (13.9 percent). Over a fifth (21.4 percent) did not respond.

Complex feelings of both faith and frustration about their children's acceptance as Mormons emerged from the interviews. Rosetta Moore Spencer's daughter Latoya was in her early teens when Rosetta was interviewed in Chicago in 1988. Rosetta commented: "I know the Lord is blessing [Latoya] to be a very strong little girl because at a time when peers and friends are so important to her she may be in a situation where she may not be in the church social group. The girls are all friendly with her, but as far as dating . . . , that's our next biggest challenge. What will she do?"[48]

Vivian Troutman especially found that her two daughters from a previous marriage suffered. Although her older teenage daughter was a class president in the church's Young Women's organization, she always felt like an outsider. But Vivian had great hopes for both daughters: "By them just coming into this [church] at the ages that they are, I feel good about it. I feel that it is going more smoothly."[49]

48. Rosetta Moore Spencer Oral History, 9, interviewed by Alan Cherry, 1988, LDS Afro-American.
49. Vivian Troutman Oral History, 18, interviewed by Alan Cherry,

When Janet Wright Rice was interviewed, her three sons were grown and living away from home. Two had served missions. "I would like to see my sons marry black girls in the church," she said, "but if there are no black girls in the church for them to marry, I'd rather them marry someone else in the church as opposed to going outside of the church looking for someone."[50]

Mary Angel Wilbur, a high school student and beauty contestant in Pittsburgh, was the only black teenager in her ward and stake. After explaining that she had dated only one member, a young black man six years her senior, she spelled out the familiar painful dilemma. Her Young Women and seminary teachers warned the class to date only members, but she explained: "I really have no choice if I want to date at all. There is no way that any guy at my church would ever ask me for a date. I have accepted that fact. . . . They see my color and not me."[51]

Martha Branigan, who converted from Catholicism as a high school student in Beloit, Wisconsin, was interviewed at BYU. Although she dated white students, the uncertain reactions of her dates was a strain: "I do think some whites are hesitant to ask black women out because they just don't know and they are afraid to take that chance. . . . There are just too many questions that haven't been answered, and they don't want to risk their eternities." She explained that she encountered a range of suggestions. One was that if she could "find someone that you feel good with, God will sanction it, and it will be okay." Others had questions and reactions that surprised her. As she tactfully put it: "I would expect them to have a deeper understanding of the gospel."[52]

Michelle Evette Wright, a student at Southern University in Baton Rouge, Louisiana, at the time she was interviewed, had been Mormon since age twelve. Lightly she said: "Whether I was a Mormon or not,

---

1985, LDS Afro-American; Larry Troutman Oral History, 15, interviewed by Alan Cherry, 1985, LDS Afro-American.

50. Janet Rice Oral History, 19, interviewed by Alan Cherry, 1988, LDS Afro-American.

51. Mary Angel Wilbur Oral History, 8, interviewed by Alan Cherry, 1986, LDS Afro-American.

52. Martha Branigan Oral History, 22, interviewed by Alan Cherry, 1987, LDS Afro-American.

I would probably have dated very little because I am very hard to please. . . . In high school . . . church standards were hard enough, not to mention the ones that I had." Her former boyfriends had not been black. One had joined the church, but she was sure it was not because of her. "I tried to make him hate me before he joined, and he joined anyway."[53]

Mary E. Smith, a Jackson, Mississippi, teenager, had been a member for a year when she was interviewed in 1987. "We're great friends," she said of her relationships with the other Mormon teens. "I get along with them." She said she was a "curiosity" with the girls. At slumber parties she noticed: "They always seem to find something new that I do that they've never seen before like roll my hair." She said her "off-the-wall" dances "amaze" the boys. One white girl was an especially close friend: "I think of her as my sister. We go places together. . . . She once told me that she would never consider not wanting to take me somewhere because I was black. She said that was silly. I can feel the same way about her." She added, "With others, we're close, but I don't see them as much as I see [her]." Still she admitted that dates were few: "The white boys seemed to say, 'You're cute,'" but "they've always sort of kept their distance."[54]

Eva Joseph, a divorced mother who had been a sales representative, explained a further complication in meeting other men: "As a black LDS I do not get invited to anyone's home. If we are given something like a dance, . . . we are not invited. No one tried to make friends with us as far as to say that we are welcome."[55] Doris Nelson Russell, another single mother and a professional singer from Los Angeles who had been a Mormon since 1980, enjoyed her callings and her participation in the southern California choir. But "sometimes I still feel a sense of loneliness. . . . There are a lot of people I love in the church, but I have not developed a lot of close friends in the

---

53. Michelle Evette Wright Oral History, 6, 10, interviewed by Alan Cherry, 1987, LDS Afro-American.

54. Mary Smith Oral History, 8-9, interviewed by Alan Cherry, 1987, LDS Afro-American.

55. Eva Joseph Oral History, 20, interviewed by Alan Cherry, 1985, LDS Afro-American.

church. I would love to."[56] Part of this distance may be caused by marital status. Reginald Allen, a married black man, observed that there were many more single black females in his ward than single black males. He sensed a natural "aloofness."[57]

Natalie Palmer-Taylor, a divorced mother with a son living in Salt Lake City, agreed that marital status was often a barrier. Activities were "always family things" and she always felt like an "outcast. I do not even go to them. I do not even pretend that I am going to go. I simply do not go because I feel like everybody is there as a family and it is just me and my son. I do not even feel comfortable in that setting. . . . I am single in a married church."[58] Eva Joseph in contrast found support as a single parent. Dismissing the "racial mess" with the acknowledgement that one finds it "every place that you go," she refused to "let that bother me." She insisted, "As far as helping and building my family and strengthening it, that is the thing I like about the church. Being a single parent, there is a place for me there."[59]

SUMMARY

Just as there are mixed reactions about how successfully the LDS church has achieved public assimilation, there are also mixed responses to private assimilation. Black Latter-day Saints who report adequate acceptance at meetings are less likely to have social interactions, friendships, and dates with white members. But responses range from blacks who claim to have never met a bigoted Mormon to the other extreme. Most simply recognize individual variations.

Single black members, whether teens or adults, face poignant problems—who will they date and marry? The two-part counsel—to marry within their race and to marry a church member—leaves a perplexingly small candidate pool. Another concern, especially for single parents, is their place within a married church. Some feel accepted; others feel excluded. Once again, much of the problem—and

---

56. Doris Nelson Russell Oral History, 30, interviewed by Alan Cherry, 1986, LDS Afro-American.

57. Reginald Allen Oral History, 19-20, interviewed by Alan Cherry, 1986, LDS Afro-American.

58. Palmer-Taylor Oral History, 12.

59. Joseph Oral History, 6.

much of the solution—lies in individual responses to the ideals of justice, love, brotherhood, and sisterhood in the mutually-shared principles of Mormon Christianity.

9.

ORGANIZATIONAL ISSUES

General and local LDS leaders have explored various organizational options for new black members, struggling to find a balance between practical and theological concerns. Practical questions deal with comfort zones where black and white members feel they can worship without restriction. But if all are brothers and sisters, as Mormon theology teaches, then are racial concerns artifical barriers?

LDS African Americans have been raised in the United States and share experiences with all other Americans. But is there something unique about the black American experience, elements of the culture which make it more satisfying for African Americans to worship together? Since the 1970s when the LDS church authorized formation of the Genesis Group for blacks in the Salt Lake City area, various solutions have been tried but none has been completely successful. The argument for ethnic wards like Samoan, native American, and Laotian units acknowledges cultural diversity in the larger Mormon community. In the case of African Americans, does this smack of segregation?

New members in inner-city black neighborhoods enhance the dilemma of whether the LDS church should sponsor separate branches and wards for black Americans. The growth of the LDS church in the United States in the last forty years has been mainly among the middle-class. This demographic pattern and land availability in growing suburban neighborhoods has resulted in new LDS chapels primarily in those areas. In places like Los Angeles and Washington, D.C., inner-city chapels were sold. In Oakland, California, the meetinghouse sat empty. This building pattern created immense logistical problems for new black members from the inner-city getting to church. With reduced bus runs or no public transportation on Sunday, some members depend on rides from white members who must drive out of their way to pick them up. Even with public transportation, time and money pose problems for some, especially those with large families.

SOCIAL GROUPS

The first group for black members was organized in Salt Lake City in 1971. LaMar S. Williams, who worked for the LDS church's Missionary Department and had promoted missionary efforts in Africa, organized socials for Salt Lake City Afro-Americans. When they asked for a formal organization, Williams advised them to contact church headquarters.[1] Ruffin Bridgeforth, Jr., Darius Gray, and Eugene Orr, all black Mormons, "call[ed] the church offices [to] see if there was some way that our people could meet together, such as the Danish and Norwegian branches." They subsequently met with Gordon B. Hinckley, Thomas S. Monson, and Boyd K. Packer, members of the church's Council of Twelve Apostles. On 19 October 1971 Hinckley set Bridgeforth apart as president of a group called Genesis with Gray and Orr as counselors. In an interview Bridgeforth explained that the apostles had asked, "What would you name the group if it were organized?" Bridgeforth responded: "We thought about it, and then the name came to us."[2]

Although Genesis had no written objectives, some implied goals were to promote missionary work among blacks and to facilitate reactivation and fellowship among the rumored 200 active and inactive black Latter-day Saints in the Salt Lake area.[3] The *Church News*

1. Lamar Williams and Nyal B. Williams Oral History, 30-32, interviewed by Gordon Irving, 6 May 1981, James Moyle Oral History Project, archives, historical department, Church of Jesus Christ of Latter-day Saints, Salt Lake City, Utah (hereafter LDS archives).

2. Peggy Olsen, "Ruffin Bridgeforth: Leader and Father to Mormon Blacks," *This People* 1 (Winter 1980): 15-16.

3. Ibid., 14; Alan Cherry Oral History (in process), interviewed by Jessie Embry, 1985, LDS Afro-American Oral History Project, Charles Redd Center for Western Studies, Archives and Manuscripts, Harold B. Lee Library, Brigham Young University, Provo, Utah (hereafter LDS Afro-Ameri-

announced vaguely that the group would be an "auxiliary program of the Liberty Stake" and "would meet and conduct Relief Society, Primary and MIA for the benefit and enjoyment of [black] members, but [they] will attend their respective Sunday . . . meetings in their home wards, where they will retain their membership."[4]

Genesis was an organization and a procedure that mimicked conventional branch structure without priesthood authority. Throughout its existence Bridgeforth served as president. Other officers changed as black leaders moved away from Utah and new people came to Salt Lake City. Although the group met weekly and sponsored a Relief Society and Primary (then weekday activities), members attended local wards on Sunday. This arrangement was similar to a German-speaking branch which met in Logan, Utah, until World War II. Unlike other ethnic branches where Latter-day Saints maintained their records, those who went to the Logan German-speaking branch also attended a Logan ward.[5] In the same way Genesis provided a chance for blacks to speak their cultural language, yet still affiliate with an ethnically-mixed congregation.

Genesis had the advantage of providing leadership opportunities for black men who, lacking priesthood, could not hold key ward positions. James Sinquefield, for instance, was grateful that Genesis gave him "an opportunity to gain experience in leadership. Brother Bridgeforth needed someone to fill the position of second counselor. I accepted it in faith that I would do the best I could."[6]

Genesis was organized at the height of the publicity given to priesthood restriction. Fearing that the group might be seen either as a Mormon positive public relations attempt or as a forum to force militant changes in the church, Genesis members were encouraged to be "cautiously conservative in their associations and avoid media

---

can); Armand Mauss, "The Fading of the Pharaoh's Curse: The Decline and Fall of the Priesthood Restriction Ban Against Blacks in the Mormon Church," *Dialogue: A Journal of Mormon Thought* 14 (Autumn 1981): 41.

4. "Salt Lake: Group Formed for Black Members," *Church News*, 21 Oct. 1971, 13.

5. Jessie L. Embry, "Little Berlin: Swiss Saints of the Logan Tenth Ward," *Utah Historical Quarterly* 56 (Summer 1988): 222-35.

6. Ibid., 13.

attention."[7] Helen Kennedy, a former Hill Field employee from Ogden, Utah, remembers that Elder Packer, speaking at the first meeting of Genesis, urged a low profile. According to Kennedy, Packer said, "Things that are young and tender need room to grow." He requested, "Those who do not belong [should] stand back, give them room. This is not a tourist attraction."[8]

Inevitably problems developed. Unlike wards and branches at the time, no minutes were kept of the meetings. With no set membership, people came and went at will, some leaving because they felt their needs had been fulfilled, others because they objected to the way the group was run.

Although sources of difficulties are not clear, in a published interview Bridgeforth remembered:

> When the group was organized, we didn't know what was ahead, but we did feel that there would be many problems. We had dissension, and we had people who were dissatisfied. "Why can't we do this?" and "Why can't we do that?" Trying to keep them calm was a constant challenge. We had the general authorities come and speak, but the dissenters would come and try to create problems. Some of them would come to the meetings and not make any outright disturbance, but would talk privately to our people. Some, of course, were vulnerable, and they would go off. It was just odd the way these things happened. We'd have some of our people get up and do some strange things.

Bridgeforth suggested that these problems happened because "Satan seemed determined to disturb our meetings."[9]

For Alan Cherry, however, Genesis's vagueness caused the quandaries. He found "having an organization that didn't have written purposes everyone could read, didn't have a definite form to follow, didn't have a means for its members to fully redress their grievances with the way we were managing our affairs . . . [made it] difficult for people . . . to effect changes."[10]

---

7. Cherry Oral History.

8. Helen Kennedy Oral History, 15, interviewed by Alan Cherry, 1986, LDS Afro-American.

9. Olsen, "Ruffin Bridgeforth," 16.

10. Alan Cherry, "California Report," Charles Redd Center for Western Studies, copy in my possession.

After the June 1978 announcement, many wondered if there was any longer a need for Genesis. Bridgeforth felt that there was still a role for the group. He explained: "We still need the social contact. I have got a black man out here at a ward. He is the only one. . . . If he has got nobody to talk to, sometimes he will just stay away."[11] Attendance dropped sharply, and it was often difficult to predict who would be at the meetings. The group continued to meet in monthly testimony meetings until 1987 when the gatherings were discontinued although never officially disbanded.[12]

Genesis was the model for two other social groups. Marva Collins joined the church in Montana within a month of the priesthood announcement. She then wrote President Spencer W. Kimball asking about other black Latter-day Saints and was referred to Genesis. She moved to Salt Lake City, attended Genesis meetings, and then moved to Oakland, California, where she started Genesis II in January 1985.[13] Three years later Genesis II was still meeting on the third Saturday of each month. An annual event was a picnic open to missionaries, black members, and anyone from the Oakland Stake. Black members from throughout the Bay area came.

Marvin Collins also started, edited, and published a newsletter to help black Latter-day Saints stay in touch. After mailing a letter in 1984, *Genesis: A New Beginning* helped the Oakland Genesis Group focus on issues of interest to Latter-day Saints. It expanded from Oakland and was mailed throughout the United States and some foreign countries. With financial help from the LDS church's Public Communications Department, Collins attempted to contact black Mormons throughout the world. The newsletter later changed its name to *Ebony Rose*. Collins explained in a 1986 issue: "I believe . . . [in] Blackness blossoming (like an Ebony Rose)." The newsletter carried news articles, recipes, personal advertisements for dates, editorials, and reprints about blacks in general but always focused on LDS

---

11. Ruffin Bridgeforth Oral History, 4, interviewed by Alan Cherry, 1985, LDS Afro-American.

12. Ruffin Bridgeforth, "All Worthy Males," KBYU television special, 9 June 1988, videotape in my possession.

13. Marva Collins Oral History, 25, interviewed by Alan Cherry, 1985, LDS Afro-American; *Ebony Rose* 21 (Oct.-Nov. 1986): 1.

blacks. Collins and her daughters Shelly and Tiombe were essentially the newsletter staff. According to the August 1986 issue, there were 1,000 subscribers.

Ebony Rose sponsored a black history conference in Salt Lake City on 21 February 1987 featuring Yochiko Kikuchi, a Japanese church leader, as keynote speaker. Collins commented in the newsletter: "It was touching that Elder Kikuchi saw the validity in *Ebony Rose* and Genesis to meet that [fellowshipping] need" of black Mormons.

The newsletter ended with an announcement in the July-August 1988 issue: "After five years we at Ebony Rose can proudly say we succeeded in our original goals to educate and bring Ebony LDS members together. Without regrets, but sadly, we say farewell and head on to new adventures."[14]

In January 1986 black members in the Washington, D.C., area asked through church channels for permission to organize a Genesis group and received permission. Drawing on the Salt Lake City group, this new organization was also called Genesis. According to Cleeretta Henderson Smiley, a home economics teacher who joined the church in 1977, its mission "was to unite the black LDS in the eastern region in valiant brotherhood and sisterhood." Smiley described Genesis as her "most significant experience in the church until her "calling to [a] public communications job." The D.C. Genesis group met for special firesides; Ruffin Bridgeforth and Alan Cherry were among the invited speakers. The group also held missionary workshops and socials but was discontinued in 1987 when no one assumed leadership.[15]

In January 1985 students at BYU and Salt Lake City Genesis co-sponsored a program honoring Martin Luther King's birthday. Emanuel Reid recalled: "The underlying factor of the program was to get people together." According to Reid, about 150 people, black and white, attended and then lingered for "a great gathering afterwards. Refreshments were served; the spirit was felt. We hope that we are

---

14. Issues of *Ebony Rose* are available in Special Collections, Lee Library.

15. Cleeretta Henderson Smiley, LDS Afro-American Symposium, 8 June 1988, videotape in my possession.

able to do things of that nature in the future."[16]

BYU black students subsequently formed a black student association. In her oral history interview, Joelle Margot Aull, president in 1987, reported that the association had "social purposes" and "educational reasons." The association sponsored a "Black Awareness Week" for several years in honor of King's birthday. Speakers included Ronald Coleman, a non-Mormon black professor of history at the University of Utah; Mary Sturlaugson Eyer, a black LDS author; and Alan Cherry. During the week the group sponsored other activities including dances and dinners to make BYU students and the Provo community more aware of black Americans.[17]

Another social group was organized with a publication in mind. The LDS African American Cultural Awareness Group (AACAG), a Utah-based non-profit organization, was formed in September 1989 by Nathaniel and Ruby Womble, Natalie Palmer-Taylor, and Nathaniel Chism, all residents of Salt Lake City. In the first issue of the association's newsletter *Let's Talk*, editor Jerri A. Harwell asked how these two separate cultures—black and white America—could come together, admitting it was "awkward at first."[18]

A later article in the newsletter reported that the Salt Lake City Genesis Group had combined with AACAG and that Ruffin Bridgeforth was serving as an officer. The author, Cara M. Billinger, continued: "Some day there may come a time when we no longer need the AACAG and similar groups, when all people are unified by gospel love and are so secure in their love that unique characteristics are celebrated and understood."[19]

This group like Genesis sought official recognition from the LDS church. Despite discussions with Apostle David B. Haight and others, that goal was not accomplished. In a highly hierarchical institution

---

16. Emanuel Reid Oral History, 22, interviewed by Alan Cherry, 1985, LDS Afro-American.

17. Joelle Margot Aull Oral History, 18-19, interviewed by Alan Cherry, 1987, LDS Afro-American.

18. *Let's Talk* 1 (Apr./May 1989): 3. Copies of the newsletter *Let's Talk* are in the library, historical department, Church of Jesus Christ of Latter-day Saints, Salt Lake City, Utah.

19. *Let's Talk* 1 (Aug./Sept. 1989): 1.

where the line between "official" and "unofficial" is sometimes perceived as the equivalent of "orthodox" and "unorthodox," this was a signficant blow to the organization. At a dinner meeting in Salt Lake City in October 1989, Joseph C. Smith, the group's president, explained that he did not want the group to be perceived as "a splinter group." According to Smith, "If the prophet told us to disband tomorrow, we would do it." Dinner speaker Apostle Haight was cautiously encouraging. After asking members to participate in their wards and branches, he commented, "It is also good for this group to meet."

At the same meeting Smith defined the organization's goals. These included sharing testimonies and being an example for other blacks. "It helps to hear a testimony from someone in circumstances similar to your own," explained Smith. Another goal was to maintain black culture in the LDS church. "One of the biggest goals of the AACAG is to dispel the fear that African Americans will have to give up their black culture in order to be accepted into the church." And these differences, according to Smith, "need not separate us. . . . In fact, those differences can strengthen us. . . . Through the gospel, all races can be united." The news article about the dinner concluded: "It is the mission of the AACAG and this newsletter alike to break down those barriers. For, as Elder Haight concluded, 'Christ atoned for all men. There are no exceptions.'"[20] The AACAG sponsored potluck dinners, musical programs, and other socials. The group later changed its name to Latter-day Saints for Cultural Awareness, although it continued to cover only African American issues. The LDS church Public Communications Department occasionally called on members to entertain black guests from other countries.

The AACAG's newsletter, *Let's Talk*, attempted to reach black members throughout the world. *Let's Talk* was edited by Jerri A. Harwell and published bimonthly. Seven issues were printed. *Let's Talk* listed its goals as the "three-fold mission of the church" defined by the First Presidency: "proclaiming the gospel," "perfecting the Saints," and "redeeming the dead." To achieve these goals the newsletter outlined specific objectives to "assist African-Americans with the transition into the gospel so they do not feel separated and lonely after

20. Ibid.

joining the Church, nor that they have to leave their culture behind to assimilate into the LDS culture," "to encourage African-Americans to open up avenues of communication and trust with their local Church leaders," and "to educate Latter-day Saints about African Americans." The newsletter cost $9.50 for a yearly subscription or $1.25 a issue. It carried historical articles and short essays.

Shortly after *Let's Talk* ceased publication in 1990, a quarterly replacement, *Uplift*, published by Latter-day Saints for Cultural Awareness, started. Now in its second volume, it continues to be published at no cost to subscribers, but it seeks advertisements and donations.

All of these groups attempted to fill social, spiritual, emotional, and cultural needs of black members, believing that there were unique aspects of the African American lifestyle which united them. None of the organizations was set up as "dating services" for single blacks nor was that a goal. George Garwood attended Genesis to associate with other LDS Afro-Americans. He explained, "I think it is good especially for blacks who need that building up and that encouragement that comes from that group."[21] Carol Edwards of Washington, D.C., found that many new members "get lost in the shuffle. . . . There is not a net to keep them in . . . long enough to realize what they should be concentrating on. That is why this [D.C.] Genesis Group is important to us now because, as they come in, we are going to try to hold them and keep them in."[22]

Clara McIlwain, Edwards' mother, noted: "Before Genesis I only knew the four [black] people that were in my ward."[23] Natalie Palmer-Taylor added, "It is just nice to know that people are all going through the same struggle and you are not alone."[24] Jerri Allene Thornton Hale, who joined the church as a student in the midwest in 1977 and

---

21. George Garwood Oral History, 20-21, interviewed by Alan Cherry, 1985, LDS Afro-American.

22. Carol Edwards Oral History, 14, interviewed by Alan Cherry, 1986, LDS Afro-American.

23. Clara McIlwain Oral History, 13, interviewed by Alan Cherry, 1986, LDS Afro-American.

24. Natalie Palmer-Taylor Oral History, 34, interviewed by Alan Cherry, 1985, LDS Afro-American.

served a mission in Texas, did not feel a need to socialize but participated in Genesis and later the AACAG because, she said, "perhaps there are other blacks who do need a social support and maybe I could help them there."[25]

Social groups have also enabled blacks to retain and enjoy cultural distinctions. Annette Reid said that she enjoyed meeting with other black Latter-day Saints because "we not only have the gospel in common, but a lot of times we have common words and lingos and traditional things that have happened in our families that are unique to that particular culture of people."[26] Genesis meetings included "Baptist music that [blacks] were brought up with. . . . It is just something to make you feel that you are with your people."[27]

James Sinquefield, at one time Ruffin Bridgeforth's counselor in Genesis, explained the group gave "black members an opportunity to worship together." Its intent, he explained, "was not to segregate them. I hope that in the future maybe more Genesis groups will be organized within the church throughout the world so that black members can worship together for culture's sake."[28] In Washington, D.C., "Negro spirituals" in special programs sponsored by Genesis exposed other LDS members to black music.

Another reason Bridgeforth and others had in starting black organizations was public relations.[29] Many people assumed that the priesthood restriction excluded blacks from membership. The D.C. Genesis, for example, volunteered to work at the Shiloh Baptist church family center, which helped improve the LDS church's image in the black community.[30]

Cherrie Lee Maples felt that support from black members allowed

---

25. Jerri Allene Thornton Hale Oral History, 39, interviewed by Alan Cherry, 1985, LDS Afro-American.

26. Annette Reid Oral History, 30, interviewed by Alan Cherry, 1985, LDS Afro-American.

27. Ruffin Bridgeforth Oral History, 21.

28. James Sinquefield Oral History, 12, interviewed by Alan Cherry, 1985, LDS Afro-American.

29. Olsen, "Ruffin Bridgeforth," 14.

30. Cleeretta Henderson Smiley, 12, interviewed by Alan Cherry, 1986, LDS Afro-American.

her to reach out to other blacks:

> To deal with families who are nonmembers, to deal with my culture which is not in the church, I need the strength and support of black LDS people to rely on. . . . My white LDS friends cannot give me that strength. They could if I totally assimilate and immerse myself in their world, but I choose not to do that because I want to be able to bring blacks into the church. To remain in my culture, I need the support of my black LDS friends.[31]

Parallels to the various Genesis groups were the church's special language units in Utah. In organizing a German-speaking ward in 1963 Apostle Spencer W. Kimball hoped that as immigrants learned English they would return to their local wards.[32] Similarly black members such as George Garwood attended Genesis for a short time and then stopped going. As he explained: "I felt that I needed not to be tied to that group because . . . you need to get used to going around with different [i.e., non-black] people."[33]

Garwood touched on one of the problems of Genesis. Darrin Davis, who occasionally attended Genesis in Salt Lake City while studying at Brigham Young University in Provo, had mixed feelings. Although he enjoyed the gathering, he also felt "a little bit distressed when black people feel that there is a need for special treatment." He advocated a less culture-conscious approach to church membership: "I think if we just take our role as regular Latter-day Saints and let our daily experiences teach one another, then things will go smoothest."[34] Being a "regular Latter-day Saint" takes time and adds meetings and callings to family and work obligations. Genesis groups were disbanded in part because they added one more layer of responsibility.

---

31. Cherrie Lee Maples Oral History, 12, interviewed by Alan Cherry, 1986, LDS Afro-American.

32. German-speaking Branch, University West Stake, Tape, 30 January 1963, LDS archives.

33. Garwood Oral History, 20.

34. Darrin Davis Oral History, 27, interviewed by Alan Cherry, 1985, LDS Afro-American.

BLACK BRANCHES

After 1978 when black men could be ordained to priesthood, black branches were organized in areas where missionary work in black neighborhoods produced significant numbers of members. The president of the California Los Angeles Mission, F. Britton McConkie, organized one of the first black branches in the Watts area of Los Angeles. The ninety-two people who attended the first meeting on 2 December 1979 sustained Robert L. Lang, a member since 1970, as branch president. During his six years as president, Lang often served with no counselors and only rarely had two, although most of the auxiliaries were completely staffed.[35] Lang insisted it was not a "black branch"; it was the Southwest Los Angeles Branch in a "predominantly black area."[36] In 1981 the 109 members were black, except for several families of mixed race and approximately ten white members.[37] Black members came from throughout the greater Los Angeles area, some traveling from as far away as Long Beach and Orange County. In 1981 Van Floyd, who was married to a white woman, lived three blocks from the Inglewood Ward but traveled miles to serve as a counselor in the branch presidency.[38] Joseph C. and Marilyn Smith and their children, who moved to California after Joseph had graduated from BYU, commuted from Orange County to attend the branch. When Lang was released, Paul Divine, a black member from Long Beach, replaced him. John Phillips, a white stake high councilor who served in the branch presidency under both Lang and Divine remembered only one white member, the wife of a black man, among the sixty to seventy members who attended regularly.[39]

The Southwest Los Angeles Branch had built-in structural problems. Members in the black neighborhoods had no transportation to

---

35. Jessie L. Embry, "Separate but Equal?: Black Branches, Genesis Groups, or Integrated Wards," *Dialogue: A Journal of Mormon Thought* 23 (Spring 1990): 19.

36. Robert Lang Oral History, 12-13, interviewed by Alan Cherry, 1985, LDS Afro-American.

37. Mauss, "Fading of the Pharaoh's Curse," 42.

38. Gayla Floyd Oral History, 7, interviewed by Alan Cherry, 1986, LDS Afro-American.

39. In conversation with John Phillips, 1988, notes in my possession.

church, and branch leaders often spent most of the time between meetings giving rides. The need for imported leadership guaranteed dependent status and a lack of full psychological independence. Ecclesiastical responsibility for the branch shifted four times in eight years from the mission to the Torrance California North Stake to the Lawndale California Stake and finally to the Downey California Stake. Teri La Rue Hall, a white woman who served in the stake Young Women's program, recalled that the branch's young women would not attend stake-sponsored activities, despite efforts to find out what displeased them about their interracial gatherings. When the branch sponsored special events, they seemed to expect and enjoy participation from other young women in the stake.[40] In 1988 the branch was disbanded. Some members had become inactive, others attended their local wards.[41]

In the mid-1980s mission president Ralph Bradley organized a similar branch in Charlotte, North Carolina, after missionary efforts in federal housing projects resulted in a large number of black converts. He hoped the branch would both solve transportation problems for new converts and ease racial and economic tensions that threatened to swamp fragile religious accords.

At first white missionary couples were in charge of the branch with the husband serving as branch president. Robert Ezell was the first black called to be branch president. He was sustained shortly before Alan Cherry conducted interviews in North Carolina in 1986. A number of white stake leaders believed Ezell had been a minister, but he had actually been an itinerant preacher who had felt a "calling." Without formal training or administrative experience, he was unprepared for the responsibility and was soon replaced by a white member. In 1988 branch membership was estimated to be 900-1,200, though only 100-200 attended regularly.[42]

The branch in Greensboro faced similar problems. Rex D. Pinegar of the area presidency asked Johnnie McKoy to help organize a black branch. At first McKoy urged him to find another solution. When Pinegar countered that there was no time to come up with another

---

40. Teri La Rue Hall, conversation, Oct. 1991.
41. Embry, "Separate but Equal?" 20.
42. Ibid., 21.

plan, McKoy agreed, though he declined to serve as branch president. He felt a white president could enlist more assistance from stake leadership. Instead he was made a counselor and involved in all decisions.

The Greensboro Bennett Branch, organized in 1986, had geographical boundaries. Because of the area's ethnic makeup, approximately 90 percent of members were black. McKoy explained that the branch averaged four baptisms a month, had a 60 percent retention rate, had reactivated about 50 percent of those who were lapsed at the time the branch was organized, and had an average attendance of sixty to seventy weekly. McKoy believed this was the equivalent of about 150 active members since most worked swing shifts and could only attend every other week.[43]

After serving in the branch presidency, McKoy was called to the high council and later became branch president. McKoy was a powerful local leader. In a 1989 *Church News* interview, McKoy said the branch was averaging two baptisms a week. With this growth he concluded: "Within a year's time . . . we're going to have a ward, and then other wards will develop. We feel this branch will be a nucleus where blacks will come. This kind of love is going to spread through the black community, and thousands will come to the church when they see the work progressing here."[44]

Like Genesis and other groups, ethnic branches met a number of needs—social, missionary, reactivation, and leadership training. Donna Chisolm decided to go to the Charlotte Sixth Branch, the name eventually given to the black branch, because she "wanted to . . . get the black LDS experience."[45] Members of these fledgling branches felt the energy of a new enterprise. Mason Anderson commented: "This is really encouraging to me to see people coming in, to be able to start from the beginning, to be able to work themselves up and be able to take part in the church. . . . I have liked the fellowship with the Saints that I have met there. I have come to know quite a few of them. . . .

---

43. Johnnie McKoy, conversation with Alan Cherry and Jessie L. Embry, 10 June 1988, notes in my possession.

44. Elayne Wells, "Our Motto is Love," *Church News*, 28 Oct. 1989, 11.

45. Donna Chisolm Oral History, 13, interviewed by Alan Cherry, 1986, LDS Afro-American.

We are trying to organize ourselves and to get the church set up."[46]

Many black members, discouraged by integrated wards, felt revitalized by ethnic branches. According to Johnnie McKoy, seventy-five of nearly 400 inactive members came back immediately. He said the branch "gave them opportunities to grow, to experience the gospel more deeply, more fully . . . because it was a close knit branch."[47] Beverly Perry recalled that some of the people who came to the Southwest Los Angeles Branch at first "sacrificed a lot to come" and "the spirit was really neat."[48]

These inner-city branches sometimes covered entire metropolitan areas. Nathaniel Womble, who had been a counselor in the presidency of the Georgia Atlanta Mission, felt that many small branches throughout the Atlanta area would make it easier for members to attend church services. Bryan Waterman, a white missionary, thought storefront churches, similar to those maintained by evangelical and rescue missions, would help some Newark members who could not afford the bus rides across town. He had heard that small congregations directed by mission presidents rather than stakes had been established in New York and Philadelphia. Waterman felt a need "to bring the church to the people" and commented: "If we are ever going to become strong and deeply rooted, then we will have to have store-front churches scattered throughout the cities to bring the church to the people."[49]

Some missions and stakes have developed the store-front churches Waterman encouraged. The Pennsylvania Philadelphia Mission worked with African Americans, Hispanic Americans, and Asian Americans living in ethnic neighborhoods. To help meet the needs of these groups, LDS general authority F. Enzio Busche organized the Philadelphia Metro District in June 1991. Two years later the mission ran the district's ten urban branches with some 500 members. In addition to holding meetings, these branches were involved in projects

---

46. Mason Anderson Oral History, 19, interviewed by Alan Cherry, 1986, LDS Afro-American.

47. McKoy conversation.

48. Beverly Perry Oral History, 30-31, interviewed by Alan Cherry, 1988, LDS Afro-American.

49. Ibid., 13-14.

to improve their members' living conditions. A Laotian woman, Viengzay Mounelasy, appreciated the opportunity to work in a small branch. She became a Primary president only six months after her baptism. She explained, "Serving has helped me grow more quickly than I would have otherwise."[50]

The Boston Massachusetts Stake organized an urban congregation, the Malden Branch, in 1989 as part of a master plan. Since then stake leaders have organized branches in Spanish, Portuguese, and Asian areas of the city. The stake originally organized the branches to deal with the three major reasons inner-city members had stopped attending church meetings: distance, language, and culture. Stake members referred to these units as "store-front" branches or "boutiques" because "they represent a street-level effort to display the beauty of the gospel before the people." One of the first orgnaized inner-city congregations, the Boston Branch, included church members originally from Haiti, Cuba, Tonga, Lebanon, Nigeria, Mexico, Trinidad, Ecuador, Asia, and El Salvador. According to the branch president, "Our branch is a neutral place; we accept people where they are. . . . We offer them peace with God and with themselves, as well as practical solutions to their everyday problems."[51]

Transportation was not the only problem facing new black members. Often if they had to travel to a suburban ward, they encountered people from different economic backgrounds. For them the advantage of economic similarity was significant. Before the creation of the Spring Garden Branch in Newark, New Jersey, members in Irvington, a poor inner-city community, were included in the Shorthills Ward. According to Waterman, this ward "was at one time the most affluent ward in the church." Sharon Davis, who immigrated from Jamaica with her mother and sisters lived in Orange, New Jersey. Her first experience at the Shorthills Ward was intimidating.[52] Waterman noticed that not only did "black members [have] a difficult time attending church

50. Ronald M. Mann, "Philadelphia, the Seedbed of a Nation," *Ensign* 23 (Aug. 1993): 76-77.

51. Don L. Brugger, "Climate for Change," *Ensign* 23 (Sept. 1993): 24-28.

52. Sharon Davis Oral History, 6, interviewed by Alan Cherry, 10 Feb. 1985, LDS Afro-American.

in Shorthills, . . . the members in Shorthills had a difficult time home teaching in Irvington."[53]

Similarly blacks in Oakland felt uncomfortable attending church with people from Piedmont, an exclusive nearby neighborhood. When asked why some black members stop attending the Mormon church, Vivian Troutman, a manager of a Kentucky Fried Chicken franchise in East Oakland, explained: "They see all these white people with all these nice cars and nice clothes. They may have one dress, and the next Sunday they don't want to wear that one dress. They don't have the funds to do better."[54]

Some see a public relations benefit of inner-city branches. John Phillips hoped the Southwest Los Angeles Branch would establish a physical presence in Watts from which wards and eventually stakes would grow.[55] Robert Lang commented that "the branch had done wonders" because the black community saw that blacks "belong to the [Mormon] church."[56]

A further benefit of black branches, like black groups, was leadership opportunities provided to new converts. As Robert Lang argued: "A black man gets baptized into a ward with another race of people. What is the chance of this particular black person getting a calling in order to learn leadership? It is kind of slim."[57] Elizabeth Pulley found her greatest opportunities to serve in the Los Angeles branch. She taught mother education and social relations in Relief Society and worked in the Primary.[58] Mason Anderson elected to attend the Charlotte branch because with his lack of education and experience, he felt, "If I went into a church that was already established[,] I would not be able to do hardly anything. . . . To be able to work is really helping me in my growth in the . . . church."[59]

---

53. Ibid., 4.

54. Vivian Troutman Oral History, 20, interviewed by Alan Cherry, 1985, LDS Afro-American.

55. Phillips conversation.

56. Robert Lang Oral History, 18.

57. Ibid., 12.

58. Elizabeth Pulley Oral History, 15, interviewed by Alan Cherry, 1985, LDS Afro-American.

59. Anderson Oral History, 20.

Yet disadvantages of ethnic branches grew from the very factors that were their strengths. New converts misunderstood church procedure and had difficulty functioning in leadership positions. Beverly Perry, who lived in San Pedro, California, commented: "Some good has come out of the Southwest Los Angeles Branch . . . but I think the leadership needs to be reinforced. In the beginning I was telling everyone to go [there to church]. . . . But now I do not think I would tell anyone to go because they are so disorganized."[60]

In North Carolina members of the Charlotte Sixth Branch soon recognized Robert Ezell's inexperience. Melonie Quick, a Baptist before she became Mormon, remembered that Ezell spoke every week and "mostly read . . . out of one of the [church] books. . . . It's kind of hard to sit and listen to someone when they really don't understand what they are saying." Even though she complained, "I don't know why they put him in that position," she was willing to work with him "so he can accomplish something and try to make it work, I guess. We are all beginners."[61]

With so many recent converts in the black branches, there was often confusion about basic church organization and teachings. Gladys Brown, a forty-year-old convert, interviewed after she had been a member for less than a year, wanted leaders to "take fifteen minutes and explain to the people what [Relief Society] is all about." She also had questions about the temple that no one took the time to answer.[62] Donna Chisolm reported other concerns about church procedure. When a Relief Society teacher's attendance became sporadic, the president asked Chisolm to teach the class instead, but she was never formally called.[63]

Naturally new members brought with them experiences from their previous churches. According to Robert Lang, people had to "unlearn" old habits.[64] Benjamin Washington, who had attended

---

60. Perry Oral History, 31.

61. Melonie Quick Oral History, 16, interviewed by Alan Cherry, 1986, LDS Afro-American.

62. Gladys Brown Oral History, 7, interviewed by Alan Cherry, 1986, LDS Afro-American.

63. Donna Chisolm Oral History, 15-16.

64. Robert Lang Oral History, 17.

Methodist, Baptist, and Holiness churches as a child, said, "I do not think there is any harm in singing good songs on Sunday, but all of that whooping and hollering . . . that fire and brimstone stuff is their biggest problem."[65] The wife of the president of the Charlotte Sixth Branch recalled a white speaker repeating the LDS platitude that "the church is the same wherever you go." From the back row one of the members called, "Amen, Brother!"[66] Such congregational interaction is rare in most Mormon worship meetings.

The most tension-fraught issue of black branches was the suspicion of segregation. Darlene Bowden, of the Charlotte Sixth Branch, noticed that there were "not a whole lot of whites going to the black church" and vice versa, and that "there is still that uncomfortable racial feeling [that is] like a thick smog."[67] Catherine Stokes, former Relief Society president of the integrated Hyde Park Ward in Chicago, adamantly opposed separate units for Chicago, pointing out the "public relations nightmare for the church. It would tend to confirm what most people think about the church, that it is racist."[68] Jerri Allene Thornton Hale living in Provo summarized the dilemma: "Some blacks need [a black ward that] . . . would serve as support," but "then you would have [people] on the other side saying that the church segregates you."[69]

ISOLATED LDS AFRO-AMERICANS

Black branches, whatever their advantages and drawbacks, cannot be organized where there are few black members. The Willises, the Jenkins, and the Rices in the St. Louis area were acquaintances before they joined the Mormon church. They meet together once a month for a dinner and social. They have deliberately limited the group size, because they feel a need to maintain these private friendships. Accord-

---

65. Benjamin Washington Oral History, 17, interviewed by Alan Cherry, 1986, LDS Afro-American.

66. Embry, "Separate but Equal?" 24-25.

67. Darlene Bowden Oral History, 12, interviewed by Alan Cherry, 1986, LDS Afro-American.

68. Catherine M. Stokes Oral History, 20, interviewed by Alan Cherry, 1988, LDS Afro-American.

69. Hale Oral History, 39-40.

ing to Eva Willis, "We're three couples that really gel. . . . We do fit well together."[70] Janet Rice explained, "I think the reason that I guarded this so carefully was because we all had common interests, we all liked each other, and we all got along so well with each other. When other people ask about joining our group, I tell them no way." This policy includes her mother who cannot come over on dinner night.[71]

Other groups are deliberately inclusive. Aurbie Rayford Johnson of Atlanta recalled that blacks would come from a hundred-mile radius to gatherings Nathaniel Womble organized. "We would just congregate together and talk about some of the problems that we would have and try to work them out. We would try to bring investigators from each area to talk to or show a film and share our testimonies."[72]

Others have more diffuse contacts, such as Mary Smith, a high school student, who said that black members in Jackson, Mississippi, were "sort of like family. We hang on to each other. We use each other for strength. We use each other for sounding boards. If there's something that is truly bothering us and that we can't talk to the white LDS about, we can always go to one of the blacks and tell them how we feel."[73] Marilyn Larine Thomas, who lived in the same city, felt less connected: "I don't have too much [contact with black Latter-day Saints] right now. When we first joined, there was just a handful. Now that the number of blacks has increased in the church, we're now trying to get to know them. We see them in church, and we talk to them. Outside of that right now, we don't have much contact with them."[74]

Many LDS African Americans are the only black members in their

---

70. Eva Willis Oral History, 9, interviewed by Alan Cherry, 1988, LDS Afro-American.

71. Janet Rice Oral History, 21, interviewed by Alan Cherry, 1988, LDS Afro-American.

72. Aurbie Rayford Johnson Oral History, 9, interviewed by Alan Cherry, 1987, LDS Afro-American.

73. Mary E. Smith Oral History, 12, interviewed by Alan Cherry, 1987, LDS Afro-American.

74. Marilyn Larine Thomas Oral History, 8, interviewed by Alan Cherry, 1987, LDS Afro-American.

area. Annie Wilbur of New Kensington, Pennsylvania, just outside of Pittsburgh, grew up in a black area and moved to a largely white neighborhood after high school. She stayed there through a marriage and a divorce and worked in a hospital operating room, where most employees and patients were white. Depressed by her singular situation after baptism, she exclaimed: "I have got to find some ward that has some black members in it. I am traveling miles to church anyhow so I might as well travel miles in another direction so I can see somebody black. I am working all day with white people; I am living in a white neighborhood; I am going to a white church. What am I doing?"[75]

Some members responded to interviews with delight because Alan Cherry was someone they could relate to. Junious Edwards Ross living in San Jose, California, was gratified to learn that Cherry was "actually doing something to let others know that you are not alone. That is a good feeling." He continued, "Once in a while I need to talk with someone who knows what I am going through. You and I can relate. We are both black and we know the problems. . . . It is kind of hard to talk with someone else about feelings I may have when they didn't grow up in a ghetto and they didn't ever experience racial problems."[76]

Carl Simmons, a Utah State University football player from West Oakland, knew only one black member, Kenneth K. Mack, a fellow football player. "I think it would be kind of fun to sit around and to talk with them and to see some of their reasons why they joined the church and why they like the church so much," he explained. "It would be a good experience just to sit down with a lot of the black LDS and just start talking about the church."[77]

The LDS Afro-American Symposium held on the tenth anniversary of the priesthood announcement, 8 June 1988, provided such an opportunity for those who could afford to come to Provo, Utah.

---

75. Annie Wilbur Oral History, 16, interviewed by Alan Cherry, 1985, LDS Afro-American.

76. Junious Edwards Ross Oral History, 10, interviewed by Alan Cherry, 1985, LDS Afro-American.

77. Carl Angelo Simmons Oral History, 17, interviewed by Alan Cherry, 1985, LDS Afro-American.

Approximately 300—white and black—attended the opening session where Apostle Dallin H. Oaks, the keynote speaker, and Alan Cherry discussed the experiences of LDS blacks. Eight LDS African Americans talked about their experiences as Mormons and the future of black Mormons. People traveled from as far away as Hawaii and Philadelphia; even some non-Mormon blacks from Salt Lake City and Ogden attended. African Americans who attended the symposium were also invited to an informal discussion group the next day. A picnic featured "nostalgia food" with fried chicken, collard and turnip greens, cornbread, and pound cake, all staples of black church socials. Participants greeted old friends, some of whom they had not seen for years, and struck up new acquaintances. Many wanted a poster from the conference and started collecting names and addresses so they could stay in touch.

NEED FOR BLACK PROGRAMS

The survey showed a division among blacks about the needs and values of black programs. Three-quarters of respondents (75.7 percent) said that having more black members would not make them more active. Over four-fifths (83.1 percent) said they "never" wanted to belong to an all-black ward/branch. An additional 7 percent "very seldom" or "seldom" felt that desire. Only 2.5 percent said they "very often" wanted to worship with only blacks; 6.5 percent "sometimes" felt such as a wish.

Respondents were more evenly divided on the need to communicate with other black Mormons. The survey asked if there should be a publication exclusively for blacks. Jerri Allene Thornton Hales Harwell, former editor of *Let's Talk,* objected to the word "exclusively," but the question was designed to measure the need for information related primarily to black Latter-day Saints. Over a third (39.5 percent) said "never"; an additional 16.4 percent said "very seldom" or "seldom." But two-fifths (44.2) said they "very often" (16.8 percent) or "sometimes" saw a need (27.4 percent). In response to another question about whether they spoke differently to blacks than whites, almost half (49.3) said they "never" speak a different language with blacks than whites and a quarter (26.4) said "seldom" did. Burgess Owens, of New York City, addressed this issue in his interview: "It doesn't really come down to a black/white issue at all. I just happen to be an LDS member that happens to be black."[78] Deborah Spearman, who grew up in Philadelphia, felt the church needed to make an effort "to understand blacks a bit. They should look at why some of them are converted but don't really stay. It is not that they should start a special program, but they should understand why it is hard for some types of blacks to convert from Baptist to Latter-day Saints because it is a totally different environment."[79]

Rosetta Moore Spencer had been dissatisfied with the Lutheran church and was thinking about the Baptist church before she met Mormon missionaries. She expressed the dilemma of dissatisfaction probably shared by others: "I do feel a need to have the church meet black people's needs specifically, and I haven't figured out how yet. . . . At the same time I sometimes feel guilty for having those feelings. I have a lot of faith in the church, and I know that all of the programs are of God. I feel that they should be meeting our needs." Yet she added, "Our cultures are different, and because of that, [blacks and whites] have different needs."[80]

Maintaining elements of black culture is important. The black church has been "the major vehicle for the preservation and interpretation of the rich heritage of Black Americans,"[81] and from these predominantly black congregations, Mormon converts were suddenly worshipping with whites. Most (61.3 percent) "strongly disagreed" and 24.6 percent "disagreed" with the statement: "I am afraid that in order to be a good member of the church, I have to 'give up my black identity.'" People were less sure about what white Latter-day Saints expected of them. When asked to respond to the statement, "I have felt that some non-black members expect me to forget my blackness and to fit into a white world," half (50.8 percent) said "never," 20.8

---

78. Burgess Owens Oral History, 24, interviewed by Alan Cherry, 1986, LDS Afro-American.

79. Deborah Spearman Oral History, 18, interviewed by Alan Cherry, 1987, LDS Afro-American.

80. Rosetta Moore Spencer Oral History, 14, interviewed by Alan Cherry, 1988, LDS Afro-American.

81. John A. Adams, Jr., *The Black Pulpit Revolution in the United Methodist Church and Other Denominations* (Chicago: Strugglers' Community Press, 1985), 1.

percent said "seldom" or "very seldom." However, 18.9 percent said that they "sometimes" felt that way and 9.7 percent said they did so "very often."

Style of worship is an area where most blacks have made enormous adjustments. Robert L. Simmons, pastor at the First United Methodist church and professor at the United Theological Seminary in Dayton, Ohio, taught a class on black music in white churches at the Gospel Music Workshop of America in Salt Lake City. He observed that Euro music is usually fast tempo and tells a story. He cited as an LDS example, "Come, Come Ye Saints," written by William Clayton as Mormons came to Utah. The song encourages the Saints to face their new adventure with "joy," describes different elements of the trip, and closes by comforting/exhorting:

> And should we die before our journey's through,
> Happy day! All is well!
> We then are free from toil and sorrows, too
> With the just we shall dwell.
> But if our lives are spared again
> To see the Saints their rest obtain,
> Oh, how we'll make this chorus swell,
> All is well! All is well!

Simmons maintained that Afro music is slower and requires voice and body movement. He argued that it was a "sin" not to have movement, either in the notes themselves or the body in the Afro tradition. Afro music focuses on the power of repeated phrases rather than on telling a story. Simmons "rewrote" "Come, Come, Ye Saints" for the closing session of Salt Lake City's Gospel Music Workshops in Afro style and gave it its original name, "All is Well." His changes added runs to the standard English tune so that the music "moved" more, repeated phrases from the Clayton verse, and eliminated the story elements. For example, the Clayton version begins, "Come, come, ye Saints, no toil or labor fear,/ But with joy wend your way." The Simmons version repeats the opening phrase "come, come, ye saints" four times. Simmons also added traditional Protestant phrases. "Gird up your loins; fresh courage take" became "lift high the cross, fresh courage take." The Mormon tradition places no special emphasis on the cross while Protestant/Catholic convention does.[82]

The survey asked how black Mormons adapted to Euro music with the statement: "I would like to hear some black gospel hymns and/or spirituals in church services." Less than a quarter (23.7 percent) said they felt that way "very often," but 43.7 percent said they "sometimes" did. The rest of the answers were divided between "seldom (11.1 percent)," "very seldom (11.6 percent)," and "never (10.0 percent)." But interviewees gave indication of ambivalence towards standard Mormon music. Alvin Alphabet, a former Baptist who joined the Mormon church with his wife Ellen in 1981 to provide a religious background for their daughter, said: "I still have to go once in a while [to the black church in the Atlanta area] and hear some good gospel singing."[83] Since the question was not specifically asked, only those who felt strongly about the music commented about it.

Bryan Waterman recalled a new black member in New Jersey who was a gospel music pianist. Shortly after he was baptized, this piano player was asked to play at a stake meeting in a white neighborhood in Caldwell. Waterman recalled when the new convert got up to play, he said, "'This probably isn't quite what you're used to hearing, but if you feel the spirit, I hope that you will get up and dance.'" Waterman observed, "That wasn't going to happen. He didn't know that, though. He also didn't know that we don't applaud in the chapel. He went through a really loud piece of stand up and get excited because 'Jesus is your Lord.' . . . No one clapped; no one . . . danced."

Waterman remembered that later the convert "told me that he was depressed the rest of that meeting." Although people complimented him after the meeting, he interpreted their restraint negatively. Waterman recalled the convert's feelings: "He said it made him feel like we didn't have the spirit because we didn't act on whatever we might have felt at the time." Employed as a pianist at other churches, he no longer attends Mormon meetings but told Waterman,

---

82. Robert M. Simmons, "Black Music in White Churches," Gospel Music Workshop of America, 14 Aug. 1991, Salt Lake City, notes in my possession; Robert M. Simmons, "All is Well," music in my possession.

83. Alvin Alphabet Oral History, 4, interviewed by Alan Cherry, 1987, LDS Afro-American.

"As soon as the church progresses to the point where they will accept his culture, then he would be the best Mormon you have ever seen." He quoted a Book of Mormon scripture to Waterman which said, "Shout praises to the Holy One of Israel," and then told Waterman, "You are not living your own scripture."[84]

The decorum at worship service seemed unnatural and subdued to Emanuel Reid of Georgia, a former Baptist, who drove sixty to seventy miles to attend the nearest Mormon church: "I was used to a lot of 'Amens' and clapping and feet patting. . . . Everything was so quiet and reverent." Despite the difference, Reid still felt "a good spirit" at Mormon meetings. He remembered: "I was hungering and thirsting after the knowledge that I knew was there."[85]

Deborah Spearman, formerly a Seventh-day Adventist, was also "not used to the quiet that is in the church." She commented, "Sometimes I enjoy the [hymns] and sometimes I can't relate because I am used to hearing gospel music."[86] She had the same reaction to the variety of speakers rather than a minister. "Sometimes I enjoy them; sometimes it just doesn't relate to me."[87]

Charles Lancaster, son of an AME minister and a former minister himself, summarized the main differences in services:

> Your LDS services are very quiet, very refined. . . . Our people are used to having a regular minister deliver a regular sermon on Sunday, whereas in the LDS church the bishop might speak and he might not. Somebody else is assigned to talk. There will be a youth speaker, then this speaker, and then that speaker. It's just a vast change in not having a full-time clergyman up there delivering this Sunday message. Sometimes we find that a little boring. I have stated to the bishop at certain times that I find that his services are boring.

He added, "I know that I wouldn't be happy anywhere else. . . . [But] I will not give up all of my traditions. I love my black music. I love the

---

84. Bryan Waterman Oral History, 9, interviewed by Jessie L. Embry, LDS Afro-American.

85. Emanuel Reid Oral History, 9, interviewed by Alan Cherry, 1985, LDS Afro-American.

86. Deborah Spearman Oral History, 2, interviewed by Alan Cherry, 1986, LDS Afro-American.

87. Ibid.

spirituals. I love to hear a good fiery sermon sometimes. I haven't heard one since I've been in the LDS church. I haven't had the opportunity to deliver one either."[88]

Other important areas of black culture involve lifestyle. William L. Cox, of Greenville, North Carolina, grew up during the 1960s. He recalled: "I get the impression that many of us [blacks] think that we have to give up our cultural heritage, our history and our background, in order to join the church. I have not changed any in the area of my diet or . . . lifestyle." He summarized: "The only thing that separated us in the early years was segregation. The only thing that separates us now is economics."[89] Sharon Davis, who was born in 1958 and grew up in Jamaica, moved to the United States as a pre-teen. She observed: "Black is not only a color. It is also a culture. Your culture is a part of you no matter where you are from. It is exciting when you can hold onto a rich heritage and enhance it with God's true church."[90]

Betty Ann Bridgeforth admitted, "I have to adjust" to the Mormon church being "a way of life, . . . not a Sunday thing that you leave after church."[91] She implied she was willing to make the change, but it was not easy. Rodney Carey, who served a mission in Oakland, where he returned to live, was uncompromising: "I think the worst problem that I have seen with black Latter-day Saints . . . . is that they carry their black culture too heavily into the church."[92] Considering this range of opinion, it is interesting that respondents did not see cultural differences as a reason for becoming inactive. When asked to respond to the statement, "I have considered leaving the church because of feeling that blacks don't fit into the social or cultural experience of the church," 63.2 percent said "never," and 21.4 percent said "seldom"

---

88. Charles Lancaster Oral History, 12-13, interviewed by Alan Cherry, 1988, LDS Afro-American.

89. William L. Cox Oral History, 29, interviewed by Alan Cherry, 1986, LDS Afro-American.

90. Sharon J. Davis Oral History, 12, interviewed by Alan Cherry, 1985, LDS Afro-American.

91. Betty Ann Bridgeforth Oral History, 20, interviewed by Alan Cherry, 1985, LDS Afro-American.

92. Rodney Carey Oral History, 35, interviewed by Alan Cherry, 1985, LDS Afro-American.

or "very seldom." Only 6 percent said "very often," and 9.5 percent said "sometimes."

At least one change in LDS publications might give many respondents a stronger feeling of belonging. Responding to the statement, "I wish more black church members were shown in film, magazines, and other church publications," 57.7 percent said "very often" and 30.6 percent said "sometimes." Only 3.1 percent said "never." Darrin Davis, a returned missionary and student at Brigham Young University in 1985, commented favorably about blacks in Bonneville Corporation's "Homefront" spots for the church. He explained: "I think it is fine. It is representative of the change that is coming about in the church." But he added: "I don't feel there should be any special programs . . . for black people [nor should their] needs . . . be catered to. . . I feel that we should fall into the rank and file of the church, do our duty, live, enjoy, bless one another's lives. As a whole the church will grow and grow. As we become more and more a multi-cultural church, there won't be problems."[93]

PARALLELS WITH OTHER ETHNIC GROUPS

Davis's point is a valid one. Mormon church membership even within the United States is becoming less European American. Native Americans, Hispanic Americans, Asian Americans, and Polynesian Americans as well as African Americans are joining the church in increasing numbers. All of these cultural groups experience adjustment transitions when they come into the church. Are their experiences different from each other? Are adjustments harder for blacks than for other groups?

Marva Collins felt the answer was yes. She wrote to Apostle David B. Haight in 1984: "Black people do not have a wide reference point in the church like the Tongan, Asian, and Latino people do."[94] She repeated the theme in an 1986 issue of *Ebony Rose*: "When other races join the Church of Jesus Christ of Latter-day Saints, they manage to keep their wonderful culture first because they don't give up their

---

93. Darrin Bret Davis Oral History, 24, interviewed by Alan Cherry, 1985, LDS Afro-American.

94. Letter to David B. Haight, 4 Mar. 1984, in *Ebony Rose*, 1 June 1984.

language." She added that while blacks speak the same language as white Americans, they have a "cultural family" they want to preserve.[95]

The Charles Redd Center for Western Studies is currently documenting how other ethnic and cultural minorities feel about their positions in the LDS church. While each group feels that their problems are unique, they are often similar. The language branches for Spanish-speaking, German-speaking, and Tongan-speaking people Collins cited as advantages did not always have a smooth existence. Other LDS ethnic groups, regardless of the group involved, identify the same advantages and challenges as do the black branches and social groups. Advantages included worshipping with people who shared a similar culture, more leadership opportunities for men and women, reduced prejudice, a visible presence in ethnic neighborhoods, and shared activities.

For example, the stated goals of the Indian Branch organized in Los Angeles in 1961 for relocated native Americans were: "to provide the Lamanite members of the church with an opportunity to become active in an organized unit of the church, to mingle with their own people, to serve in positions of responsibility, to grow in the gospel, and to have an opportunity to socialize and progress under the influence of the church."[96]

These goals closely match those of black organizations and branches, and were shared by other ethnic groups. In a Spanish-speaking branch in Oakland an elderly sister who was illiterate in both English and Spanish, could participate in meetings, something that had been impossible in an English ward. The clerk of a Samoan branch in the Long Beach Stake declared with pride when the branch was organized in 1966: "Now we are taught in our own mother tongue."

Esmeralda Meraz, a Mexican American from Southern California, explained why her parents decided to attend a Spanish-speaking branch: "Even though my dad speaks English, he has not mastered the English language and he can't communicate very well. He is not a very educated man as far as schooling is concerned. My mom has had less schooling than he has. . . . I think [my dad] felt that

95. Ibid.
96. Indian Branch, Los Angeles, California, 23 September 1961, Manuscript History, LDS archives.

he would get more out of it and so would his family if we attended the Spanish branch."[97]

But just as the goals are similar, so are the problems. There are organizational and staffing difficulties when members are inexperienced in church administration and doctrines. Smaller branches cannot offer the full church program some members would like to experience. All ethnic branches have difficulties with members who have not been socialized to fill callings dependably or to certain standards.

According to Omaha Joseph Harlan, who served as branch president in Macey, Nebraska, "Without the numbers, you can't really have all of the programs in the church and all of the auxiliaries. You get a watered down version of the gospel. You have to do a lot of independent study to really get the meat of the gospel." Meraz had similar experiences in Southern California. When her family moved from Mexico to California and attended a Spanish-speaking branch, she had a hard time adjusting. She explained,

> [In Mexico] I was used to attending these ward meetings separating into my classes, and seeing my friends. [In California, however] I felt like we weren't really part of what was going on. It was kind of discouraging to see only ten people, twelve people in the meetings. It was also discouraging not to see any youth. We were the only kids that were attending church. . . . We didn't really have any teachers in Primary or Young Women's. . . . We always had a feeling of not being complete and of not having everyone there that needed to be there to make it a successful experience for us every Sunday.

She explained that the Spanish branch "didn't have the leaders. It didn't have people that were strong in the gospel. . . . There weren't people there who were examples of returned missionaries . . . or people who had been outside of El Centro or the Imperial Valley."[98]

Whether they were German-speaking Americans, Hispanic Americans, native Americans, or Polynesian Americans, they repeated similar challenges and satisfactions. Navajo Robert Hatch used to attend the Alma Lamanite Branch in Farmington, New Mexico, and stopped

---

97. Jessie L. Embry, "Ethnic Groups and the LDS Church," *Dialogue: Journal of Mormon Thought* 25 (Winter 1992): 86.

98. Ibid., 91.

attending church when the Lamanite Branch was dissolved in the 1980s. "I just miss it so much. It was joyous. It was always a friendly feeling to go there. . . . It's really sad to see it interrupted now." Yet when asked what he would do for Navajos if he were the stake president, he was hesitant to reinstate such a branch: "I don't know that I'd make such a big deal about Indians or Navajos. . . . Maybe our Lamanite Branch that we used to have wasn't such a good idea. It kept us separate for all these years for no reason really. . . . While I'm sad that Alma Branch is gone, I think it's good that we're all mixed in like this."

The dilemma for Hatch was simultaneously achieving integration and retaining ethnic identity. "I'd like the Indians to be proud of themselves," he insisted. "I wouldn't want them to hide that. I'd like them to blend in, but, at the same time, be individuals. . . . I just think that we don't need to bury our heritage, bury our skin color. We don't need to raise it on a flagpole either. We just need to be somehow more aware of who we are but it's not a big deal to anybody. I don't think we need to glorify it, just be content." He admitted, "I don't know what a program like that would be."[99]

SUMMARY

Black Latter-day Saints are in a unique position since they are the only group that has historically been excluded from priesthood and temple worship. Still, like other ethnic groups, they want to retain their culture and maintain contact with other blacks, but organizational efforts to achieve both goals have shown mixed success—whether it has been social groups like Genesis and its offshoots, inner cities branches with mostly black memberships, black publications, or less formal networks. Those responding to the survey are divided on whether these programs are needed. Because there are no easy solutions, the topic of how to blend diversity without assimilation will continue to be debated for blacks as well as other ethnic groups.

---

99. Robert Hatch Oral History, 9, 11-12, interviewed by Ernesteen Lynch, 1989, LDS Native American Oral History Project, Charles Redd Center for Western Studies, Archives and Manuscripts, Lee Library.

10.

WITHIN THE BLACK COMMUNITY

It would be both impossible and undesirable for black Latter-day Saints, having joined what is perceived to be a white church, to sever all ties with the black community. Even though they have changed religion and thereby entered a new culture, many LDS African Americans continue to live in a mostly black world. Over a third of survey respondents (36.8 percent) live in mostly black neighborhoods. About a quarter (23.4 percent) live in integrated neighborhoods. The rest (38.3 percent) live in mostly nonblack areas. They all continue social and collegial associations with black friends and relatives. Many maintain ties precisely because they want to talk about their new church with other blacks. Despite their best intentions, they sometimes feel ostracized, often misunderstood, as though they are hovering between two worlds but belong to neither.

REACTIONS OF BLACK CONVERTS

Black friends and neighbors possess many of the stereotypes about Mormons being a Jim Jones-type cult,[1] or a polygamous group.

---

1. In late 1978 the world learned about the demise of the Peoples Temple at Jonestown, Guyana, South America, a utopian community established by Jim Jones. Some 914 residents of the Peoples Temple Agricultural Project died in a mass murder-suicide, most from drinking poisoned Kool-Aid. This event had such an impact on Americans that families of Mormon converts remembered and connected it with all unknown sects. For more information, see David Chidester, *Salvation and Suicide: An Interpretation of*

Some knew the church had denied priesthood to black men. How did nonmembers react to their close associates joining the Mormon church? To try to assess that, the survey asked about reactions of family members and friends. For example, the survey asked how often "my black friends tell me that I am a traitor to 'my people' because I am a member of the church." Only 8.5 percent stated that their friends reacted this way "very often," but 16.6 percent said it happened "sometimes." Nearly half (49.2 percent) said it "never" happened; 10.1 percent said "seldom" and 15.6 percent "very seldom."

The survey asked for agreement or disagreement with the statement, "I think many black members of the church are leaving the church because of pressures from their black friends." The survey did not define "pressure," leaving both persuasion to return to black culture and insistence to return to former lifestyles as possible interpretations. Here 10.8 percent said "very often," almost a fifth (19.0 percent) said "sometimes," and 70.2 percent said "seldom," "very seldom," or "never." Over a third of those (37.4 percent) said "seldom."

People who were interviewed again provided more details. Over three-fifths (62.3 percent) of those interviewed mentioned family responses to their LDS church membership. No two responses were exactly the same, but nearly all answers fell into four categories. Of those, over a quarter (27.7 percent) said their families were pleased and supportive, slightly less (24.7 percent) had both positive and negative reactions, and only 8.4 percent saw their families as antagonistic but accepting. A very small percentage, 2.3 percent, claimed they were disowned or lost contact with their family.

A higher percentage of friends than family members was upset. Half (50.7 percent) mentioned the reaction of friends and neighbors as generally antagonistic. Responses fell into five general categories. Only 4.7 percent had a positive reaction from their friends, 8.5 percent said their friends were curious, 19.7 percent had positive and negative responses, 10.8 percent were antagonistic but supportive, and 7.5 percent were hostile and disassociated.

DeNorris Bradley, who grew up first in a Holiness church and then

Jim Jones, the Peoples Temple, and Jonestown (Bloomington: Indiana University Press, 1988).

a non-denominational black church, phrased his response in almost the same words as the survey: "If they don't say it with words, they say it with actions. 'You are a traitor. You have relinquished . . . all of our heritage and our culture. You have joined a white church.'"[2] Deborah Taylor's brothers and sisters asked: "Why a white church? Are you turning your back on your race? . . . Do you think you are better than me now? . . . Have you forgotten where you came from?"[3] Barbara Lancaster's father-in-law was an AME minister. Her in-laws and her husband's children from a previous marriage "were going to kidnap us and have us deprogrammed because they thought we had been brainwashed."[4] Mary Smith, a high school student from Mississippi, said a black date cancelled when he discovered she was LDS because he said, "You're betraying my black heritage."[5] She added: "A lot of black teens oppose you because they say you are going to a 'white' church. If you want to hang out with them, you've got to do what they do. If you don't want to do what they do, then you're kind of left out in the cold."[6]

Complete tolerance was rare. Margaret and Willie J. Carter lived in a white neighborhood in Danville, California, when they were interviewed in 1985. Members for a year, Margaret reported: "We weren't taught to hate the white man. We were taught to love our fellowman. I think maybe this is why my parents accepted it and why no one has squeaked about us becoming LDS."[7] Willie's family had "no reactions." He explained: "When we were growing up, no one even thought anything different about LDS. We did not realize that some LDS members feel constantly persecuted." In fact his sister's

---

2. DeNorris Clarence Bradley Oral History, 35, interviewed by Alan Cherry, 1986, LDS Afro-American Oral History Project, Charles Redd Center for Western Studies, Archives and Manuscripts, Harold B. Lee Library, Brigham Young University, Provo, Utah (hereafter LDS Afro-American).

3. Deborah E. Taylor, letter to Jessie Embry, 18 Nov. 1988.

4. Barbara Lancaster Oral History, 7-8, interviewed by Alan Cherry, 10 Mar. 1988, LDS Afro-American.

5. Mary Smith Oral History, 9, interviewed by Alan Cherry, 1987, LDS Afro-American.

6. Ibid., 4.

7. Margaret Carter Oral History, 25, interviewed by Alan Cherry, 1986, LDS Afro-American.

bland reaction was, "I guess the only thing that is different is that they do not object to using lipstick and things like that."[8]

For most built-in prejudice seemed inevitable. Candance Kennedy said her friends in California warned her, "The Mormons believe the black man is cursed, and the black man can't get to heaven."[9] Deborah Taylor's family asserted: "They will always think they are better than you are. They may give you a job in the church, but you will never hold a high office. They will keep you right where they want you."[10]

John W. Phoenix, a pharmacist from Washington, D.C., said blacks would "throw . . . in our faces that we couldn't become a leader in the church" because of the priesthood restriction.[11] Marvin Arthur Jones, who was a missionary in Utah when he was interviewed, said his father had investigated the church before the 1978 announcement and would not join because of the restriction. When Marvin wanted to become a Mormon, his father, who was involved in Civil Rights, thought that "the church is just trying to change their views just so they can get more blacks." Jones conceded, "I guess even if I were him and I grew up in his time period, I would probably have some hard feelings in the same ways. I can understand where he is coming from."[12]

Interestingly many of the interviewees had not been aware of the priesthood policy until they started investigating the church. When some joined, they were unaware that they could not have participated fully before 1978. For example, Alan Cherry asked Benjamin Washington, a truck driver from Charlotte, North Carolina, "What do you know about the past situation of priesthood restriction in the LDS church?" In his reply Washington exposed his lack of information: "I hope I have got the right meaning of it. You have to give up all of your

---

8. Willie J. Carter Oral History, 16-17, interviewed by Alan Cherry, 1985, LDS Afro-American.

9. Candance Kennedy Oral History, 3, interviewed by Alan Cherry, 1986, LDS Afro-American.

10. Taylor letter.

11. John W. Phoenix Oral History, 9, interviewed by Alan Cherry, 1986, LDS Afro-American.

12. Marvin Arthur Jones Oral History, 2, interviewed by Alan Cherry, 1985, LDS Afro-American.

old habits if you want to advance in the priesthood."[13] After recognizing that neither missionaries nor church leaders had discussed priesthood restriction with these new converts, Cherry realized that it would take too much time to explain the policy and even when he attempted, it was so foreign to them that their answers did not add to the interviews.

A more widespread perception was that the LDS church was a cult. Emanuel Canaday, who grew up in St. Louis, said his family thought the church was "making me run off to a South American country and drink poison Kool Aid."[14] Others warned black investigators that Mormons worshipped Joseph Smith or another prophet in Salt Lake City, still practiced polygamy, or were members of the Ku Klux Klan.

Edwin Burwell, who lived in Greensboro, North Carolina, when he was interviewed in 1986, had been a member for about a year. An aunt denounced him because he "had left God." Many friends felt that "Mormons are a cult. They do not believe the Mormons serve God. When you tell them that they believe in the Father, the Son, and the Holy Ghost, they go, 'They just started because they used to worship this man in Salt Lake City.'"[15] Burwell's wife Retha also reported that friends attacked her: "Why did you join that church? It is a cult. You know that, don't you? They do not worship Christ; they worship Joseph Smith."[16] "I lost a lot of friends," she continued, "I can count my black friends on my hand, three. . . . It is like, 'This child has a disease. We do not want to be around her any more.' It was hard because I am so used to having friends."[17]

Doris Russell, a divorcee from Pennsylvania and Virginia, had been a Baptist but was praying for more religion when missionaries

13. Benjamin R. Washington Oral History, 15-16, interviewed by Alan Cherry, 1986, LDS Afro-American.

14. Emanuel M. Canaday Oral History, 7, interviewed by Alan Cherry, 1988, LDS Afro-American.

15. Edwin Allen Burwell Oral History, 7-8, interviewed by Alan Cherry, 1986, LDS Afro-American.

16. Retha Burwell Oral History, 21, interviewed by Alan Cherry, 1986, LDS Afro-American.

17. Ibid., 20.

came to her home. She explained: "I met so many black people who were anti-Mormon and some who really just got downright indignant with me about my membership. Some of my friends just shied away from me, and I was not close to any of the members. I think my family was really perturbed with us becoming members of this church. It was kind of lonely for awhile."[18]

Delphrine Young said his uncle believed Mormons "have multiple wives" and warned that "they are the Ku Klux Klan. . . . I was told I was set to be killed."[19] Young's father had been killed by a white policeman for "resisting arrest." Johnnie McKoy, a brick mason, was also told the church was "a cult" and "full of Klansmen."[20]

Some friends were dismayed that LDS Afro-Americans would leave traditional black churches. David E. Gathers commented: "You have it on both ends. You have the white Mormons. A lot of them do not believe that you should belong. They feel you are inferior. Then you have the blacks that feel that you are overstepping yourself and how dare you not be a Baptist or how dare you not be a Methodist."[21] Virginia Johnson of Los Angeles, whose mother was a lapsed Baptist because her minister had been so strict, countered her mother's arguments by asking: "Didn't they hang black folks in the South in the name of Christianity? Your good old Baptist Christians, didn't they do that in the name of Christianity?"[22]

Brenda Sanderlin, who had been in the military and a Roman Catholic nun before joining the Mormon church, told of calling her mother and telling her: "Mom, you've always wanted me to be happy. Now I have a full joy. I am now a member of the Church of Jesus Christ of Latter-day Saints." Her mother said, "A cult." Brenda said it could not be a cult if it used the name of Jesus Christ. "That gave her some

---

18. Doris Russell Oral History, 28, interviewed by Alan Cherry, 1986, LDS Afro-American.

19. Delphrine Gracia Young Oral History, 20, interviewed by Alan Cherry, 1985, LDS Afro-American.

20. Johnnie McKoy Oral History, 8-9, interviewed by Alan Cherry, 1986, LDS Afro-American.

21. David E. Gathers Oral History, 23, interviewed by Alan Cherry, 1986, LDS Afro-American.

22. Virginia Johnson Oral History, 18, interviewed by Alan Cherry, 1985, LDS Afro-American.

peace, but not much." Now when she talks to her mother, she "keeps commenting, 'Brenda, you sound so happy.' I am glad it sounds like that because underneath everything I am. That is what the gospel has been doing for me."[23]

Like Sanderlin, others reported that their families and friends softened as they saw positive changes. Barbara Lancaster said her stepchildren eventually accepted their conversion: "I think they thought we were going to change and we were going to be something other than what they thought we were. They see that their father still loves them. They see that he still has a love for the Lord. Even though he doesn't have his own church and pastoring every Sunday, he still has a ministry that he has to fulfill."[24]

Melvin D. Mitchell, who was born in 1937, grew up in Columbus, Ohio, and joined the marines in the 1950s, said his mother told him that it didn't matter what church he belonged to as long as he had some religion in his life. For him "joining the church . . . brought my family closer to me even though I am a Latter-day Saint and my family isn't. We are able to talk scriptures and talk about the Bible. It was very interesting because I didn't think they would accept me when I joined the church. But they have seen the change it has made in me."[25]

Sarah Kaye Gripper grew up in the Union Baptist church in her hometown of Springfield, Illinois. When she was baptized, her mother told her it didn't matter what church she belonged to. But then "I found out that my mom and my sister had been laughing behind my back." She confronted her mother: "I believe in God, and we believe in the same things basically." Gripper stated that with time her mother could "see a growth in me as far as the religion goes. She sees how active I am in the church also. She hasn't had a lot of comments lately."[26]

Winston Wilkinson said his mother-in-law hesitantly attended the

23. Brenda Sanderlin Oral History, 12, interviewed by Alan Cherry, 1985, LDS Afro-American.

24. Barbara Lancaster Oral History, 10.

25. Melvin D. Mitchell Oral History, 2, interviewed by Alan Cherry, 1988, LDS Afro-American.

26. Sarah Kaye Gripper Oral History, 8, interviewed by Alan Cherry, 1988, LDS Afro-American.

baptism of his eight-year-old son. "She had these preconceived notions about the church, [but] once she got in the church and she saw that she was welcome and Mormons didn't have devil ears and horns, her own attitude towards us changed."[27] Florita Davis's family also saw positive changes in her, and because of that she said the family members "have kind of a gratitude towards the church."[28] Davis who grew up in the Los Angeles area as a Catholic had also attended the Baptist and Jehovah's Witness churches as a teenager before joining the LDS church in 1980.

J. Joseph Faulkner of Gadsden, Alabama, reported that people told him "we had joined a cult. I guess they thought that we had joined a Jim Jones sort of a situation where eventually we were all going to drink some poison and die and that we had to sign all the property that we had over to the church." When Faulkner "started doing my genealogy, and I shared with [my brother information about] our grandparents that he didn't know," his brother's feelings became warmer. "He has made a vast change that he is willing to at least listen to me talk about the church."[29]

A rare reaction was that of Beverly Latimer's mother, who was indifferent at first, but "then . . . she saw that we were serious because we would go to church every Sunday. . . . One day she said, 'Did you know that they don't like black folks?'" In contrast her husband, Randolph E. Latimer, Jr., an attorney from New York City who shifted from the Baptist church to the Pentecostal tradition with his mother as a child, encountered no opposition when he joined the LDS church. His mother saw their baptisms as "moving towards where she wants us to move anyway—which is serving God."[30]

Virginia Johnson of Los Angeles found acceptance from some relatives but not from others: "The part of my family that are Catholic

---

27. Winston A. Wilkinson Oral History, 6, interviewed by Alan Cherry, 1986, LDS Afro-American.

28. Florita Davis Oral History, 9, interviewed by Alan Cherry, 1985, LDS Afro-American.

29. J. Joseph Faulkner Oral History, 10-11, interviewed by Alan Cherry, 1987, LDS Afro-American.

30. Randolph E. Latimer, Jr., Oral History, 15, interviewed by Alan Cherry, 1986, LDS Afro-American.

accepted my baptism without any problem. That is my stepmother [and] my natural father's side of the family. . . . They came to my baptism and some of the lessons. . . . From the Sunday school classes, they told me that the doctrine was not that much different from their Catholic upbringing. My Baptist side of the family were against it 100 percent. They could not understand why I had to be baptized again." Johnson said that she "wanted to share [the gospel] so much that I was becoming over-excited. Then when they would condemn it, I would become overly defensive. . . . I had to learn to tone myself down." She said with time her family started asking her questions. Her sisters thought she wouldn't last, but since she has they seem to say, "'I love her; we better accept it.'"[31]

Thomas Taylor, a former Baptist who lives in Chesterfield, Virginia, joined the church in 1980. His family had mixed reactions. Some "were happy that I am an LDS member. The rest of them kind of frown, . . . think it's some kind of a hoax" and "shy away from me when we get to talking about religion."[32]

Some black converts reported no waning in family members' attitudes. Sherrie Honore Franklin said when she, her husband Harvey, and her children converted in New Orleans, "we became . . . outcasts in our family." She overheard her mother say snippily to her daughter: "Your mama must be on the phone with one of her church members. I can tell because her whole speech changes." Sherry was irritated that her mother made comments to her daughter. She went on to explain: "Whenever it comes down to something for the church, it's always a negative tone. She can't find anything right with it."[33]

PROSELYTING

By joining the LDS church, African Americans become part of an active proselyting movement with the slogan "every member a mis-

---

31. Virginia Johnson Oral History, 8-9, interviewed by Alan Cherry, 1985, LDS Afro-American.

32. Thomas Taylor Oral History, 4, interviewed by Alan Cherry, 1986, LDS Afro-American.

33. Sherrie Honore Franklin Oral History, 8, interviewed by Alan Cherry, 1987, LDS Afro-American.

sionary." Many want to share their newly found knowledge, yet black converts see relatively few blacks joining the Mormon church. Alan Cherry asked people why they did not feel missionary efforts were more successful in black communities. The responses can be divided into six categories:

1. The "white" image of the LDS church

Nearly all interviewees agreed that the LDS church is considered a white church. Marie Edington Chisolm, whose father was a Presbyterian minister in Tennessee, asserted that blacks "feel . . . Mormons are not interested in bringing black members into the church. I have heard some say that Mormons did not welcome black membership until after the nation as a whole started doing something about civil rights. Then the church got on the bandwagon and started doing it too."[34]

Clement Biggs, who had served as a branch president in Birmingham, Alabama, felt that anti-Mormon literature and stories followed missionaries into black neighborhoods: "You go and visit them the first time, and they are all happy and excited about the gospel and what you have to say. You go back the next time and they don't want to talk about it. They don't want to see you because they've been told by their friends something on the contrary to what you were teaching." Biggs felt such pressures accounted for inactivity as well: "We've had some pretty big disappointments in this area lately. We get people baptized in the church. They remain in church a couple of Sundays. Then their family or friends get to them."[35]

Michelle Evette Wright, a college student in Baton Rouge, expressed frustration about changing the negative image. She wished "there [could] just be a statement or something that the church can do to let people know that they are not prejudiced." One possiblity she suggested was the church could help "in a disaster that just happened in a black community." Then, more realistically, she added:

---

34. Marie Edington Chisolm Oral History, 9, interviewed by Alan Cherry, 1986, LDS Afro-American.

35. Clement Charles Biggs Oral History, 10, interviewed by Alan Cherry, 1987, LDS Afro-American.

"But the church doesn't act that way. They are not just going to come out and try to do something to get black people to join the church." She rationalized: "Those are just signs I guess. Some people need to have something that they can see."[36]

Several *Church News* articles report similar kinds of community outreach programs. Danny Boyle, a Young Men's president, noticed that the Holy Temple church of God in Christ in Mesa, Arizona, needed repair. He and the pastor, Rev. B. E. Dansie, had been on the track team in high school. When Boyle offered the services of LDS young men and women, Dansie willingly accepted. "Both groups were surprised," said Boyle. "We found that regardless of color and denomination, we are the same people, people who like to laugh and talk and work."[37]

Another article reported missionaries starting a scout troop for deaf boys on the south side of Chicago.[38] Peter Gillo, who is African American, was asked to help. It was his first encounter with Mormonism, and he joined the LDS church in 1983.[39] Cleeretta Henderson Smiley of Maryland observed that the Washington, D.C., Genesis Group's service projects with the Shiloh Baptist church provided a positive Mormon presence in the black community.[40]

Bryan Waterman recalled that the airing of a "Homefront" television public service announcement impressed African Americans in the area where he was working. He commented: "From what I understand—this might be a myth of our mission—Newark had the highest response in the United States for free copies of the Book of Mormon. When the first large-scale media blitz took place the Christmas of 1989, in one day our mission office received three hundred referrals from it. . . . Part of the appeal might have been that they were free and

---

36. Michelle Evette Wright Oral History, 17, interviewed by Alan Cherry, 1987, LDS Afro-American.

37. "Service—LDS Youths Help Spruce Up Other Church's Meetinghouse," *Church News*, 2 June 1982, 9.

38. J. Malan Heslop, "Deaf Scout Troops Build Solid Citizens," *Church News*, 6 Feb. 1983, 10-11.

39. Peter Tabani Gillo Oral History, 3, interviewed by Alan Cherry, 1988, LDS Afro-American.

40. Cleeretta Henderson Smiley, 12, interviewed by Alan Cherry, 1986, LDS Afro-American.

definitely the appeal was Jesus. When we talked to people, they were most interested in Jesus."[41]

Edward J. Harris, who grew up in Pike County, Missouri, during the 1930s and 1940s where he experienced discrimination, reported a critical, yet helpful comment of a woman who wanted to come to church because she saw an LDS advertisement. Pointing out an obvious but overlooked approach, Harris said: "If you were to do something like that where you have a high density of black population, [use] the same kind of spot with a black face saying the same thing in a black idiom."[42]

2. Inability to explain priesthood restriction

Several people interviewed struggled with the historic priesthood restriction policy. Although they had accepted it themselves, they felt uncertain about providing a persuasive explanation to others. Nathleen Albright, who had read accounts of hostile demonstrations at Brigham Young University athletic events, asked missionaries about it when they came to her home in Virginia in 1971. Later she could not remember what they told her, "but I do remember that whatever they said it was enough to soothe me. . . . My only problem, after I became a member, was explaining to other people. . . . So I had to just bear my testimony when I was asked."[43]

Florita Davis felt blacks "feel kind of shy to go and preach to our own people because we are going to be looked at as, 'You fell for that?' because of all the bad traditional things that people have put on the church, because we are black, because of not having the priesthood."[44] William Johnson, who joined the church after the 1978 priesthood announcement, agreed. "A lot of times I'm afraid to take the gospel to other blacks," because "I'm somewhat embarrassed about the past.

---

41. Bryan Waterman Oral History, 3, interviewed by Jessie Embry, 1991, LDS Afro-American.

42. Edward J. Harris Oral History, 21-22, interviewed by Alan Cherry, 1988, LDS Afro-American.

43. Nathleen Albright Oral History, 3, interviewed by Alan Cherry, 1985, LDS Afro-American.

44. Florita Davis Oral History, 12, interviewed by Alan Cherry, 1985, LDS Afro-American.

. . . Overcoming that is a barrier for me, and I'm sure it is for a lot other blacks. Perhaps there's an attitude that no one likes the idea of being thought of as an Uncle Tom."[45]

3. Past church experiences

Many blacks come from strong religious backgrounds. While they are willing to discuss religion with Mormon missionaries and often accept return visits, they generally feel satisfied with the spiritual life in their own churches. Julius Ray Chavez, a Navajo who served in the Virginia Roanoke Mission, recalled, "They [blacks] always want to hear a message about God or hear a message about Jesus. You're welcomed into their homes. . . . The majority want you to come back." Yet, he said, the missionaries' "duty . . . was to teach people and to baptize them."[46] Why should blacks leave the church of their childhood, steeped in tradition, for an unknown religion with a recent track record of black consciousness? What can a young missionary say in response to this kind of objection? Indeed, what is the proper response?

Barbara Lancaster of Barberton, Ohio, acknowledged this dilemma: "It's really hard to proselyte in this area because the majority of the blacks here are Baptists or Methodists. Their parents and their relatives have always been Methodist or Baptist, and they have no desire to change." She continued: "Had I not been praying and searching, I'm not so sure I would have let [the missionaries] come into my home so eagerly either."[47]

4. Need for black missionaries

The most common response on how to improve LDS missionary work among blacks was to increase the number of black missionaries. The comments of Janis Parker, who grew up in Chicago, are typical.

---

45. William T. Johnson Oral History, 17, interviewed by Alan Cherry, 1987, LDS Afro-American.

46. Julius Ray Chavez Oral History, 16, interviewed by Odessa Neaman, 1990, Native American Oral History Project, Charles Redd Center for Western Studies, Archives and Manuscripts, Lee Library.

47. Barbara Lancaster Oral History, 14.

She said: "[If] two clean-cut white boys come into an all-black neighborhood, people are going to automatically say, 'These people are from a church.'" Parker thought people would be "automatically turned off."[48] Brenda Elaine Combs, who grew up in the St. Louis, Missouri, area where her parents were active in the Church of God in Christ, explained that "black missionaries . . . on the streets" would diffuse a common reaction to white missionaries: "'That's the white folks' religion, and I don't want to be bothered.'"[49]

Mavis Odoms, who served a mission to the Philippines, agreed: "I think it would be easier to be taught by a black missionary than it would be a white missionary. I think a black missionary would understand a little better the problems they would be going through conversion wise." She added, "I do not think a lot of people understand the feelings that black people go through their entire life being called names all the time and being denied so much."[50]

Linda Cooper of Oakland, successively a Baptist, a Jehovah's Witness, and Baptist again before joining the LDS church in 1982, felt, "The white missionaries that they sent out into the field cannot relate to where the blacks are coming from."[51]

Kenneth Bolton added, "When they see two white guys knocking on their door, some people, especially older people, are very skeptical about it."[52]

Black Mormon missionaries reported a range of experiences working with blacks. George Garwood was one of the first black missionaries in the California Oakland Mission in 1979. When his mission president asked if he would like to work with a black companion, Garwood resisted: "It would have been just too obvious putting two black missionaries together in a predominantly black

48. Janis Parker Oral History, 27, interviewed by Alan Cherry, 1988, LDS Afro-American.

49. Brenda Elaine Combs Oral History, 9, interviewed by Alan Cherry, 1988, LDS Afro-American.

50. Mavis Odoms Oral History, 13-14, interviewed by Alan Cherry, 1985, LDS Afro-American.

51. Linda Cooper Oral History, 13, interviewed by Alan Cherry, 1985, LDS Afro-American.

52. Kenneth Bolton Oral History, 12, interviewed by Alan Cherry, 1987, LDS Afro-American.

area. . . . That is not the makeup of the church. When the people go to church, they are going to see a different group. I think they need to be exposed to that as they are being taught the gospel."[53] The mission president agreed and furthermore did not have blacks work in black neighborhoods simply because of their color. As a result Alan Cherry spent most of his mission in Walnut Creek, a largely white community.

Ollie Mae Lofton, who served in the Los Angeles area, explained: "When you go door to door, you just don't really know whether it is going to be somebody black. We had a variety of people to work with, but I was really fortunate in being able to have experiences with a lot of black brothers and sisters that did join the church."[54] Jerri Allene Thornton Hale, who served in the Texas Houston Mission, recalled one ward in which the mission leader decided, "Maybe the blacks are just not ready for the gospel yet" and asked missionaries to go to a white area. After two weeks she reported: "The only two callbacks we had were from blacks." Although her color may have been an entree in some cases, she did not feel it protected her. "I wouldn't even go" into a black area of Wharton, she commented. "It was very rough. I just didn't have the spirit that felt there was anyone there to be taught so we just basically left it alone."[55]

Most black missionaries were not sent to exclusively black neighborhoods. Marvin Jones, called to the Utah South Mission, did not mention teaching blacks on Salt Lake City's west side. He next worked in Vernal and Cedar City, both small Mormon communities with few ethnics other than native Americans.[56] Cherrie Lee Maples worked with Southeast Asian refugees in the California Fresno Mission.[57] Paul Staples, who grew up in southern California during the 1960s, worked with Spanish-speakers in the Washington Spokane Mission.[58] Obvi-

---

53. George Garwood Oral History, 13, interviewed by Alan Cherry, 1985, LDS Afro-American.

54. Ollie Mae Lofton Oral History, 11, interviewed by Alan Cherry, 1985, LDS Afro-American.

55. Jerri Allene Thornton Hale Oral History, 21, 22-23, interviewed by Alan Cherry, 1985, LDS Afro-American.

56. Jones Oral History, 8-9.

57. Maples Oral History, 5.

ously mission leaders did not feel it was necessary to call blacks to work with blacks, and missionaries had not expressed a desire to work only with African Americans.

5. Need for black members to work with missionaries

Several people suggested leveraging techniques such as having black members accompany missionaries and actively discuss Mormonism with friends and relatives. But Janet Rice, a former Catholic teacher, expressed frustration at the closed system: "You've got to get them in first before they can talk to their friends and relatives. It's a cycle. I know the missionaries don't go out looking for black people, so I don't know the answer."[59] Rice added: "I think that Heavenly Father prepared certain black people for the church because I don't think that all black people are ready to accept [Mormonism]. . . . Blacks will listen to blacks as opposed to sometimes listening to whites. . . . I feel we [black members] have a purpose in the church to set examples and to carry the gospel to other blacks who will relate with us as opposed to the whites."[60]

Several others agreed. Florita Davis felt that "in a black community you want to accept someone that is your race. You feel automatically like they understand. You are more acceptable to them." People are impressed with the clean-cut Mormon missionaries, but black missionaries "make you even more proud. They are going somewhere; they are doing something. I think the black communities will accept them because they automatically know, 'There is not a racist thing there.'"[61]

Alfonza Day from Charlotte, North Carolina, said more black members "can reach out and touch people if they set their minds and hearts to it. They know the circumstances in which they are living, so they know more or less what they would need to encourage them to

---

58. Paul Staples Oral History, 6-7, interviewed by Alan Cherry, 1986, LDS Afro-American.

59. Janet Rice Oral History, 20, interviewed by Alan Cherry, 1988, LDS Afro-American.

60. Ibid., 19.

61. Florita Davis Oral History, 14, interviewed by Alan Cherry, 1985, LDS Afro-American.

pick up the cross and walk with it."[62]

Members who had assisted missionaries generally felt good about the results. Hattie Soil and her daughter Lenora, members of the Hyde Park Ward in Chicago, found "we had a lot of doors open" when they accompanied white sister missionaries going door-to-door. "Maybe it's because of the black and white situation," she continued. "I think that the members, especially the black members, need to help the missionaries out a little bit more . . . because I certainly know black people better than the missionaries do."[63]

Kenneth Bolton, a twenty-seven-year-old member in Jackson, Mississippi, was not pleased when missionaries asked him to visit only black investigators with them, but his attitude soon changed: "Believe it or not, the fact that I'm black and the fact that they're black does make a difference. There is a common bond there; there is a tie there."

In contrast William B. Jenkins, a retired federal government worker, refused when white missionaries wanted him to call on black families: "The attitude when I go with you is that I'm a token. You automatically los[e] the minute you walk in there with me. . . . Just like you have got your inside jokes, we've got our inside jokes. Once they figure I'm just a token, then you've got a sound bit of hostility from then on about coming into the church."[64] George Garwood also felt that blacks saw tokenism when two whites came initially and came back with an African American.[65]

6. Need to change missionary approach

Several thoughtful members pointed out the need for adaptation in missionary approaches in black neighborhoods. Alan Cherry tried to help his mission president realize the subconscious message presented by the flipchart. In the 1970s and early 1980s missionaries

---

62. Alfonza Day Oral History, 6, interviewed by Alan Cherry, 1986, LDS Afro-American.

63. Hattie Soil Oral History, 13-14, interviewed by Alan Cherry, 1988, LDS Afro-American.

64. William B. Jenkins Oral History, 16, interviewed by Alan Cherry, 1988, LDS Afro-American.

65. Garwood Oral History, 13.

commonly used hand-held illustrations to give a quick introduction to the church. The photographs were all-white faces with dress and hair styles from the 1950s. The message was ultra-conservative. "It meant that we weren't representing the church as it is," summarized Cherry. "It didn't mean that we needed a flipchart full of black faces because when a black person would come to church they wouldn't find a church full of black people. We needed something, I felt, more representative of what these people would experience as they went. We needed to show them what they would be experiencing in the church and we didn't."[66]

Janis Parker, a journalist from Chicago, also felt the limitations of the all-white lifestyle portrayed in church videos: "You can't have a generic presentation; you have to talk to people in ways that they will understand."[67] Bryan Waterman said he quickly learned which videos worked in a black community. "Together Forever," which included a black couple, was especially successful. But he stopped showing "Our Heavenly Father's Plan" after a few tries because it "would create an uncomfortable situation. A lot of times I would be asked if there were any blacks in our church at the end of that film."[68]

Sarah Kaye Gripper, a working single mother from Illinois, hoped to see the lesson plans "revamped." When she went with elders to teach a black woman, she was "not embarrassed" but dismayed by the discussion format. "After they said something, then they'd reword it and ask the question back. It's just kind of repetitive. It kind of insulted my intelligence."[69] It reminded her of "sales training."

Not all missionaries were equally successful in black neighborhoods. Alan Cherry explained:

> Taking a young man from Idaho and submerging him into an Oakland, California, black neighborhood is easy enough to do and the Spirit of the Lord will attend him. But the Spirit of the Lord might not teach him all that might help him ease the communication if he knew certain things. . . . A white face in a black neighborhood in a dark suit may seem all right

66. Alan Cherry Oral History (in process), interviewed by Jessie Embry, 1985, LDS Afro-American.
67. Parker Oral History, 27-28.
68. Waterman Oral History, 3.
69. Gripper Oral History, 10-11.

in the designing rooms of the missionary committee in Salt Lake City, but in Oakland, he will look like he is an FBI agent perhaps, a bill collector, or someone that is not a welcomed image.[70]

Bryan Waterman agreed. In Newark, New Jersey, most people thought missionaries were from a federal agency charged with caring for abused children, and he commented, "A lot of people wouldn't open their doors to us."[71]

Because of his cultural conditioning, Alan Cherry realized one way missionaries could avoid problems was to say they were ministers. Because of the high regard most blacks have for ministers, such an approach would give missionaries entree whereas identifying them-selves as representatives of the Mormon church would not.[72] Bryan Waterman said his senior companions had taught him that if a problem developed to "say we were ministers. Immediately, we were treated with respect, and there was no problem."[73]

CHURCH GROWTH AMONG BLACKS

African American Mormons anticipate large numbers of blacks joining the LDS church in the future. Referring to the influence that a minister has in a black Baptist church, Ollie Mae Lofton explained: "The way the black communities are structured is that they have a lot of strong black leadership within the community. . . . When one person within that community or that church joins that is a strong leader, they will be very influential in bringing in many. . . . I know if my father [a Baptist minister] were to join the church today, he would bring in many, many people with him because he is an influential leader in the community."[74]

A member of a stake presidency in Virginia wanted to form a branch in Petersburg, a largely black community, for basically the same reason. He felt that if the church had a presence in the city,

70. Cherry Oral History.
71. Waterman Oral History, 2.
72. Alan Cherry, in conversation.
73. Waterman Oral History, 2.
74. Ollie Mae Lofton Oral History, 14, interviewed by Alan Cherry, 1985, LDS Afro-American.

whole congregations of black churches would join just as British converts had during the early Mormon period in England in the 1830s and 1840s.[75] Elijah Jackson, a former Ricks College and BYU-Hawaii basketball player who had been a Jehovah's Witness before he became a Latter-day Saint, adapted a Mormon scripture to explain what he felt would happen: "There is a saying that the fields are white, the harvest is white and ready to pick. I . . . say, 'The harvest is black and ready to be picked' because the blacks are going to be a massive flock in the church in the upcoming years."[76]

SUMMARY

For most blacks, joining the LDS church meant they now worshipped with whites but continued to maintain contact with black family and friends, whose reactions ranged from accepting to hostile and frequently changed over time. For most LDS converts, these reactions did not affect their views of Mormonism. People responding to the survey felt that negative reactions might discourage LDS Afro-Americans from remaining members. Like other members black Latter-day Saints were eager to share their new faith with peers, and most had thought about ways to improve missionary work among blacks. In their attempts to share their new religion, LDS African Americans who participated in the survey and who were interviewed demonstrated how they have now entered a new culture.

---

75. Lidge Johnson, telephone conversation, 1988, notes in my possession.

76. Elijah Jackson, Jr., Oral History, 23, interviewed by Alan Cherry, 1986, LDS Afro-American.

11.

THE FUTURE OF
LDS AFRICAN AMERICANS

In their own way LDS African Americans are as much pioneers as the early Mormons who crossed the Great Plains in the nineteenth century. Virginia Johnson of Los Angeles, who joined the Mormon church in 1981 after a "black power" phase, articulated the black pioneer theme well: "We did not come from the pioneer stock or Utah stock, but we are . . . pioneers in our own right because we are laying down the ground work for the future of blacks in the Mormon church. . . . The more blacks that become . . . strong in the church . . . by their sheer example and being able to testify to others, it will be a positive thing."[1] Johnson is a product of the Civil Rights movement and a new era in Mormon history.

In many ways LDS African Americans are "firsts." They are the first Mormons in their families, the first blacks in an all-white congregation, or the first blacks to hold the priesthood. In all of these circumstances, they are setting a pattern for future members. The LDS church's historic discrimination against blacks—barring men from priesthood and men and women from temple ordinances—may not have been a unique religious practice. But as official policy it was often

---

1. Virginia Johnson Oral History, 18, interviewed by Alan Cherry, 1985, LDS Afro-American Oral History Project, Charles Redd Center for Western Studies, Archives and Manuscripts, Harold B. Lee Library, Brigham Young University, Provo, Utah (hereafter LDS Afro-American).

branded as discriminatory both within and outside of the Mormon church, particularly in the 1960s and 1970s.

This policy affected the church's contact with African Americans in a variety of ways. Although the LDS church is known as one of the most missionary-oriented churches in the United States, few blacks joined. This was not only because of the discrimination policy. The LDS church's geographical isolation combined with embarrassment, concern about recrimination, and prejudice on the part of at least some members resulted in an unofficial tradition of not proselyting blacks. If they wanted to investigate the church, blacks had to request the information. Since the Mormon church lifted the restriction in 1978, increased missionary efforts in black neighborhoods have led to a growing presence of African Americans in the church.

Although there are still relatively few LDS Afro-Americans, their experiences demonstrate the range of possibilities for blacks in a predominately white church. The LDS *Church News* consistently reports optimistic anecdotes about blacks and whites working together. Yet the church's image has been that it is racist. The lack of contact of many Utah Mormons with African Americans sometimes fulfills expectations on insensitivity and cultural clumsiness. In reality the experience of most LDS Afro-Americans lies between the extremes of aversion and acceptance.

Most black Americans who have joined the LDS church experience genuine and heartfelt acceptance; at the same time they have concerns over the past priesthood exclusion and latent forms of racism and prejudice exhibited by some white members. While fractional minorities of black Mormons reported only acceptance or only discrimination, most experienced both from white Mormons. Many were not concerned about the dual messages since the pattern is similar to that found in the larger American society. Both those interviewed and survey respondents had mixed reactions about continued connections with the larger black community. They are unsure about their relationships with other black Mormons, as well. And they all must decide how to adapt to the new Mormon culture and still retain their African American identity.

Time will tell how well the Mormon church, its leaders, and individual members succeed at welcoming into full fellowship the increased black membership. Undeniably prejudice remains, yet it seems likely that as Euro-Americans have more contact with blacks and members of other ethnic groups, stereotypes will fade. Instead of having a single image of all African Americans, for example, they will meet "John Brown" and "Jane Jones" who will not match perceived ideas. The same holds true for LDS Afro-Americans who interact with white Mormons. Overcoming racial prejudices takes time, and the LDS church will change as black and white children are raised as Mormons in common wards and accepted as necessary ingredients in a beef-and-potato stew rather than a puree of bland uniformity.

The survey asked the respondents to agree or disagree with the statement: "When I look at my future in the church, I am very hopeful." Over half (56.0 percent) "strongly agreed" and about one-quarter (25.5) "agreed" that they were hopeful about their future as Mormons. Thus more than three-quarters of black Mormons thought there was a place for them in the LDS church. But about a fifth (18.5 percent) did not share these hopes. Questions in both the survey and interviews attempted to probe the needs of black Latter-day Saints and determine how well they were being met by the LDS church. The questions elicited several positive themes as well as some negative ones.

POSITIVE ELEMENTS

The survey asked an open-ended question about what black Latter-day Saints "enjoy most about their experiences as Mormons." Of course, there was no single answer. Two-fifths (40.9 percent) said that learning about the LDS gospel was the most positive aspect of Mormonism. The next three highest responses were relationships with other Mormons (16 percent), relationship with God (14.4 percent), and LDS teachings (12.2 percent).

These responses were echoed in the interviews. Despite cultural misunderstandings, most members felt their church had a positive influence on their lives. The common themes included:

1. Developing a personal relationship with God and understanding the LDS plan of salvation

For Vivian Collier, Mormonism "was just not a church" where people attended meetings. She reported: "If you're really striving, you really come to understand better who Heavenly Father is, who

Jesus Christ is, who you are, and how you fit in the realm of things. You develop a personal relationship with Jesus and Heavenly Father."[2] Thomas Taylor, who was born in 1951 in Virginia and raised as a Baptist, also believed that the church "really opened my mind up as far as why I'm here and what I'm supposed to do here. If I continue to do this, I believe that I'll return to be with Heavenly Father."[3]

Doris Marie Wilson, who joined the church in 1981 at age forty-seven, stated: "[The church] has changed our lifestyle. . . . Our black friends certainly don't understand. We have a greater goal in mind."[4]

Delphrine Young recalled his enthusiasm when missionaries "began teaching me the truthfulness of the gospel. . . . They made me understand things that I had never understood before. They had brought a light into my life."[5]

2. Personal growth

While joining the church did not remove problems, it helped some black members cope. Margie Ray White commented that the two years she had been a member had "been the happiest two years of all my life. I know the Lord didn't say we would have sunshine every day. He didn't promise us a bed of roses every day. Things are still hard; things still get complicated. But now there is something that I have to always go back on."[6]

Samuel Coggs, a Baptist until he was fourteen, attended college, served in Vietnam, worked for the Department of Labor, and was baptized in Chicago in 1987 at age forty-seven. Something was "miss-

---

2. Vivian Collier Oral History, 3, interviewed by Alan Cherry, 1986, LDS Afro-American.

3. Thomas Taylor Oral History, 2-3, interviewed by Alan Cherry, LDS Afro-American.

4. Doris Marie Wilson Oral History, 2, interviewed by Alan Cherry, 1986, LDS Afro-American.

5. Delphrine Garcia Young Oral History, 4, interviewed by Alan Cherry, 1985, LDS Afro-American.

6. Margie Ray White Oral History, 7, interviewed by Alan Cherry, LDS Afro-American.

ing from my life," he said, but baptism "filled that void." He added, "I . . . look forward to growing."[7]

Deborah E. Taylor explained that in five years of membership "my family and friends tell me how happy I am and how contented I am with my life. . . . I want to tell them about how special the church is, the peace I have now, joy, happiness, and how the pure love of Christ has lifted my inner soul and set me on a burning fire for his presence to be with me at all times."[8]

Janet Brooks of St. Louis was working several jobs to support herself and her one child living at home. Yet she said: "I floated for two weeks. I don't feel like I have a heavy building inside me anymore. Everything seems so light. Even though I've had heartaches, trials, and tribulations, they don't feel like they used to." Despite a stroke, a difficult marriage, threats of losing her home, and "all types of problems that were heavier than I thought, . . . I never felt them because the burdens were light."[9]

William B. Jenkins, a retired military and civil servant, found a new perspective after his baptism in 1981 at age sixty-seven: "Things that used to upset me don't anymore. I seem to have more patience and to have a better understanding of human beings."[10] Charles Frazier Chisolm, who grew up in the Methodist-Episcopal and the Episcopal churches, summarized his feelings about the LDS church: "I have been blessed by my involvement in the Mormon church. It is the lighthouse of my life and the power that keeps me going."[11]

3. Relationship with Family

Along with personal growth one of the most dramatic changes black members reported was improved relationships with family mem-

---

7. Samuel Coggs Oral History, 13, interviewed by Alan Cherry, 1988, LDS Afro-American.

8. Deborah E. Taylor to Jessie L. Embry, 18 Nov. 1988.

9. Janet Brooks Oral History, 4, interviewed by Alan Cherry, 1988, LDS Afro-American.

10. William B. Jenkins Oral History, 5, interviewed by Alan Cherry, 1988, LDS Afro-American.

11. Charles Frazier Chislom Oral History, 7, interviewed by Alan Cherry, LDS Afro-American.

bers. According to Thomas Taylor, a truck driver from Chesterfield, Virginia, who joined the LDS church in 1980, the concept of eternal families helped strengthen bonds.[12] Winston Wilkinson described his former personality as cold, considering it a sign of weakness to hug his children. But as he watched other Mormon men hugging their wives and children, he tentatively followed suit. His oldest son was confused by the change, but in time, Wilkinson said, the physical closeness brought them closer in many other ways. "I now believe that in raising kids you must keep them talking, and I have to be more than just a father. I have to be their friend."[13]

James Johnson's marriage had ended in divorce partly because of his rowdy lifestyle. He commented: "Before when I was drinking, [my children] would not come and see me. . . . [They] are just overwhelmed with me being a member. . . . They said, 'Daddy, we are so proud of you.' . . . They are prouder of me now than they were when I was at home because the things I was doing at home they did not half approve of, especially when I got drunk and had fights. This quiet life and good life that I am living now is what they wanted when I was at home."[14]

4. Relationship with other church members

Many African Americans felt that church membership had helped them overcome their own prejudices and hoped that the entire church would become less color-conscious than society in general. For example, Mary Angel Wilbur felt that many of the blacks at her high school were prejudiced and "afraid to get close to white people." She believed they would feel differently if they would come to her Young Women classes or ward dances. Despite prejudice from some members, she said she felt "such a closeness" in her ward. "It is almost like a family."[15]

---

12. Taylor letter, 3.

13. Winston A. Wilkinson Oral History, 6-7, interviewed by Alan Cherry, 1986, LDS Afro-American.

14. James Johnson Oral History, 22-23, interviewed by Alan Cherry, 1986, LDS Afro-American.

15. Mary Angel Wilbur Oral History, 12, interviewed by Alan Cherry, 1986, LDS Afro-American.

5. Changed goals

Converts identified changed goals as an effect of their baptism. With the emphasis on families, many developed goals to be sealed in eternal marriage in a Mormon temple. Many wanted to serve full-time missions, especially as retired couples. Others found a new emphasis on family and spiritual activities over career ambitions.

When asked about her goals, Janis E. Parker explained that she had earned a B.A. at age twenty-two, worked for a Chicago newspaper, and married. When she joined the church in 1986, her husband did not. She remarked:

> If you had asked me this question five years ago, I would have answered it in terms of career. . . . Now I have found through the church and also by having a child, that a job is a job is a job. My goal is to be a righteous person, to be a good mother, to be an understanding and patient wife, to be a good daughter, to be a loving sister, and a wonderful friend. . . . One day you may turn on CBS and you may see me. You may not, and that is not important. I have found out that the time and the energy that you give to a job or to a career is not as important as being home at all.[16]

Similarly Annie Wilbur, raised a Baptist but looking for another religion when missionaries contacted her in 1983, said her new faith immediately made her feel "better about myself. I did not have the bitterness. I had a desire to change my life. . . . I did not hate my [former] husband any more, and I did not hate the [white] people at work. I did not have this hostile attitude. I knew that it had something to do with this religion."[17]

6. Different views about money

Alan Cherry specifically asked, "How have LDS values influenced the role money plays in your life?" Over three-fourths (78.6 percent) said that their views of money had changed. A third (34.8 percent) mentioned the impact of paying 10 percent of their income as tithing. The next most common responses were that they had learned how to

---

16. Janis E. Parker Oral History, 34, interviewed by Alan Cherry, 1988, LDS Afro-American.

17. Annie Wilbur Oral History, 7-8, interviewed by Alan Cherry, 1985, LDS Afro-American.

budget better (21.6 percent) and that money occupied a less important place in their values (22.2 percent).

Catherine Stokes commented that the gospel "had a lot of influence because when you pay tithing you have to figure out how to be a better steward with the rest of it. . . . I believe in the law of tithing. I have a testimony of it. I think that's the basis for whatever financial security you're going to have."[18]

Delphrine Young painted a vivid picture of his financial plight when he first met the missionaries: "I had fourteen credit cards, and I had charged on thirteen of them. I had a first and a second [mortgage] on a home. I was really heavy in debt and was terribly depressed. . . . A couple of years after I joined the church, I was able to pay off my credit cards and pay off all my debts except the [mortgage] on my home. . . . My life was totally straightened out and totally put in order."[19]

7. Outreach to other blacks

Because of the positive changes that Mormonism has made in their lives, black Latter-day Saints expressed a desire to share these same values with other African Americans. Carol Edwards, formerly a member of the Shiloh Baptist church, exclaimed: "You know what I see the gospel as? I see it as freedom for our people. . . . The values and that doctrine are going to help clean up people to be able to go to the celestial kingdom, to gain eternal life."[20]

Darryl Kenneth Gaines felt that blacks "are being led in all different kinds of directions. They are just wasting their lives away." To prevent that he said, "I hope to serve a mission and spread the word to more black people."[21]

Cecelia Johnson, baptized in Pennsylvania with her husband,

---

18. Catherine M. Stokes Oral History, 21, interviewed by Alan Cherry, 1988, LDS Afro-American.

19. Young Oral History, 4.

20. Carol Edwards Oral History, 12, interviewed by Alan Cherry, 1986, LDS Afro-American.

21. Darryl Gaines Oral History, 11, interviewed by Alan Cherry, 1986, LDS Afro-American.

saw fellow blacks "hold[ing] grudges." The gospel, she believed, would teach them "how to progress and how to forgive others."[22]

Victor Soil saw economic as well as psychological hope for blacks: "LDS principles, to me, are the only salvation for black Americans. . . . Ninety percent of the people I work with in the four schools I service are on welfare. Eighty or ninety percent have one parent. With the emphasis that we place on family and the emphasis we place on economic development and self-improvement, the principles of the church are the only way to go. . . . We have to develop pride in ourselves. We have to develop the work ethic."[23]

Some black members saw hope in the gospel for what has widely been called a crisis in black families. Peter Gillo, a teacher in Chicago described a bleak picture: "Many . . . men will not accept responsibility. Many women and men do not get married. They just have children. The men go away, and the women are left with the kids. But the church teaches us that the families stay together. Families are forever. That's a very good value. If they use that, women have to be strong and men have to be strong."[24]

Diane Amelia Hughes was born in 1961 to a black father and a Panamanian mother and felt discrimination both in Panama and in the United States. After joining the LDS church in Belgium where she was serving in the U.S. Navy, she felt that the gospel had the answer to the quest of the "black race . . . for an identity" that would give them "unity" and let them "feel proud." She explained, "The unity is in Jesus Christ," and without it "black Americans . . . will be drowned, literally."[25]

She was not alone in her hope that her church held the answer to bigotry. Ruby Ann Womble spoke of the *de facto* isolation of blacks and whites in Atlanta that resulted in some blacks "feeling that white

---

22. Cecelia Johnson Oral History, 14, interviewed by Alan Cherry, 1986, LDS Afro-American.

23. Victor G. Soil Oral History, 9, interviewed by Alan Cherry, 1988, LDS Afro-American.

24. Peter Tabani Gillo Oral History, 8, interviewed by Alan Cherry, 1988, LDS Afro-American.

25. Diane Amelia Hughes Oral History, 11, interviewed by Alan Cherry, 1987, LDS Afro-American.

people are better than they are. The gospel will help them overcome that. They will no longer feel that 'they are better than I am' but 'we're equal; we're all the same.'"[26] Edwin Burwell agreed: "LDS principles have made me see a ray of hope. If we all can get together and keep our heritage but remember that we are all the same we can stop having the dividing line" between whites and blacks. "I am looking forward for a day when you could move next door to somebody and they do not get upset because you are one color, because you talk differently, or because your hair is not straight. You can go to church and worship with that person and there is no problem."[27]

NEGATIVE ELEMENTS

Nevertheless, not all is well in the new Zion these converts have found. Even blacks who expressed hope about their future in the Mormon church listed negative aspects. And a fifth of survey respondents saw a bleak future. The survey asked the open-ended statement: "What I enjoy least about my membership in the LDS church is." The most common negative answers were prejudice (20.5 percent), a sense of not belonging (15.7 percent), and not knowing the music and other parts of LDS church worship and procedure (13.4 percent). The survey included an open-ended question: "The most serious church-related problems I face currently are." Of the 127 answering that question, dating was a problem for 19.7 percent. Prejudice (12.6 percent), unfriendly members (11.8 percent), and trouble obeying the commandments were also seen as problems. The survey also included a more impersonal question: "The most serious church-related problems of black members of the church are." Among the 142 who responded, prejudice (19 percent) and lack of fellowship (16.2 percent) were again the most common answers.

How do blacks respond to these problems? Almost certainly many withdraw. The survey asked the open-ended question: "I know black members who have become inactive because of." Of 140 responding to the question, the most common answers were racial discrimination

---

26. Ruby Ann Womble Oral History, 7, interviewed by Alan Cherry, 1987, LDS Afro-American.

27. Edwin Allen Burwell Oral History, 9, interviewed by Alan Cherry, 1986, LDS Afro-American.

(26.4 percent), inability to adapt to another culture (14.3 percent), and problems of adapting to a white church (7.1 percent). Only 5 percent said problems existed because there were no other black members.

Personal voices illustrate many of the same concerns. Prejudice has already been discussed. But prejudice is often subtle. Eva Joseph, a single mother in Oakland who was not attending meetings regularly, explained that African Americans

> are very sensitive and we are very easy to pick up where we are wanted and where we are not. I can walk into a room and from the atmosphere I know that the people there accept me. . . . But if I walk into a room and I do not feel good in that room, then I know I am not wanted. This is something I guess you could call a sixth sense that we have. . . . [White Latter-day Saints] do not have to speak with words because we know without your even opening your mouth.[28]

David E. Gathers from Pineville, North Carolina, identified slow-growing testimonies as a hindrance for his daughter and son-in-law: "They still are not fully embedded in the [LDS] gospel as I feel they should be. But maybe in time something will happen that will explain to them that the gospel is true and will not leave any doubt in their minds." For them, belief was far from instantaneous, and they had protested, "How do you expect us to see you do a ninety degree turn from one religion to another and expect us to make a fast transition like that?"[29]

One participant in the interviews, William Thompson of Decatur, Georgia, felt that callings "put too much pressure on a person in the beginning." He commented that if he were a new convert and were called "to go and home teach somebody that I knew had been a member for a long time, it would put extra pressure on me because what am I going to tell these people when I get there?"[30] Callings are paradoxical. Too much pressure on the one hand, or feeling left out on the other; either situation can lead to inactivity.

---

28. Eva Joseph Oral History, 21, interviewed by Alan Cherry, 1985, LDS Afro-American.

29. David E. Gathers Oral History, 21, interviewed by Alan Cherry, 1986, LDS Afro-American.

30. William Thompson Oral History, 21, interviewed by Alan Cherry, 1987, LDS Afro-American.

Dan Mosley explained that some blacks felt that by joining a white church they were "losing their identity."[31]

Others, according to Angela Brown, "are just not used to being around whites. They may not feel comfortable so they don't come."[32]

Mary Angel Wilbur, a teenager, found no Latter-day Saint young men willing to date her. New Latter-day Saints, she observed wryly, "think members are perfect, and then it is hard when they find out . . . members are just normal people." The adjustment was painful: "I guess I kind of resented Heavenly Father for a while because I thought, 'If these people are righteous and they're doing what Heavenly Father wants to do, how can He be good?'" She concluded: "I wouldn't want anyone to feel the way I did, or go through any of the depression and have that resentment. . . . It is really self destructive."[33]

Although some respondents became inactive, others sought different solutions. Betty Ann Bridgeforth compared the church to home. "Leaving home . . . is not the way to build it up. You stay and work at it and you make home better."[34] Suggestions for possible courses of action were solicited in an open-ended question in the survey that asked, "With regard to helping black members of the church feel a more integrated part of the church, non-black members need to. . . ." Of 151 respondents, over half said whites could be more accepting (55.4 percent). Others said there needed to be greater fellowshipping (16.6 percent) and greater understanding of black culture (10.8 percent).

Ways were identified to help whites see the needs of blacks. Elizabeth Pulley, who attended school and church with only blacks, pled for more acceptance by "knowing that our white brothers and sisters can love us and accept us as children of our Heavenly Father

---

31. Dan Mosley Oral History, 20, interviewed by Alan Cherry, 1985, LDS Afro-American.

32. Angela Brown Oral History, 15, interviewed by Alan Cherry, 1986, LDS Afro-American.

33. Mary Angel Wilbur Oral History, 16.

34. Betty Ann Bridgeforth Oral History, 31, interviewed by Alan Cherry, 1985, LDS Afro-American.

and be able to learn about us and understand us. They can really show that they really care and that they can really shake my hand without rubbing it off. They can really give me a hug and be sincere. They can cry when I cry and share experiences in their lives that have helped them."[35] Eva Joseph asked white members to "accept us for who we are and be real to us."[36]

It was not white prejudice but white "ignorance" that bothered Sharon Davis. "I don't think we need to just accept ignorance," she asserted. "I think we need to teach the members of the church through examples that there isn't a difference between us and them spiritually."[37]

Others recommended simple interaction to defuse ignorance. Vincent Lewis of Pittsburg, California, suggested the church have "a cultural class or something. Sometimes when some of them first meet you, they are kind of afraid of you. They are kind of leery because they do not know exactly where you are coming from. You could be this big black demon coming from some place. Maybe one time you could have a soul-food dinner and invite the white LDS members or have some classes together to be able to interact."[38] A black member in Detroit agreed that sharing food made a simple bridge: "When we invite[d] some of our [white] friends over, . . . we had a good time with chittlings. There's a difference, but nothing so deep it can't be crossed."[39]

Such positive and negative experiences are just a sampling of the odyssey of interviewees and survey respondents. Each has a unique story about his or her life as a Latter-day Saint. What is impressive is that although they come from all walks of life from the uneducated to Ph.D.s, all reported they found something they could enjoy in the

---

35. Elizabeth Pulley Oral History, 13, interviewed by Alan Cherry, 1985, LDS Afro-American.

36. Eva Joseph Oral History, 21, interviewed by Alan Cherry, 1985, LDS Afro-American.

37. Sharon J. Davis Oral History, 11-12, interviewed by Alan Cherry, 1985, LDS Afro-American.

38. Vincent Lewis Oral History, 11, interviewed by Alan Cherry, 1985, LDS Afro-American.

39. Jerri A. Harwell, "An Inner City Detroit Branch Organized," *Let's Talk* 1 (Feb./Mar. 1990): 6.

Church of Jesus Christ of Latter-day Saints. It has provided a religious home for them.

Yet, as Virginia Johnson stated, black Mormons face new adjustments. While they were not driven from their homes in Missouri and Illinois, as were traditional Mormon pioneers, their trials are just as real. Their isolation can have the same effect as being forced from one's home. And the occasional prejudice, slights, and discrimination from their new religious community are as traumatic as federal marshals invading nineteenth-century Utah territory to stamp out polygamy. The lack of acceptance they sometimes experience comes through in both interviews and the survey as all-too-common experiences.

The interviews were conducted between 1985 and 1989. In the time that has passed, the interviewees' lives have changed. While no attempt has been made to maintain formal contacts, the "Mormon grapevine" and informal methods of communication have brought news that some of the most active have stopped attending Mormon meetings for a variety of reasons: returning to a former way of life, not feeling accepted, feeling unachieved spiritual and social needs, being under pressure from friends and family, and yearning for reimmersion into a black church and culture. Their description of their experiences when they were participating Latter-day Saints, however, communicate their individual uniqueness and their relationships with God. Whatever their current status, those insights are valid and can help increase interracial understanding, eliminate stereotypes, promote cultural awareness and acceptance, and strengthen the religious community not only within the LDS church but also in the black and white American communities.

APPENDIX

INTERVIEWS BY ALAN CHERRY

Name	*Date*	*Place*
Nathleen Albright	23 Oct. 1985	Lake Los Angeles, CA
Reginald Allen	25 Sept. 1986	Brooklyn, NY
Alvin Alphabet	30 May 1987	Carrollton, GA
Ellen M. Alphabet	30 May 1987	Carrollton, GA
Mason Anderson	21 Jan. 1986	Charlotte, NC
Dexter Andrews	5 June 1987	Jackson, MS
Sylvia V. Arnold	18 Oct. 1986	Richmond, VA
Leo Arrington	7 Nov. l986	Honolulu, HI
Joell Aull	12 Feb. 1987	Provo, UT
Alva Baltimore	13 Oct. 1986	Washington, D.C.
Elizabeth Baltimore	12 Oct. 1986	Washington, D.C.
Mary Lucile Bankhead	11 Apr. 1985	Salt Lake City, UT
Betty Wright Baunchand	10 June 1987	Baker, LA
Clement Charles Biggs	3 June 1987	Birmingham, AL
Lula M. Biggs	3 June 1987	Birmingham, AL
Kenneth Bolton, Sr.	6 June 1987	Jackson, MS
Darlene Bowden	18 Jan. 1986	Charlotte, NC
Denorris Clarence Bradley	24 Jan. 1986	Winston-Salem, NC
Martha Branigan	17 Feb. 1987	Provo, UT
Betty Ann Bridgeforth	23 Mar. 1985	Salt Lake City, UT
Ruffin Bridgeforth	16 Mar. 1985	Salt Lake City, UT
Janet Brooks	15 Mar. 1988	St. Louis, MO
Angela Brown	25 Jan. 1986	Greensboro, NC
Gladys Brown	20 Jan. 1986	Charlotte, NC
Norman Lee Brown	25 Jan. 1986	Greensboro, NC
Robert Coleman Brown	10 Oct. 1986	Beltsville, MD
Samuella Brown	12 Mar. 1988	Columbus, OH

Wesley Jennings Brown	9 June 1987	Baton Rouge, LA
Calvaline Burnett	2 June 1987	Birmingham, AL
Edwin Allen Burwell	25 Jan. 1986	Greensboro, NC
Retha Burwell	25 Jan. 1986	Greensboro, NC
Emanuel Canaday	15 Mar. 1988	St. Louis, MO
Rodney Carey	14 Oct. 1985	Oakland, CA
Margaret Carter	12 Oct. 1985	Danville, CA
Vanessa A. Carter	15 May 1985	Ogden, UT
Willie Carter	11 Oct. 1985	Danville, CA
Gilmore H. Chappell	4 Oct. 1986	Philadelphia, PA
Charles Frazier Chisolm	23 Jan. 1986	Asheville, NC
Donna Chisolm	18 Jan. 1986	Charlotte, NC
Marie Edington Chisolm	23 Jan. 1986	Asheville, NC
Crystral Clark	26 Jan. 1986	Raleigh, NC
Matt Clark	24 Jan. 1986	Raleigh, NC
Samuel Coggs	5 Mar. 1988	Chicago, IL
Vivian Collier	18 Oct. 1986	Richmond, VA
Marva Collins	3 Oct. 1985	Salt Lake City, UT
Sonya Isilma Collins	13 Sept. 1985	Salt Lake City, UT
Linda Cooper	14 Oct. 1985	Oakland, CA
William L. Cox	1 Feb. 1986	Greenville, NC
Bobby Darby	16 Jan. 1986	Charlotte, NC
Darrin Bret Davis	9 Jan. 1985	Provo, UT
Florita Davis	20 Oct. 1985	Los Angeles, CA
Sharon J. Davis	10 Feb. 1985	Provo, UT
Alfonzo Day	21 Jan. 1986	Charlotte, NC
Emma J. I. Dickerson	7 Oct. 1986	Philadelphia, PA
Anita Durphey	16 Mar. 1988	St. Louis, MO
Carol Edwards	10 Oct. 1986	McLean, VA
J. Joseph Faulkner	1 June 1987	Gadsden, AL
James Ashley Fennell II	1 Feb. 1986	Greenville, NC
Ruth Fields	28 Oct. 1985	Chandler, AZ
Gayla Floyd	6 Nov. 1986	Laie, HI
Sean Floyd	6 Nov. 1986	Laie, HI
Van E. Floyd	9 Nov. 1986	Laie, HI
Sherrie Honore Franklin	13 June 1987	New Orleans, LA
Darryl K. Gaines	18 Jan. 1986	Rock Hill, SC
Janis R. Garrison	10 May 1985	Provo, UT
George Garwood	1 May 1985	Ogden, UT
David Diamond Gathers	18, 22 May 1985	Salt Lake City, UT
David E. Gathers	28 Jan. 1986	Pinebluff, NC
Mazie Gathers	27 Jan. 1986	Pinebluff, NC

Romona Gibbons	30 Aug. 1985	Orem, UT
Peter Gillo	7 Mar. 1988	Chicago, IL
Sarah Gripper	18 Mar. 1988	Springfield, IL
Jeri Allen Thornton Hale	14 Feb. 1985	Provo, UT
Keith Norman Hamilton	26 Aug. 1985	Provo, UT
Edward Harris	15 Mar. 1988	St. Louis, MO
Gehrig Harris	10 June 1987	White Castle, LA
Mary Harris	17 Mar. 1988	St. Louis, MO
Gayle Harrison	12 June 1987	New Orleans, LA
Donald L. Harwell	1 May 1985	Salt Lake City, UT
Chester Lee Hawkins	1 Mar. 1985	Provo, UT
Betty Jean Hill	7 Sept. 1985	Provo, UT
Leonard Hill	4 Mar. 1988	Chicago, IL
Diane Amelia Hughes	16 June 1987	Gulfport, MS
Elijah Jackson, Jr.	7 Nov. 1988	Laie, HI
Lester Jefferson	5 Mar. 1988	Chicago, IL
Hazel Mary Jenkins	3 Mar. 1988	Chicago, IL
Pauline Jenkins	16 Mar. 1988	St. Louis, MO
William Jenkins	15 Mar. 1988	St. Louis, MO
Aurbie Rayford Johnson	28 May 1987	Lithonia, GA
Cecelia Johnson	6 Oct. 1986	Philadelphia, PA
James Johnson	20 Jan. 1986	Monroe, NC
Juanita Johnson	7 Mar. 1988	Chicago, IL
Richard Johnson	6 Oct. 1986	Philadelphia, PA
Thomas Harrison Johnson	7 Oct. 1987	Philadelphia, PA
Virgina Johnson	22 Oct. 1985	Los Angeles, CA
William T. Johnson, Jr.	17 June 1987	Norcross, GA
Dorothy Gray Jones	7 Oct. 1986	Philadelphia, PA
Marvin Arthur Jones	9 Aug. 1985	Cedar City, UT
Eva Joseph	12 Oct. 1985	Oakland, CA
Ethel Ann Kelly	29 Sept. 1986	New York City, NY
Candace Kennedy	28 June 1986	Los Angeles, CA
Helen Kennedy	11 Apr. 1986	Ogden, UT
Raymond W. Keys	14 Oct. 1986	Richmond, VA
Barbara Lancaster	10 Mar. 1988	Masillon, OH
Charles Calvin Lancaster	10 Mar. 1988	Masillon, OH
Delores Lang	19 Oct. 1985	Los Angeles, CA
Robert Lang	21 Oct. 1985	Los Angeles, CA
Beverly Latimer	27 Sept. 1986	East Elmhurst, NY
Randolph E. Latimer	28 Sept. 1986	East Elmhurst, NY
Carol Elaine Lawrence	25 Feb. 1985	Provo, UT
Vincent Lewis	15 Oct. 1985	Pittsburg, CA

Ollie Mae Lofton	27 June 1985	Provo, UT
Richard Lowe	7 Nov. 1986	Hauula, HI
Cleolevia Lyons	9 Mar. 1988	Jackson, MI
Kenneth K. Mack	29 Apr. 1985	Logan, UT
James Mallory	28 May 1987	Stone Mountain, GA
Cherrie Lee Maples	12 Oct. 1986	Washington, D.C.
Melvin McCoy	11 Mar. 1988	Barberton, OH
Sharon McCoy	11 Mar. 1988	Barberton, OH
Clara Evans McIlwain	11 Oct. 1986	McLean, VA
Johnnie McKoy	24 Jan. 1986	Greensboro, NC
Gloria McLaughlin	12 Jan. 1986	Charlotte, NC
Alfred McNair	14 June 1987	Gautur, MS
Melvin Mitchell	12 Mar. 1988	Columbus, OH
Carrie Elizabeth Morris	18 Oct. 1986	Richmond, VA
Arlene Mosley	30 May 1987	Decatur, GA
Dan Mosley	26 Oct. 1985	Phoenix, AZ
Joan Mosley	28 Oct. 1985	Phoenix, AZ
Mavis Odoms	15 Oct. 1985	Fremont, CA
Bonita O'Neal	12 Mar. 1988	Columbus, OH
Burgess Owens	29 Sept. 1986	Melville, NY
Esther B. Owens	13 Oct. 1986	Richmond, VA
Josephine Owens	26 Sept. 1986	Melville, NY
Robert A. Owens	13 Oct. 1986	Richmond, VA
Natalie Palmer-Taylor	15 Mar. 1985	Salt Lake City, UT
Janis E. Parker	2 Mar. 1988	Chicago, IL
Wilie Perry Perkins	1 Feb. 1986	Greenville, NC
Beverly Perry	21 Oct. 1985	San Pedro, CA
John W. Phoenix	10 Oct. 1986	Arlington, VA
Audrey Marie Pinnock	16 May 1985	Salt Lake City, UT
Barbara Ann Pixton	5 Nov. 1986	Honolulu, HI
Lois W. Poret	13 June 1987	New Orleans, GA
Frank Porter	4 Mar. 1988	Chicago, IL
Tom Porter	9 Mar. 1988	Chicago, IL
Martha A. Poston	29 May 1987	Dunwoody, GA
Arthur Preston	1 Mar. 1988	Chicago, IL
Drianda Preston	1 Mar. 1988	Chicago, IL
Elizabeth Pulley	19 Oct. 1985	Los Angeles, CA
Melonie Quick	20 Jan. 1986	Charlotte, NC
Annette A. Reid	20 Feb. 1985	Provo, UT
Emanuel Lenard Reid	13 Feb. 1985	Provo, UT
Linda Reid	12 Feb. 1987	Provo, UT
Janet Rice	18 Mar. 1988	St. Louis, MO

Leonard Rice	18 Mar. 1988	St. Louis, MO
Debra Dionne Gooden		
Rodriguez	13 June 1987	New Orleans, LA
Junious Edwards Ross	16 Oct. 1985	San Jose, CA
Elijah Royster	10 Nov. 1986	Kula, Maui, HI
Doris Russell	27 June 1987	Los Angeles, CA
Brenda Sanderlin	16 Oct. 1985	San Jose, CA
Ed Scroggins	26 Oct. 1985	Phoenix, AZ
Rhonda Shelby	25 Feb. 1985	Provo, UT
Carl Angelo Simmons	16 May 1985	Logan, UT
James Henry Sinquefield	30 Mar. 1985	Salt Lake City, UT
Cleeretta Henderson Smiley	10 Oct. 1986	Silver Spring, MD
Gabriele Smith	26, 27 Sept.,	Provo, UT
	2 Oct. 1985	
Gwendolyn Lucille Jones Smith	13 June 1987	New Orleans, LA
Joseph C. Smith	12 Mar. 1985	Provo, UT
Marie Smith	4 Mar. 1988	Chicago, IL
Marilyn Smith	12 Mar. 1985	Provo, UT
Mary E. Smith	6 June 1987	Jackson, MS
Hattie Soil	7 Mar. 1987	Chicago, IL
Victor Soil	7 Mar. 1987	Chicago, IL
Deborah Spearman	7 Oct. 1987	Philadelphia, PA
Boris Spencer	17 May 1985	Logan, UT
Rosetta Spencer	3 Mar. 1988	Chicago, IL
Paul Staples	6 Nov. 1986	Honolulu, HI
Robert Lee Stevenson	31 May 1987	Carrollton, GA
Ardelia Stokes	2 Sept. 1985	Salt Lake City, UT
Catherine M. Stokes	6 Mar. 1988	Chicago, IL
Rosa Lee Green Taylor	26 Oct. 1985	Phoenix, AZ
Rose S. Taylor	17 Oct. 1986	Chesterfield, VA
Thomas Earl Taylor	18 Oct. 1986	Chesterfield, VA
Marilyn Larine Thomas	5 June 1987	Jackson, MS
Natalia Thompson	5 Mar. 1988	Chicago, IL
William Thompson	28 May 1987	Decatur, GA
Larry Troutman	14 Oct. 1985	Oakland, CA
Vivian Troutman	14 Oct. 1985	Oakland, CA
Burl Turner, Jr.	11 June 1987	Baton Rouge, LA
Gloria Turner	11 June 1987	Baton Rouge, LA
Susan Walker	2 Mar. 1988	Chicago, IL
Karen Tonette Ward	6 June 1987	Jackson, MS
Maxine Wardlaw	22 Jan. 1986	Charlotte, NC
Katherine Warren	12 June 1987	New Orleans, LA

Benjamin R. Washington	15 Jan. 1986	Charlotte, NC
Lee Washington	23 Oct. 1985	Pasadena, CA
Jerry Watley	2 June 1987	Birmingham, AL
Phillip Webb	16 Mar. 1988	St. Louis, MO
Margie Ray White	16 Jan. 1986	Monroe, NC
Annie Wilbur	11 Aug. 1985	Provo, UT
Mary Angel Wilbur	1 Oct. 1986	New Kensington, PA
Winston A. Wilkinson	10 Oct. 1986	Olney, MD
Emma Williams	23 Jan. 1986	Hickory, NC
Linda Williams	3 Mar. 1988	Chicago, IL
Cynthia Willis	17 Oct. 1985	Sunnyvale, CA
Eva Willis	17 Mar. 1987	St. Louis, MO
Jerry Willis	14 Mar. 1987	St. Louis, MO
Albert L. Wilson	2 Oct. 1986	Williamsport, PA
Doris Marie Wilson	2 Oct. 1986	Williamsport, PA
Nathaniel Womble	29 May 1987	Atlanta, GA
Ruby Womble	27 May 1987	Atlanta, GA
Dorothy Mae Wright	9 June 1987	Baton Rouge, LA
Dunk Wright	9 June 1987	Baton Rouge, LA
Jess Wright, Jr.	1 June 1987	Gadsden, AL
Michelle Evette Wright	9 June 1987	Baton Rouge, LA
Richardo Wright	21 Oct. 1986	Aldie, VA
Shirley Walker Wright	11 June 1987	Baton Rouge, LA
Van C. Wright, Sr.	10 June 1987	Baton Rouge, LA
Virginia K. Wright	14 Oct. 1986	Richmond, VA
Delphrine Garcia Young	22 Oct. 1985	Los Angeles, CA

INTERVIEWS BY JESSIE L. EMBRY

Name	*Date*	*Place*
Alan Cherry	24, 25 Apr. 1985	Provo, UT
Charles W. Smith, Jr.	17 Mar. 1988	Provo, UT

SELECTED READINGS

AMERICAN RELIGIONS

Adams, John A., Jr. *The Black Pulpit Revolution in the United Methodist Church and Other Denominations*. Chicago: Strugglers' Community Press, 1985.

Ahlstrom, Sydney E. *A Religious History of the American People*. New Haven, CT: Yale University Press, 1972.

Carroll, Jackson W., Douglas W. Johnson, Martin E. Marty. *Religion in America, 1950 to the Present*. San Francisco: Harper and Row, Publishers, 1979.

Dolan, Jay P. *The American Catholic Experience: A History from Colonial Times to the Present*. Garden City, NY: Doubleday and Company, 1985.

Greeley, Andrew M. *Religious Change in America*. Cambridge, MA: Harvard University Press, 1989.

Hoge, Dean R. and David A. Roozen, eds. *Understanding Church Growth and Decline, 1950-1978*. New York: Pilgrim Press, 1970.

Launius, Roger D. *Invisible Saints: A History of Black Americans in the Reorganized Church*. Independence, MO: Herald Publishing House, 1988.

Lincoln, C. Eric and Lawrence H. Mamiya. *The Black Church in the African American Experience*. Durham, NC: Duke University Press, 1990.

Liptak, Delore. *Immigrants and Their Church*. New York: MacMillan Publishing Company, 1989.

Marty, Martin E. *Modern American Religion, Volume 1: The Irony of It All, 1893-1991*. Chicago: University of Chicago Press, 1986.

————. *A Nation of Behavers*. Chicago: University of Chicago Press, 1976.

Mays, Benjamin E. "The Black Experience and Perspective." *American Religious Values and the Future of America*, Rodger Van Allen, ed. Philadelphia: Fortress Press, 1978.

Ochs, Stephen J. *Desegregating the Altar: The Josephites and the Struggle for Black Priests, 1871-1960*. Baton Rouge: Louisiana State University Press, 1990.

Roof, Wade Clark and William McKinney. *American Mainline Religion: Its Changing Shape and Future*. New Brunswick: Rutgers Press, 1987.

254 / Selected Readings

Schaefer, Richard T. *Racial and Ethnic Groups*. Boston: Little, Brown, and Company, 1979.

Stark, Rodney and Charles Y. Glock. *American Piety: The Nature of Religious Commitment*. Berkeley: University of California Press, 1970.

LDS CHURCH HISTORY AND BELIEFS

Albrecht, Stan L. "The Consequential Dimension of Mormon Religiosity." *Brigham Young University Studies* 29 (Spring 1989).

————— and Tim B. Heaton, "Secularization, Higher Education, and Religiosity." *Review of Religious Research* 26 (Sept. 1984): 43-58.

Alexander, Thomas G. *Mormonism in Transition: A History of the Latter-day Saints, 1890-1930*. Urbana: University of Illinois, 1986.

Allen, James B. and Glen M. Leonard. *The Story of the Latter-day Saints*. Salt Lake City: Deseret Book Company, 1976.

Arrington, Leonard J. and Davis Bitton. *The Mormon Experience: A History of the Latter-day Saints*. New York: Alfred A. Knopf, 1979.

Brugger, Don L. "Climate for Change." *Ensign* 23 (Sept. 1993): 24-28.

Cornwall, Marie et al. "The Dimensions of Religiosity: A Conceptual Model with an Empirical Test." *Review of Religious Research* 27 (Mar. 1986).

Embry, Jessie L. "Ethnic Groups in the LDS Church." *Dialogue: A Journal of Mormon Thought* 25 (Winter 1992).

—————. "Little Berlin: Swiss Saints of the Logan Tenth Ward." *Utah Historical Quarterly* 56 (Summer 1988): 222-35.

Florence, Giles H., Jr. "City of Angels." *Ensign* 22 (Sept. 1992).

Foster, Lawrence. *Religion and Sexuality: The Shakers, the Mormons, and the Oneida Community*. Urbana: University of Illinois Press, 1984.

Hansen, Klaus J. *Mormonism and the American Experience*. Chicago: University of Chicago Press, 1981.

Jensen, Richard L. "Mother Tongue: Use of Non-English Languages in the Church of Jesus Christ of Latter-day Saints, 1850-1983." *New Views of Mormon History: A Collection of Essays in Honor of Leonard J. Arrington*, Davis Bitton and Maureen Ursenbach Beecher, eds. Salt Lake City: University of Utah Press, 1987, 273-303.

Kimball, Edward L., ed. *The Teachings of Spencer W. Kimball*. Salt Lake City: Bookcraft, 1982.

Kimball, Spencer W. "The Evil of Intolerance." *Improvement Era* 57 (June 1954): 423-24.

Mann, Ronald M. "Philadelphia, the Seedbed of a Nation." *Ensign* 23 (Aug. 1993): 76-77.

McConkie, Bruce R. *Mormon Doctrine*. Salt Lake City: Bookcraft, 1966.

Mulder, William. *Homeward to Zion: The Mormon Migration from Scandinavia*. Minneapolis: University of Minnesota Press, 1957.

O'Dea, Thomas F. *The Mormons*. Chicago: University of Chicago Press, 1957.

Shipps, Jan. "In the Presence of the Past: Continuity and Change in the Twentieth-Century Mormonism." *After 150 Years: The Latter-day Saints in Sesquicentennial Perspective*, Thomas G. Alexander and Jessie L. Embry, eds. Provo, UT: Charles Redd Center for Western Studies, 1983.

Whittaker, David J. "Mormons and Native Americans: A Historical and Bibliographical Introduction." *Dialogue: A Journal of Mormon Thought* 18 (Winter 1985): 33-64.

LDS CHURCH AND BLACKS

Allen, James B. "Would-Be Saints: West Africa before the 1978 Priesthood Revelation." *Journal of Mormon History* 17 (1991): 207-47.

Bringhurst, Newell G. *Saints, Slaves, and Blacks: The Changing Place of Black People Within Mormonism*. Westport, CT: Greenwood Press, 1981.

Bush, Lester E., Jr., and Armand L. Mauss, eds. *Neither White Nor Black: Mormon Scholars Confront the Race Issue in a Universal Church*. Midvale, UT: Signature Books, 1984.

Carter, Kate B. *The Story of the Negro Pioneer*.

Cherry, Alan Gerald. *It's You and Me, Lord!* Provo, UT: Trilogy Arts Publication, 1970.

Ebony Rose. Special Collections, Harold B. Lee Library, Brigham Young University, Provo, Utah.

Embry, Jessie L. "Separate but Equal?: Black Branches, Genesis Groups, or Integrated Wards." *Dialogue: A Journal of Mormon Thought* 23 (Spring 1990).

Grover, Mark L. "The Mormon Priesthood Revelation and the Sao Paulo, Brazil Temple." *Dialogue: A Journal of Mormon Thought* 23 (Spring 1990).

Hartley, William G. "Samuel D. Chambers." *New Era* 4 (June 1974): 47-50.

Let's Talk. LDS Church Library, Historical Department, Church of Jesus Christ of Latter-day Saints, Salt Lake City, Utah.

Mauss, Armand. "The Fading of the Pharaoh's Curse: The Decline and Fall of the Priesthood Restriction Ban Against Blacks in the Mormon Church." *Dialogue: A Journal of Mormon Thought* 14 (Autumn 1981): 41.

———. "Mormonism and Secular Attitudes Toward Negroes." *Pacific Sociological Review* 8 (Fall 1966).

McConkie, Bruce R. "All Are Alike unto God," an address to a Book of Mormon Symposium for Seminary and Institute teachers, Brigham Young University, 18 Aug. 1978.

———. "The New Revelation on Priesthood." *Priesthood*. Salt Lake City: Deseret Book Company, 1981.

Newell, Linda King and Valeen Tippetts Avery. "Jane Manning James." *Ensign* 9 (Aug. 1979): 26-29.

Olsen, Peggy. "Ruffin Bridgeforth: Leader and Father to Mormon Blacks." *This People* 1 (Winter 1980): 15-16.

Shipps, Jan. "The Mormons: Looking Forward and Outward." *The Christian Century*, 16-23 Aug. 1978, 762.

Stokes, Catherine M. "'Plenty Good Room' in Relief Society." *Dialogue: A Journal of Mormon Thought* 21 (Winter 1988).

Sturlaugson, Mary Frances. *A Soul So Rebellious*. Salt Lake City: Deseret Book Company, 1981.

Wolfinger, Henry J. "A Test of Faith: Jane Manning James and the Origins of the Utah Black Community." *Social Accommodations in Utah*. Salt Lake City: American West Center Occasional Papers, University of Utah, 1975.

INDEX

A

Abel, Elijah, 23, 24, 38-39, 40, 43
Abel, Mary Ann Adams, 38
African Americans, growth of
LDS church among, 231-32;
image of LDS church, 234;
LDS missionary efforts, 57-
59, 229-31; music, 204-206; religious commitment, 95-118;
religious beliefs, 96-99; role
of religion, 225; Utah during
World War II, 24, 33
African-American churches, attendance by African Americans,
87; civil rights movement,
1960s, 7, 8; conditions of,
1950s-90s, 8; founding of, 3;
role in black communities, 6-
9; 203; worship, 99-102; 204
African-American Latter-day
Saints, African-American community reaction to conversion, 213-21; African-
American congregations, 192-
99; appealing elements of
LDS church, 90, 92-94; assimilation, 123; beliefs, 96-99;
church attendance, 86;

church positions, 107-17, 134;
church publications, 208; contact with non-LDS African
Americans, 240; contact with
whites, 87-89; dating, 168; discrimination, 144-57; eco-
nomic backgrounds, 88-89;
educational levels, 89-90; ethnic congregations, 181, 192-
99; ethnic Latter-day Saint
comparison, 208-211; experiences, 234-45; family devotion, 104-107; family prayer,
105-107; family relationships
as Latter-day Saints, 237-38;
fellowshipping, 228-29; future
as Latter-day Saints, 234; geographical location, 85-86; genealogy, 102; goals as
Latter-day Saints, 239; growth
as Latter-day Saints, 236-47;
marriage, 168; marital status,
85; members after 1978 priesthood announcement, 59-62;
members prior to 1978 priesthood announcement, 37-57;
missionaries, 225-27; missionary work, 228-29; missionary